CONSTITUTIONS
and
CONSTITUTIONALISM

Edited and with an Introductory Essay by
WILLIAM G. ANDREWS
Tufts University

THIRD EDITION

D. VAN NOSTRAND COMPANY, INC.
Princeton, New Jersey

Toronto   London

New York

VAN NOSTRAND REGIONAL OFFICES
New York, Chicago, San Francisco

D. Van Nostrand Company, Ltd., *London*
D. Van Nostrand Company (Canada), Ltd., *Toronto*
D. Van Nostrand Company Pty. Ltd., *Melbourne*

Copyright © 1961, 1963, 1968, by
D. VAN NOSTRAND COMPANY, INC.
Published simultaneously in Canada by
D. Van Nostrand Company (Canada), Ltd.

Library of Congress Catalog Card No. 68–26690

PRINTED IN THE UNITED STATES OF AMERICA

PREFACE TO THE FIRST EDITION

This book is designed to make available in convenient form the texts of the principal constitutional documents of four major world powers and to place them in the framework of a theoretical discussion of constitutionalism and constitutions. The translation of the French Constitution is original. I agree with Professor Pickles that the official version is "a caricature." My attention was first drawn to the need for a collection of this sort by Professor Mario Einaudi of Cornell University. He and Professor Arthur Wilson of Dartmouth College have read portions of the manuscript and given valuable advice. I am also grateful to my wife, Solange, for assistance in proofreading and other editorial chores; to Mrs. Joan Grosjean, Miss Lucille Flanders, and Miss Mary Read for typing portions of the manuscript, and to the Faculty Research Committee of Dartmouth College for financial assistance.

February 1961

PREFACE TO THE SECOND EDITION

The British Emergency Powers (Defence) Act of 1939 has been added to the Second Edition. The 1961 revised Statutes of the Communist Party of the Soviet Union have been included. All amendments to the Constitutions up to date have been incorporated. The translation of the French Constitution has been polished up. Professors Henry W. Ehrmann, Julian Towster, Marshall D. Shulman, Nicholas Wahl, John P. Vloyantes, and Martin Harrison have made suggestions. The library staffs of Tufts and Harvard Universities, the *Institut d'études politiques* of Paris, and the Embassy of the Federal Republic of Germany in Paris supplied materials. My thanks go to all of them.

Paris
February 1963

3

PREFACE TO THE THIRD EDITION

A statistical appendix has been added to this edition. It also incorporates the more than forty amendments to the Statutes of the CPSU that were ordered by the Twenty-third congress of the CPSU and the thirty-six amendments to the constitutions of France, West Germany, and the Soviet Union that were enacted between April 15, 1963, and June 15, 1968. Mr. Richard McDowell of Tufts University compiled the Appendix. Mr. Vasyl Luchkiw and Mrs. Eliese Hetler of SUC, Brockport, helped translate the Soviet and 1968 German amendments, which have not been published in English previously. The staffs of Widener and the Russian Research Center libraries at Harvard University, of the West German consulates in Boston and New York, and of Inter-Nationes in Bonn helped locate the material. Miss Diane Ballard, Miss Helen Markert, and Miss Sherian Bull helped assemble the manuscript. To all of them and to the political science teachers whose continued use of this little handbook has made a new edition possible, I extend my thanks.

WILLIAM G. ANDREWS

Brockport

4

CONTENTS

	PREFACES	3
	CONTENTS	5
1.	CONSTITUTIONALISM AND CONSTITU-TIONS	9
	A. Consensus	9
	B. Consensus and Constitutionalism	11
	C. Constitutionalism	13
	D. Natural Law and Constitutionalism	14
	E. Evolution of Constitutionalism in Practice	18
	F. Constitutionalism and Constitutions	21
	G. Other Functions of Constitutions	23
	H. Conclusion	26
2.	THE UNITED STATES OF AMERICA	27
	A. American Constitutionalism	27
3.	GREAT BRITAIN	29
	A. British Constitutionalism	29
	B. British Constitutional Documents	31
	1. Magna Carta, 1215	31
	2. Petition of Right, 1628	36
	3. Habeas Corpus Act, 1641	38
	4. Bill of Rights, 1689	40
	5. The Act of Settlement, 1701	43
	6. The Act of Union with Scotland, 1707	46
	7. Parliament Act, 1911 and 1949	48
	8. Re-election of Ministers Act, 1919	50
	9. Ministers of the Crown Act, 1937	51
	10. Emergency Powers (Defence) Act, 1939	55
	11. Statutory Instruments Act, 1946	58
	12. Representation of the People Act, 1948	64
	13. Life Peerages Act, 1958	65
4.	FRANCE	67
	A. French Constitutionalism	67
	B. French Constitutional Documents	69
	1. Declaration of the Rights of Man and of the Citizen, 1789	69

      2. Preamble to the Constitution of the
         Fourth French Republic, 1946   71
      3. Constitution of the Fifth French Re-
         public, 1958   73
5. GERMANY   98
  A. German Constitutionalism   98
  B. Basic Law of the Federal Republic of
     Germany, 1949   99
6. THE SOVIET UNION   152
  A. Constitutionalism and the Soviet Union   152
  B. Soviet Constitutional Documents   155
      1. Constitution of the Union of Soviet
         Socialist Republics, 1936   155
      2. Statutes of the Communist Party of
         the Soviet Union, 1961   179
  ADDENDUM   205
  STATISTICAL APPENDIX   213

CONSTITUTIONS
and
CONSTITUTIONALISM

— 1 —

CONSTITUTIONALISM AND CONSTITUTIONS

Man's unending search for the widest freedom to pursue his own ends within ordered society explains his acceptance of government. He tolerates gentle fetters from the State to escape the heavy chains of anarchic chaos and to gain the opportunities for collective action and division of labor that, in the modern world, are available only within the State. Yet, a State powerful enough to maintain order may also be strong enough to suppress liberty. Because of his fear that Leviathan might become a Frankenstein monster, Man equips the machinery of government with brakes as well as a motor. The manifestation of that fear in theoretical, institutional, and documentary forms is the subject of this essay and provides the substance of this book.

A. CONSENSUS

The members of a political community have, by definition, common interests which they seek to promote or protect through the creation and use of the compulsory political mechanisms we call the State. They agree that the State is preferable to any likely alternative. Consensus on this question is essential to the existence of the State. If general agreement on the desirability of the survival of the State breaks down, civil war or revolution may result. This happened, for instance, in 1789 in France; 1776 in America; and 1917 in Russia. Awareness of that possibility favors the retention of political systems that might not be accepted freely otherwise. Tyranny may be preferred to anarchy. Only when the existing system is regarded by a substantial part of the community as less tolerable than civil strife is it abandoned. But to survive it must have at least tacit support from more than a simple majority of the members of a community. The determined hostility of a substantial minority will so impede its operation as to render it useless for the attainment of the goals sought by the majority. For instance, if 40 or 45 percent of the citizens of a State adamantly refused to pay taxes, the problem of punishing this defiance would require so much effort on the part of the other 55 or 60 percent that it would disrupt government and impair, if not completely prevent, the individual pursuit of private goals. Realization of the vulnerability of the State to this form of opposition led Henry David Thoreau to advocate civil disobedience and Mahatma Gandhi to employ it so effectively. Thoreau and Gandhi preferred the disappearance of the State to its continued existence in the form they knew. Socrates in the *Crito* deals with the same problem, recognizes the alternatives clearly, and concludes that not only defiance, but even evasion of the authority of the State undermines its utility and jeopardizes its existence. In his view, this result would be less desirable than the injustice of the existing system.

In most political communities consensus covers much more than the bare minimum of agreement that the State should survive. It may embrace the form of the institutional structure or of the specific institutions. It may include such general policy goals as the even distribution of wealth, the maintenance of racial segregation or *apartheid,* national unity, or the freedom of the individual to conduct his personal and business affairs without direct State interference. There often is consensus on more limited policy goals such as raising the minimum wage law, forming a given military alliance, or nationalizing a certain industry. Consensus on solutions to *specific* problems is not essential in the way it is on the answer to the question of whether the State should exist. The will of the majority is accepted because to do otherwise would sap the authority of the State, thereby producing a greater evil, one opposed by consensus.

Although agreement in such depth is not essential, it

is desirable, for it makes more efficient, satisfactory government possible. The greater the number of questions on which there is accord, and the broader its popular base, the more quickly and efficiently government can move to resolve the questions on which there is no consensus. It is to the breadth and depth of consensus that the success of British government is sometimes attributed. One reason for the failure of the Fourth French Republic was the deep dissension on so many public questions.

Qualitative factors are also significant in appraising political consensus in societies. Not only the number, but also the types of questions on which accord prevails are important. Agreement on procedures is prerequisite to agreement on substance. Agreement on means is pointless without common goals. General policy matters require wider acceptance than specifics, and consensus is more necessary on questions that touch the vitals of society than on those that concern frills. Stability of opinion is also important. Many governmental policies require considerable time to bear fruit. If public sentiment shifts frequently, successive programs may never develop to the point of producing results, and a strong feeling of frustration and dissatisfaction may arise among the governed.

It may be seen from these comments that an assessment of the role of consensus in political society is very difficult, and that an evaluation of the correlation between it and political satisfaction and stability in any given political system is equally complex. Consideration of only one type of consensus or of consensus on only one question or in one area cannot provide a complete answer. Many forms of consensus on many questions, in many areas, and at many levels must be measured for breadth, depth, and intensity and evaluated for importance before a clear picture of this phenomenon in a given society will emerge.

B. CONSENSUS AND CONSTITUTIONALISM

The matter of consensus has an important bearing on constitutionalism. Order may be imposed through force, violence, and arbitrary action by a dictator or oligarch even if the extent and intensity of consensus in a community are low. But it is unlikely that only a modicum of cohesion will be able to sustain a government that seeks to impose its will primarily through law and constitutional rule. Every government uses force against those within it who oppose its will. The size and intensity of the opposition usually determine the amount of that force. At an indefinable point along the continuum from complete discord to unanimity, cohesion in the society becomes so broad and strong that force is needed by the regime only in exceptional circumstances rather than as a matter of course or of policy. This situation is a precondition for constitutionalism. Consensus on the form of its institutions and procedures is especially important to constitutional government. If large numbers of citizens feel that the design of the machinery of government operates unjustly to their disadvantage, they may not accept its facilities for the resolution of social conflict, thereby undermining its authority.

Agreement must also exist on the desirability of the rule of law as the basis of government. In some situations there is consensus against constitutionalism. A leader may appear, especially in troubled times, who seems to have such extraordinary wisdom and competence that the community prefers to strike the fetters of constitutionalism from his talents. Plato would have done this for his philosopher-kings. The German people did this for Adolf Hitler in 1933 and the French did it for Charles de Gaulle in 1958, though, in the latter case, the forms of constitutionalism were retained. Other reasons may produce consensus against constitutionalism. The State and the ordered society it enfolds may be so severely imperiled by internal or foreign danger that the people lose confidence in the orderly procedures of constitutionalism. To combat the danger, they may insist on or acquiesce in mobilization of the full resources of the State without regard to the restraints and prescriptions[1] of constitutionalism. This was the case in

[1] Throughout this essay, I use "prescription" in the contemporary, familiar sense of "directive, guide," rather than the Burkeian sense of legal acquisition through long usage.

the United States during the Civil War and, to a lesser extent, during both World Wars. It was true in wartime Britain.

A third consensual element usually provides part of the foundation for constitutionalism. This is agreement on the general goals of society or, to put it another way, general acceptance of the same philosophy of government. This is not so important as the other two factors discussed, for, as long as consensus prevails on procedure and on acceptance of constitutionalism, adjustment and accommodation of goals can be negotiated. On the other hand, the absence of agreement on goals produces strains and tensions that may endanger the concord in the other areas. A final element is concurrence in lesser goals and on specific policy questions. This hardens the cement of constitutionalism but is not an essential ingredient.

C. CONSTITUTIONALISM

Let us now take a closer look at the constitutionalism that rests on the consensual foundation we have prepared for it. If one were to attempt a description of this complex concept in two words, he might call it "limited government". Under constitutionalism, two types of limitations impinge on government. *Power is proscribed and procedures prescribed.* That is, there are libertarian and procedural aspects of constitutionalism. In the first place, authority to take certain actions regarding the members of the community is withheld. The State is forbidden to trespass in areas reserved for private activity. It is this type of restraint that was imposed on the national government by the first ten amendments to the United States Constitution. In the second place, directives are set forth determining the manner in which policy shall be formulated and implemented within the area of jurisdiction of the State. Governmental institutions are established, and their functions, powers, and interrelationships are defined. If these arrangements are short-circuited or contravened, the government's action is not legitimate. The obligation imposed on the governors to adhere to prescribed procedures makes it possible for opponents of proposed action, whether they be within the governmental structure or outside it, to manifest their opposition systematically and as effectively as their abilities and the merits of their case permit.

Constitutionalism, then, governs two separate but related types of relationship. First, there is the relationship of government to citizen. Second, there is the relationship of one governmental authority to another. The dichotomy is not sharp, for the latter type of relationship is regulated largely as a means of increasing the effectiveness of the control imposed on the former type. It is useful, however, for analytical purposes.

D. NATURAL LAW AND CONSTITUTIONALISM

Having considered the dual nature of constitutionalism, we may now examine the authority on which the limitations rest. It might seem that the people, in all their corporate glory, provide this authority. In a sense they do in most modern constitutional systems. The Constitution of the United States opens with, "We, the people . . .", for instance, and the Constitution of the Fifth French Republic begins, "The French people . . .". Furthermore, it is usually within the power of the people or their elected representatives to alter the scope of authority of government or change its procedures. Finally, we have seen that constitutionalism cannot exist without wide support among the people. Nevertheless, this close relationship of constitutionalism to the people is not narrowly derivative.

Constitutionalism transcends the people and claims for itself the sanctity of a higher law. It has attached itself to that great stream of natural law concepts that has swept through the history of political theory at least since the time of the ancient Greeks. At times, belief in natural law has been widespread and deep; at others, it has withdrawn to scholarly cloisters, but always it has excited sophisticated imaginations. In times of trouble and disorder it has shimmered elusively in the distance; in more settled periods it has attracted the confident grasp even of sober idealists. Key concepts of natural law, as George H. Sabine has said, "were built solidly into the moral consciousness of the European peoples" by the Ancient Greeks. "However much they might be disregarded or violated in the letter, they were too deeply rooted to be destroyed." [2] The modern constitutional State at the time of its origins was justified and, to a large extent, legitimized in terms of natural law theory. More recently, it has grown theoretical roots of its own and can be defended on a positivist basis. Nevertheless, the mainstream of theories of constitutionalism still flows in the bed of higher law. Though constitutionalism owes a great deal to natural law, the former is only one aspect of the latter. Natural law thinking has other implications not directly relevant to the question of constitutionalism which will not even be touched on here.

The Ancient Greeks—among them Sophocles, Heraclitus, Plato, and Aristotle—contributed much to the emergence and development of the concept of a divinely-inspired, universal, immutable, eternal natural law. They wrote, for instance, that "all human laws are sustained by the one divine law, which is infinitely strong, and suffices, and more than suffices, for them all." [3] Plato's theory of human law as an imperfect replica of an ideal form that exists only in the world of Ideas is another expression of much the same view. [4] But for Plato and the Greeks in general the law of nature was "no more than a basis of comparison . . . an intellectual standard" [5] and "does not serve as a means for concrete juridical decisions." [6]

[2] A History of Political Theory, Henry Holt and Company, New York, 1955, p. 144.

[3] Heraclitus; cited in Maurice LeBel, "Natural Law in the Greek Period," in Edward F. Barrett, editor, University of Notre Dame Natural Law Institute Proceedings, University of Notre Dame Press, Notre Dame, 1949, Vol. II, pp. 16-17.

[4] The Statesman, J. B. Skemp trans., Routledge and Kegan Paul, London, 1952, 297d-297e, p. 203. See Glenn R. Morrow's analysis of this point in "Plato and the Law of Nature," in Milton R. Konvitz and Arthur E. Murphy (editors), Essays in Political Theory: Presented to George H. Sabine, Cornell University Press, Ithaca, 1948, p. 23.

[5] Charles Howard McIlwain, Constitutionalism: Ancient and Modern, Cornell University Press, Ithaca, 1940, pp. 37-8.

[6] Sir Paul Vinogradoff, Outline of Historical Jurisprudence, Oxford University Press, London, 1922, Vol. II, p. 42.

It remained for the Stoics in Greece after 300 B.C. and later in Rome to erect on this philosophical base an authentic natural law theory. Cicero, the great Roman jurist and orator, summed up the views of the Stoics in a famous passage in the *Republic:*

> There is in fact a true law—namely, right reason— which is in accordance with nature, applies to all men, and is unchangeable and eternal. By its commands this law summons men to the performance of their duties; by its prohibitions it restrains them from doing wrong . . . To invalidate this law by human legislation is never morally right, nor is it permissible ever to restrict its operation, and to annul it is impossible. Neither the senate nor the people can absolve us from our obligation to obey this law, and it requires no Sextus Aleius to expound and interpret it. It will not lay down one rule at Rome and another at Athens, nor will it be one rule today and another tomorrow. But there will be one law, eternal and unchangeable, binding at all times upon all peoples; and there will be, as it were, one common master and ruler of men, namely God, who is the author of this law, its interpreter, and its sponsor. The man who will not obey it will abandon his better self, and, in denying the true nature of a man, will thereby suffer the severest of penalties, though he has escaped all the other consequences which men call punishment.[7]

The Stoics gave natural law binding authority and sanctions; the Catholic Schoolmen in following centuries supplied it with a purpose and drew tighter its bond with God. For them, natural law was divine in origin yet rationally determined, for man as a "rational creature . . . has a share of the Eternal Reason . . . and this participation of the eternal law in the rational creature is called the natural law." [8] Through this device of eternal reason, the Schoolmen fused the elements, separate in Cicero, of God and reason. It also

---

[7] Sabine and Smith translation, Ohio State University Press, Columbus, 1929, pp. 215-216 (Book III, 22).

[8] St. Thomas Aquinas, *Summa Theologica* (translated by Fathers of the English Dominican Province) R. & T. Washbourne, Ltd., London, 1915, Part II, First Part, Third Number, Question 91, Art. 2, p. 11.

imparts purpose to natural law. All kinds of law, they argued, have the purpose of providing God with a means to instruct us in good.[9] Man, because he partakes of Eternal Reason, has "an inclination" to act in a manner compatible with his nature. It is the purpose of natural law to instruct in "the proper acts and ends" deriving from that nature. That is, it prescribes that which is good for him in his capacity as a man.[10]

The Schoolmen joined natural law to Christian theology by giving it a basis in Divine Will and thereby implanted it firmly in medieval political thought. The task accomplished by the early modernizers of natural law theory in the 16th and 17th centuries, and especially Hugo Grotius and Samuel Pufendorf, was almost the reverse. By extracting God from natural law they made it the foundation of the modern, secular, constitutional State. They constructed a theory of natural law that would "carry conviction in an age in which theological controversy was gradually losing the power to do so," thereby making the "existence of God perfectly superfluous" to the doctrine.[11]

As the divine element waned, the place of the individual human being waxed. Natural law became increasingly just a platform on which natural rights and, ultimately, the libertarian aspects of modern constitutionalism were rested. Through John Locke's handling in the late 17th century, the natural law "concept undergoes . . . almost complete dissolution . . . into the natural rights of the individual." [12] In effecting this transformation, Locke defined in great detail the origin, nature, and extent of the natural law limits on government in its relations with individuals, that is, the proscriptions on government. At the same time, he also attached great importance to the observance of procedural regularity—

[9] *Ibid.*, Question 90, p. 1.
[10] *Ibid.*, Question 91, Art. 2, p. 11.
[11] Alessandro Passerin d'Entrèves, *Natural Law: An Introduction to Legal Philosophy*, Hutchinson's University Library, London, 1952, pp. 52-53.
[12] Edward S. Corwin, *The "Higher Law" Background of American Constitutional Law*, Cornell University Press, Ithaca, 1955, p. 61.

the institutional side of constitutionalism—insisting on the need to base the relationships among the institutional components of government on natural law.

It is on these twin pillars of proscribed power and prescribed procedures that modern constitutional government has been built. John Locke provided the richest store of theoretical justification for it, as shown by the constant citation of him by the 18th and 19th century Whigs on both sides of the Atlantic (and on both sides of the English Channel, as Elie Halévy has pointed out).[13]

Many writers since Locke have bolstered his theories in its weak spots and have filled in numerous details. Montesquieu and the writers of *The Federalist,* in particular, did much to bring to flower the seeds of the theory of procedural prescription planted by Locke. Yet, when all is said and done, all theory on constitutionalism written since Locke has been little more than adornment of the framework he constructed.

E. Evolution of Constitutionalism in Practice

The evolution of political institutions that occurred contemporaneously with the long growth of the theory just described was at least as important a foundation for modern constitutionalism. The imaginations of even our most gifted thinkers are able to spring only a short distance from the events of their times and places. History is seen but dimly through the screen of personal experience. The more one studies Rousseau, for instance, the more one realizes that *Citoyen de Genève* on the frontispiece of his works describes both the man and his thought. Montesquieu's rambling discourse also acquires more meaning if read less as a description of strange and exotic ways the world over and more as a nostrum for his France. Whether Locke's *Second Treatise* is read, as formerly, as an apology for the Glorious Revolution or, as recent scholarship has shown it to have been, an attack on the *ancien régime,* it was, nevertheless, closely linked to the events of 1688. So it has been, generally, with the theories of natural law and constitutionalism.

[13] *The Growth of Philosophic Radicalism* (trans. by Mary Morris), Beacon Press, Boston, 1955.

Political philosophers have, in most cases, reflected, abstracted, articulated, and generalized the ideals of living political movements or communities. Plato blended Athenian respect for education with Spartan discipline. The natural law theories of Cicero and the Stoics spun a theoretical web for Roman universalism. Aquinas and the Schoolmen, with their thought, extended the temporal hierarchy of Church and Prince upward into the Heavens, downward into the nether regions, and outward into the plant, animal, and mineral kingdoms. The Church's sword from the "doctrine of the two swords," * corroded and shattered by the Reformation, was buried by Bodin, Grotius, and Hobbes only to re-emerge 40 years after *Leviathan,* burnished by natural rights and wielded with a flourish simultaneously by Locke's theoretical "legislative" and by the newly-ascendant British Parliament. In brief, the evolution of political institutions closely paralleled the evolution of the doctrine of constitutionalism.

No attempt to survey the history of constitutionalism in practice can be made in this short eassy.[14] A few comments may, nevertheless, be in order to help round out the picture. The procedural aspect of constitutionalism was well developed by the Ancient Greeks, as numerous writings show, but none was more authoritative than Aristotle's *Politics.*[15] The Greek city-states had well-articulated constitutions, in the broad sense of the word, and the procedures for the enactment and implementation of public policies were clearly established. There was less regard among the Greeks for sharply drawing or constitutionalizing the line of authority between

* According to medieval Scholastics, the Church and the secular authorities had co-ordinate powers.

[14] The reader is referred to the McIlwain, *op. cit.;* Francis D. Wormuth, *The Origins of Modern Constitutionalism,* Harper, New York, 1949; Andrew C. McLaughlin, *The Foundations of American Constitutionalism,* New York University Press, New York, 1932; and the standard political and constitutional histories for the periods and countries concerned.

[15] See also Victor Ehrenberg, *The Greek State,* Barnes and Noble, New York, 1960, pp. 42-52.

rulers and ruled. This latter aspect began to take shape in the Roman Republic and, in the form of customary rights of the subject, was carried through the medieval period, even when the monarch was largely unbridled as far as procedures were concerned. The medieval Church always supplied a certain institutional check on the king and the feudal system of nobility was another. Where there is such joint participation in the exercise of sovereignty, the establishment of regular procedures is necessary. Concurrent rule would be ineffective if it did not entail mutual checks among the organs of authority. Such checks could hardly operate if the respective organs were not functioning in accordance with predetermined and regular procedures. We sometimes identify constitutionalism with democratic government. But, in view of the above, it is not surprising that the roots of modern constitutionalism can actually be found in the medieval system. Institutionalized power counterbalanced institutionalized power, each limiting the scope of the other and imposing on it standards of regular behavior. The weakness of these regimes, as far as constitutionalism is concerned, lay in the fact that the countervailing forces had no common temporal foundation. All derived their legitimate authority from the Will of God as expressed through natural law, but the delphic quality of its strictures left the way open for definitive interpretation by the most powerful interpreter. So long as faith in One Universal Church was deeply rooted in both subject and prince, and so long as difficulties of communication prevented tight centralization, no power was able to gain absolute ascendancy over the others. This condition had largely come to an end by 16th century Britain and 17th century France.

There ensued a period in those countries and in others on the Continent in which genuine, effective constitutionalism was gravely undermined. The royal power gathered into its hands full authority, and the medieval house of cards tumbled with the imbalance. Henry VIII and the Sun King ruled virtually unbridled. The absolutist break in Britain was neither as deep nor did it last as long as elsewhere. Yet, revolutions were required in both Britain and France before constitutionalism was placed on its modern footing. This new foundation, the instrument for the reconciliation of constitutionalism with the modern centralized state, was the establishment of a common temporal interpreter of natural law. The new sovereign, replacing the medieval competing centers of power and the absolute monarchs, was the people. Whether the new constitutional regimes separated powers (as Montesquieu proposed and the American Founding Fathers did), or only functions (as became the case in the fully-evolved parliamentary regimes), the arbiter was a broad, popular electorate.

F. CONSTITUTIONALISM AND CONSTITUTIONS

We may now turn to a consideration of the relationship between constitutionalism and Constitutions.* With final authority for interpreting the higher law transferred from one or another of a limited number of competing, institutionalized centers of power to the mass of the governed, it became useful to inscribe on parchment the limits and procedures believed by them to be imposed by natural law on the governors. The people wanted to have before them that which they were to interpret. Not only did documentary Constitutions ease the task of popular interpretation; they also made the directives of the governed to the governors concrete and explicit, on the basic natural law questions. Constitutions provided standards against which governors could measure their performance and could be measured by the governed. In Great Britain, where the transfer of sovereignty took place in a series of steps over a relatively long period of time, the standards were incorporated in a series of documents that may properly be regarded collectively as a Constitution. In France, the United States, and elsewhere where sovereignty was shifted suddenly, single documents laying down the norms were often struck off. Everywhere, however—not only in Great Britain with its series of constitutional documents, but in the United States and in all other constitutional systems as well—many of the norms of con-

---

* When capitalized, "Constitution" refers to the constitutional document or documents; "constitution" refers to the structure of the government and its relationships.

stitutionalism remained outside the documentary framework. Government was restrained only where restraint was believed necessary. Rights not endangered were not protected. On the procedural side, as the new regimes were set into operation, unforeseen institutional kinks developed and the solutions to them were incorporated into the structure of constitutionalism although not necessarily written into the documents. Thus, political parties developed generally outside the documentary framework but well within the structure of constitutionalism. So did a two-term limit on presidential office-holding in the United States. It was not until 164 years after the U. S. Constitution was drafted and eleven years after this provision of the American constitution had first been violated that prescription became text as the Twenty-second Amendment.

The same process occurs with respect to the limitations on government. As the views of the electorate change with the passage of time the unwritten constitution is altered. Whether those alterations will manifest themselves in documentary form is another matter. For instance, during the 19th century the view that the government should not intervene directly in economic affairs became an integral feature of the American constitution, but it was not until the "due process" clause of the Fourteenth Amendment that it found documentary expression and, even then, in rather ambiguous terms. Since then, the unwritten constitution has evolved again; governmental supervision of the economy has come to be expected as a legitimate and necessary function. Yet, the "due process" clause remains unchanged and no emendations have been made in the Constitution to reflect this new shift.

Not only are Constitutions often incomplete, they are sometimes quite misleading. In the last two centuries constitutionalism has become established in a position of co-legitimacy with democracy. Documentary Constitutions have come to be identified with constitutionalism. But many regimes in the world today have Constitutions without constitutionalism. Tyrants, whether individual or collective, find that Constitutions are con-

venient screens behind which they can dissimulate their
despotism. As pointed out in the note on constitutionalism and the Soviet Union, provisions that seem to be restraints can be employed to rationalize the arbitrary use
of power. Apart from these sham limitations, Constitutions can perform other pseudo-constitutional functions in despotic States. They may contribute to
the stability of those regimes and guide political action
through the channels desired by the despots by explicit
description of the machinery of government. That is,
they may present the procedural forms of the State in a
descriptive manner, rather than the directive, pre-
scriptive manner of the true constitutional State, and, in
this way, they tend to regularize and stabilize its
comportment to some extent without articulating genuine restrictions.

G. OTHER FUNCTIONS OF CONSTITUTIONS

If, as we have seen, Constitutions rarely or never embrace all the constitutional principles, neither are they
restricted to this role. Constitutions and constitutionalism
are not congruent on one side where the principles extend beyond the document. On another side, the document outreaches principles and performs other functions.

For one thing, there is a reverse face to the coin of
governmental power. As we have seen there is a side,
like the obverse of a 25-cent piece, inscribed "LIB-
ERTY" and "IN GOD WE TRUST", bearing the likeness
of the Father of the country to symbolize the higher law of
metaphysics and history as protection for freedom. But
there is also a side inscribed "E PLURIBUS UNUM"
and bearing the likeness of the eagle, with wings out-
stretched, and armed, signifying the power and authority
of the State. The Constitution imposes restraints on government as a function of constitutionalism; but it also
legitimizes the power of the government. It is the documentary instrument for the transfer of authority from
the residual holders—the people under democracy, the
king under monarchy—to the organs of State power.

The Constitution may also perform a function as a

national symbol. As Tom Paine hinted in *Common Sense*,[16] it may serve instead of the king in that ceremonial fuction of exemplifying the unity and majesty of the nation. Or it may exist alongside the monarch, embodying in parchment what he incarnates. It is in this symbolic capacity that Constitutions are trundled about the country in shiny aluminum railroad trains under armed guard and exhibited to all comers. It is this aspect of Constitutions that soldiers are sworn to defend and public servants to uphold. A newly-independent nation may have its birth registered through admission to the United Nations, but a Constitution is normally required as a baptismal certificate. A nation may exist without one, but there will be doubts concerning the likelihood of it passing through the Pearly Gates into the Heavenly City of political stability. The local nationalist leader in the ex-colonial territory may have no intention of observing constitutionalism or the provisions of the Constitution he may have drafted himself, but he cannot forego the document without smudging his country's credentials of nationhood.

As Constitutions are baptismal certificates to newly-independent nations, so are they marriage contracts for federations. They are convenient and necessary instruments for spelling out the rights and obligations of separate political units that are merging into one State structure. The pie of public authority is sliced up between national and regional governments, and their relationships are prescribed. Constitutions assign some powers to the component units and some to the national government; others are shared or denied to both. The federation may bring together previously independent States or it may simply recognize substantial cultural or historical differences among several geographic areas of an existing State.

In addition to the functions discussed so far, all of which are intended to describe present reality, Constitutions may also be given prospective functions. They may articulate the ideals or the intentions of the communities they serve. Some Constitutions describe social

[16] *Political Works*, Belfords, Clark and Co., Chicago, 1879, p. 33.

or economic aims that are still beyond the grasp of the community. The Indian Constitution does this in portraying the Indian economy as socialist, though implementation of this provision is deferred, for fear its initial effect would be economic disruption. States, such as West Germany, that regard parts of other States as alienated portions of their nations, may include in their Constitutions provisions applicable to the missing territory with full knowledge that they cannot be implemented.

Another form of prospective provision is the type that directs the government to take positive action of one variety or another. Constitutions rarely perform according to expectations, but this type of performance is most difficult of all to dictate in advance. It is much easier to forbid a government to trespass in a given area than to instruct it in the substance of policy formulation or execution. In the area of human rights, for instance, it is much easier for a Constitution effectively to deny the government the power to restrict freedom of speech than to succeed in requiring it to set up printing plants in order that all political groups might have the means to disseminate their opinions. On governments, as on fractious horses, reins are easier than spurs to use effectively.

Because Constitutions are often more difficult to alter than statutes, groups wishing to prevent the easy amendment or repeal of legislative measures will sometimes attempt to include them in Constitutions, even though they do not concern the organization of or limitations on government. A prominent example of this was the Prohibition Amendment in the United States. Another is Article 25a of the Swiss Constitution which forbids the slaughter of animals by drawing blood without previous benumbing. Many American state Constitutions contain similar legislative provisions. Although Constitutions provide a means for this type of measure, it is not properly part of the document. Legislation should not be considered a legitimate function of Constitutions.

H. Conclusion

Written Constitutions, then, are both more and less than the documentary embodiment of constitutionalism in national governmental systems. Constitutionalism, deriving its authority from the belief in transcendent principles of justice and right, controls government by limiting its authority and establishing regular procedures for its operation. Constitutions are frequently used as a means of articulating those limitations. But the effectiveness of the restrictions depends largely on the condition of constitutional consensus and, conversely, limitations may be imposed by consensus and yet not be inscribed in Constitutions. On the other hand, some Constitutions manifest constitutionalism only in appearance, and nearly all perform functions not integrally related to constitutionalism. It is a mistake, therefore, to attribute to Constitutions a more active role in the establishment and maintenance of constitutional government than they do or can perform. Even the best of them are no more than manifestations of constitutionalism and not its generators. In the headnotes introducing the constitutional documents in the following pages, Constitutions and constitutionalism in leading contemporary States will be discussed and related to the general propositions that have been advanced in this essay.

THE UNITED STATES OF AMERICA

AMERICAN CONSTITUTIONALISM*

The American Constitution has survived for more than 170 years with only minor alterations. Only five of those changes affected procedures directly. This suggests a high degree of procedural regularity, despite tremendous changes in the country's area and population and in economic, social, political, international, technological, and communications conditions. In fact, however, the American Constitution has changed more than the stability of the documentary basis indicates. For instance, the mode of designating the President is quite different from that envisaged by the Founders, having been altered by the rise of national political parties and the extension of the suffrage. Also, if one may judge by the professed desire of the Framers to emulate what they believed to be the legitimate British practices of the time and by Alexander Hamilton's effort to establish himself as President Washington's "prime minister", our system has moved from what was an embryonic parliamentary regime to a straight presidential one. During periods of Congressional dominance, such as the "Era of Good Feeling" and the Reconstruction Period, we have come close to practicing the parliamentary principle of executive responsibility to the legislature without departing from the constitutional framework.

Because of the flexibility possible within the terms of the Constitution, we must look behind the document to evaluate the extent to which procedural constitu-

* Because of its ready availability elsewhere, the text of the Constitution of the United States is not included in this book.

tionalism has been observed in the United States. Throughout our history allegations have been made that one or another officer or governmental organ was violating either the documentary or the customary Constitution. Some examples taken at random include the charges that Andrew Jackson was exercising powers not attributable to the Presidency, Woodrow Wilson's claims before he acceded to high political office that Congress and especially Congressional committees had acquired more power than had been intended, and the New Deal allegations that the Supreme Court before 1937 was acting *ultra vires*. Many of the allegations of this sort have had a large measure of validity. The breaches to which they point are evidence of a living, vital, evolving society. But they are not proof of a lack of procedural constitutionalism. Procedural regularity is not stagnation or even rigidity.

In fact, the tendency for political controversies to be cloaked in constitutional arguments is an indication of the pervasiveness and depth of public consensus on the desirability of maintaining established constitutional norms. Furthermore, cogent constitutional arguments can be raised only if a firm constitutional foundation is available as a fulcrum. In other words, the appeal of constitutional arguments depends on the existence of a highly developed sense of procedural constitutionalism. In no major modern country has this type of appeal been as strong as in the United States.

The effectiveness of the maintenance of the line between governmental power and private rights has varied significantly over time and geography, by social and ethnic groups, and from one aspect of liberty to another. In times of stress the area of private right has constricted. Legislation such as Jim Crow laws has interfered with the personal relationships of the inhabitants of some states to an extent that has not been tolerated elsewhere. Furthermore, such laws have restricted the private rights of certain groups of persons (in this case, Negroes) more than others. At some times, such as the recent McCarthyite period, some types of expression, notably that of religion, have been less restricted than others, such as political.

This libertarian aspect of constitutionalism is probably less highly developed in the United States than in Great Britain and certainly less so than in France. Also, it is less deeply implanted in the United States than is procedural constitutionalism. Nevertheless, the general lines between public and private right are quite clearly and rigidly drawn. The departures from this standard, while not uncommon, remain exceptional.

— 3 —

GREAT BRITAIN

A. British Constitutionalism

Both aspects of the concept of constitutionalism are highly developed in the British political consciousness, yet the application of neither has been articulated in a single documentary Constitution. Since before the days of the Magna Carta the English people have jealously defended their rights as subjects. The line between royal (that is, governmental) power and private right has shifted substantially from time to time, but never has it been obliterated. During the past 300 years or so, the expansion of the area of personal, though not economic, liberty has expanded fairly steadily.

Evidence of the importance attached to personal liberty by the British is provided by the continuing effectiveness of the question period in the House of Commons in this matter. An almost certain way to obtain relief for a clear breach—however trivial—of traditional English personal rights is to make it the subject of a question directed against the responsible minister during the daily question period of the House of Commons. Even supporters of the government do not hesitate to defend their constituents through this means when other avenues have failed. In contrast, it is a very rare occasion indeed when the government will alter a general public policy as a result of a parliamentary debate or a question period. The effectiveness of a question period lies in the publicity focused on it by the mass media and thus, ultimately, it depends on the public attitude toward the issue. The British consider arbitrary government more evil than foolish government and are more likely to be roused to enduring hostility by evidence of trespass on private rights than of mistaken policies. Governments act accordingly.

The regularity of procedures in the British system is not so visible. Some procedures are sanctioned by official public documents, but many more derive their authority from nothing more than the consensus of the political elite and the electorate. This is the ultimate sanction for procedures in any constitutional system, but often the consensus is transformed into parchment. The British prefer to leave it largely in the more abstract sphere. More specifically, when the government consciously and deliberately effects a change in constitutional procedure, it usually takes documentary form; but change in Britain more often occurs as the gradual adjustment of practice to meet changing conditions. In the latter case, the changes are rarely ratified by documents. The relationships between monarch, First Lord of the Treasury (now also Prime Minister), and the rank-and-file members of the House of Commons changed drastically from the time of Montesquieu and our Founding Fathers to that of Walter Bagehot in the third quarter of the 19th century, and again between that time and the present. But the changes were not made consciously and deliberately. They resulted from alterations in political society, chiefly the broadening of the franchise, and were rarely made the subject of statutory action. Despite this relative lack of a documentary focus for consensus, disagreement on constitutional interpretation among those responsible for the operation of the political system, on both government and opposition benches, has been rare.

The failure of the British to bring together in one document the principal elements of their constitution makes any selection of constitutional documents somewhat arbitrary. The guiding principle in the selection and abridgement of the documents presented below has been to include those documentary elements, insofar as possible, as are usually contained in a single Constitution. Therefore, I have tried to include the most important provisions of the major constitutional instruments since the Magna Carta that still have validity and significance in expressing the relationship of government to governed and of one governmental organ to another.

B. British Constitutional Documents

1. MAGNA CARTA, 1215

JOHN, by the grace of God, king of England, lord of Ireland, duke of Normandy and Aquitaine, count of Anjou to the archbishops, bishops, abbots, earls, barons, justiciars, foresters, sheriffs, reeves, servants, and all bailiffs and his faithful people greeting. Know that by the suggestion of God and for the good of our soul and those of all our predecessors and of our heirs, to the honor of God and the exaltation of holy church, and the improvement of our kingdom, by the advice of . . . [twenty-seven barons and church lords] . . . and others of our faithful.

1. In the first place we have granted to God, and by this our present charter confirmed, for us and our heirs forever, that the English church shall be free, and shall hold its rights entire and its liberties uninjured; and . . . that the freedom of elections, which is considered to be most important and especially necessary to the English church . . . we will observe and . . . we will shall be observed in good faith by our heirs forever.

We have granted moreover to all free men of our kingdom for us and our heirs forever all the liberties written below . . .

12. No scutage or aid shall be imposed in our kingdom except by the common council of our kingdom, except for the ransoming of our body, for the making of our oldest son a knight, and for once marrying our old-

est daughter, and for these purposes it shall be only a reasonable aid; in the same way it shall be done concerning the aids of the city of London.

13. And the city of London shall have all its ancient liberties and free customs . . . Moreover, we will and grant that all other cities and boroughs and villages and ports shall have all their liberties and free customs.

14. And for holding a common council of the kingdom concerning the assessment of an aid otherwise than in the three cases mentioned above, or concerning the assessment of a scutage we shall cause to be summoned the archbishops, bishops, abbots, earls, and greater barons . . . and . . . all those who hold from us in chief, for a certain day . . . and for a certain place; and in all the letters of that summons, we will express the cause of the summons, and . . . the business shall proceed on the appointed day, on the advice of those who shall be present . . .

17. The common pleas shall not follow our court, but shall be held in some certain place.

18. The recognition of *novel disseisin, mort d'ancestor,* and *darrein presentment* shall be held only in their own counties and in this manner; we, . . . will send two justiciars through each county four times a year, who with four knights of each county, elected by the county, shall hold in the county, and on the day and in the place of the county court, the aforesaid assizes of the county.

19. And if the aforesaid assizes cannot be held within the day of the county court, a sufficient number of knights and freeholders shall remain from those who were present at the county court on that day to give the judgments . . .

20. A free man shall not be fined for a small offence, except in proportion to the measure of the offence; and for a great offence he shall be fined in proportion to the magnitude of the offence, saving his freehold; and a merchant in the same way, saving his merchandise; and the villain shall be fined in the same way, saving his wainage, if he shall be at our mercy; and none of the above fines shall be imposed except by the oaths of honest men of the neighborhood.

21. Earls and barons shall only be fined by their peers, and only in proportion to their offence.

22. A clergyman shall be fined, like those before mentioned, only in proportion to his lay holding . . .

30. No sheriff or bailiff of ours or anyone else shall take horses or wagons of any free man for carrying purposes except on the permission of that free man.

31. Neither we nor our bailiffs will take the wood of another man for castles, or for anything else which we are doing, except by the permission of him to whom the wood belongs.

32. We will not hold the lands of those convicted of a felony for more than a year and a day, after which the lands shall be returned to the lords of the fiefs. . . .

34. The writ which is called *praecipe* shall not be given for the future to anyone concerning any tenement by which a free man can lose his court.

35. There shall be one measure of wine throughout our whole kingdom, and one measure of ale, and one measure of grain, . . . and one width of dyed cloth and of russets and of halbergets . . . ; of weights, moreover it shall be as of measures.

36. Nothing shall henceforth be given or taken for a writ of inquisition concerning life or limbs, but it shall be given freely and not denied. . . .

38. No bailiff for the future shall put anyone to his law on his simple affirmation, without credible witnesses brought for this purpose.

39. No free man shall be taken or imprisoned or dispossessed, or outlawed, or banished, or in any way destroyed, . . . except by the legal judgment of his peers or by the law of the land.

40. To no one will we sell, to no one will we deny, or delay right or justice.

41. All merchants shall be safe and secure in going out from England and coming into England and in remaining and going through England, . . . free from all evil tolls, by the ancient and rightful customs, except in time of war, and if they are of a land at war with us . . .

42. It is allowed henceforth to anyone to go out from our kingdom, and to return, safely and securely,

by land and by water, saving their fidelity to us, except in time of war for some short time, for the common good of the kingdom; excepting persons imprisoned and outlawed according to the law of the realm, and people of a land at war with us . . .

45. We will not make justiciars, constables, sheriffs or bailiffs except of such as know the law of the realm and are well inclined to observe it. . . .

54. No one shall be seized nor imprisoned on the appeal of a woman concerning the death of any one except her husband.

55. All fines which have been imposed unjustly and against the law of the land, and all penalties imposed unjustly and against the law of the land are altogether excused, or will be on the judgment of the twenty-five barons of whom mention is made below in connection with the security of the peace, or on the judgment of the majority of them, along with the aforesaid Stephen, archbishop of Canterbury, if he is able to be present, and others whom he may wish to call for this purpose along with him. . . .

61. Since, moreover, for the sake of God, and for the improvement of our kingdom, and for the better quieting of the hostility sprung up lately between us and our barons, we . . . concede to them the security described below; that is to say, that they shall elect twenty-five barons of the kingdom, whom they will, who ought with all their power to observe, hold, and cause to be observed, the peace and liberties which we have conceded to them, and by this our present charter confirmed to them; in this manner, that if we or our justiciar, or our bailiffs, or any one of our servants shall have done wrong in any way toward any one, or shall have transgressed any of the articles of peace or security, and the wrong shall have been shown to four barons of the aforesaid twenty-five barons, let those four barons come to us . . . laying before us the transgression, and let them ask that we cause that transgression to be corrected without delay. And if we shall not have corrected the transgression . . . within a period of forty days . . . the aforesaid four barons shall refer the matter to the remainder of the twenty-five barons, and let these twenty-

five barons with the whole community of the country distress and injure us in every way they can; that is to say by the seizure of our castles, lands, possessions, and in such other ways as they can until it shall have been corrected according to their judgment, saving our person and that of our queen, and those of our children; and when the correction has been made, let them devote themselves to us as they did before. And let whoever in the country wishes take an oath that in all the above-mentioned measures he will obey the orders of the aforesaid twenty-five barons . . . All those, moreover, in the country who of themselves and their own will are unwilling to take an oath to the twenty-five barons as to distressing and injuring us along with them, we will compel to take the oath by our mandate, as before said. And if any one of the twenty-five barons shall have died or departed from the land or shall in any other way be prevented from taking the above-mentioned action, let the remainder of the aforesaid twenty-five barons choose another in his place . . . In all those things, moreover, which are committed to those five and twenty barons to carry out, if perhaps the twenty-five are present, and some disagreement arises among them about something, or if any of them when they have been summoned are not willing or are not able to be present, let that be considered valid and firm which the greater part of those who are present arrange or command, just as if the whole twenty-five had agreed in this; and let the aforesaid twenty-five swear that they will observe faithfully all the things which are said above, and with all their ability cause them to be observed. And we will obtain nothing from any one, either by ourselves or by another by which any of these concessions and liberties shall be revoked or diminished; and if any such thing shall have been obtained, let it be invalid and void, and we will never use it by ourselves or by another. . . .

63. Wherefore we will and firmly command that the Church of England shall be free, and that the men in our kingdom shall have and hold all the aforesaid liberties, rights and concessions, well and peacefully, freely and quietly, fully and completely, for themselves and their heirs, from us and our heirs, in all things and

places, forever, as before said. It has been sworn, moreover, as well on our part as on the part of the barons, that all these things spoken of above shall be observed in good faith and without any evil intent. Witness the above named and many others. Given by our hand in the meadow which is called Runnymede, between Windsor and Staines, on the fifteenth day of June in the seventeenth year of our reign.

2. PETITION OF RIGHT, 1628

To the King's Most Excellent Majesty.

Humbly show unto our Sovereign Lord the King, the Lords Spiritual and Temporal, and Commons in Parliament assembled, that whereas . . . by . . . the good laws and statutes of this realm, your subjects have inherited this freedom, that they should not be compelled to contribute to any tax, tallage, aid, or other like charge, not set by common consent in Parliament: . . .

II. Yet nevertheless, of late divers commissions . . . have issued, by means whereof your people have been in divers places . . . required to lend certain sums of money unto your Majesty . . .

IV. And in the eight and twentieth year of the reign of King Edward the Third, it was declared and enacted by authority of Parliament, that no man . . . should be put out of his lands or tenements, nor taken, nor imprisoned, nor disherited, nor put to death, without . . . due process of law:

V. Nevertheless . . . divers of your subjects have of late been imprisoned without any cause showed, and when . . . they were brought before your Justices, . . . no cause was certified, but that they were detained by your Majesty's special command, . . . and yet were returned back to several prisons, without being charged with anything to which they might make answer according to the law.

VI. And whereas of late great companies of soldiers and mariners have been dispersed into divers counties . . . and the inhabitants . . . have been compelled to receive them into their houses . . .

VII. And . . . also by authority of Parliament, in

the 25th year of the reign of King Edward the Third, it is declared and enacted, that no man shall be forejudged of life or limb against the form of the Great Charter, and the law of the land . . . ; or by Acts of Parliament . . . nevertheless of late . . . certain persons have been assigned and appointed Commissioners with power and authority to proceed . . . against such soldiers and mariners or other dissolute persons joining with them . . . and them to cause to be executed and put to death, according to the law martial:

VIII. By pretext whereof, some of your Majesty's subjects have been by some of the said Commissioners put to death . . .

IX. And also sundry grievous offenders . . . have escaped the punishments due to them by the laws and statutes of this your realm . . . upon pretence that the said offenders were punishable only by martial law . . .

X. They do therefore humbly pray your Most Excellent Majesty, that no man hereafter be compelled to make or yield any gift, loan, benevolence, tax, or such like charge, without common consent by Act of Parliament; and that none be called to make answer, or take such oath, or to give attendance, or be confined, or otherwise molested or disquieted concerning the same, or for refusal thereof; and that no freeman, in any such manner as is before-mentioned, be imprisoned or detained; and that your Majesty will be pleased to remove the said soldiers and mariners, and that your people may not be so burdened in time to come; and that the aforesaid commissions for proceeding by martial law, may be revoked and annulled; and that hereafter no commissions of like nature may issue forth to any person or persons whatsoever . . .

XI. All which they most humbly pray of your Most Excellent Majesty, as their rights and liberties according to the laws and statutes of this realm . . .

[Which Petition being read the 2nd of June 1628, the King's answer was thus delivered unto it:

The King willeth that right be done according to the laws and customs of the realm; and that the statutes be put in due execution, that his subjects may have no cause to complain of any wrong or oppressions, contrary to their just rights and liberties, to the preservation whereof he holds himself as well obliged as of his prerogative.

On June 7 the answer was given in the accustomed form, *Soit droit fait comme il est desiré*.]

3. HABEAS CORPUS ACT, 1641

Whereas by the Magna Carta many times confirmed in Parliament, it is enacted that no freeman shall be taken or imprisoned, or disseized of his freehold or liberties or free customs, or be outlawed or exiled or otherwise destroyed, and that the King will not pass upon him or condemn him but by lawful judgment of his peers or by the law of the land; and by another statute . . . no man shall be attached by any accusation nor forejudged of life or limb, nor his lands, tenements, goods nor chattels seized into the King's hands against the form of the Great Charter and the law of the land; and by another statute . . . none shall be taken by petition or suggestion made to the King or to his Council, unless it be by indictment or presentment of good and lawful people of the same neighborhood where such deeds be done, in due manner or by process made by writ original at the common law, and that none be put out of his franchise or freehold unless he be duly brought in to answer and forejudged of the same by the course of the law, and if anything be done against the same, it shall be redressed and holden for none; and by another statute . . . no man of what estate or condition soever he be shall be put out of his lands or tenements, nor taken nor imprisoned nor disinherited without being brought in to answer by due process of law; and by another statute . . . it is enacted, that no man be put to answer without presentment before Justices or matter of record, or by due process and writ original according to the old law of the land, and if anything be done to the contrary, it shall be void in law and holden for error; and by another statute . . . all pleas which shall be pleaded in any Courts before any of the King's Justices, or in his other places, or before any of his other ministers, or in the Courts and places of any other Lords within the realm, shall be entered and enrolled in Latin;

and whereas by the statute made in the third year of King Henry the Seventh, power is given to the Chancellor, the Lord Treasurer of England for the time being, and the Keeper of the King's Privy Seal, or two of them, calling unto them a Bishop and a Temporal Lord of the King's most honorable Council, and the two Chief Justices of the King's Bench and Common Pleas for the time being, or other two Justices in their absence, to proceed as in that Act is expressed for the punishment of some particular offences therein mentioned; and by the statute made in the one-and twentieth year of King Henry the Eighth, the President of the Council is associated to join with the Lord Chancellor and other Judges in the said statute of the third year of Henry the Seventh mentioned: but the said Judges have not kept themselves to the points limited by the said statute, but have undertaken to punish where no law doth warrant, and to make decrees for things having no such authority, and to inflict heavier punishments than by any law is warranted;

II. Forasmuch as all matters examinable or determinable before the said Judges, or in the Court commonly called the Star Chamber, may have their proper remedy and redress, and their due punishment and correction, by the common law of the land, and in the ordinary course of justice elsewhere; and forasmuch as the reasons and motives inducing the erection and continuance of that Court do now cease; and the proceedings, censures and decrees of that Court have by experience been found to be an intolerable burden to the subjects, and the means to introduce an arbitrary power and government; and forasmuch as the Council Table hath of late times assumed unto itself a power to intermeddle in civil causes and matters only of private interest between party and party, and have adventured to determine of the estates and liberties of the subject, contrary to the law of the land and the rights and privileges of the subject, by which great and manifold mischiefs and inconveniences have arisen and happened, and much uncertainty by means of such proceedings hath been conceived concerning men's rights and estates: for settling whereof and preventing the like in time to come:

III. Be it ordained and enacted by the authority of this present Parliament, that the said Court commonly called the Star Chamber, and all jurisdiction, power and authority belonging unto or exercised in the same Court, or by any of the Judges, Officers or Ministers thereof, be . . . clearly and absolutely dissolved, taken away, and determined; . . . and that all and every Act and Acts of Parliament . . . by which any jurisdiction, power or authority is given . . . unto the said Court . . . shall . . . be . . . repealed and absolutely revoked and made void.

IV. And be it likewise enacted, that the like jurisdiction now used and exercised in the Court before the President and Council in the Marches of Wales; and also in the Court before the President and Council established in the northern parts; and also in the Court commonly called the Court of the Duchy of Lancaster . . . ; and also in the Court of Exchequer of the County Palatine of Chester . . . ; shall . . . be also repealed and absolutely revoked and made void . . . ; and that from henceforth no court, council, or place of judicature shall be erected, ordained, constituted, or appointed within this realm of England or dominion of Wales, which shall have, use or exercise the same or the like jurisdiction, as is or hath been used, practised or exercised in the said Court of Star Chamber.

V. Be it likewise declared and enacted by authority of this present Parliament, that neither His Majesty nor his Privy Council have or ought to have any jurisdiction, power or authority by English bill, petition, articles, libel, or any other arbitrary way whatsoever, to examine or draw into question, determine or dispose of the lands, tenements, hereditaments, goods or chattels of any the subjects of this kingdom, but that the same ought to be tried and determined in the ordinary Courts of Justice and by the ordinary course of the law.

4. BILL OF RIGHTS, 1689

Whereas the lords spiritual and temporal and commons assembled at Westminster lawfully, fully and freely representing all the estates of the people of this realm, did . . . present unto Their Majesties, . . . William and Mary, . . . a certain declaration . . . in the words following viz.:

Whereas the late king James the Second by the assistance of divers evil counsellors, judges and ministers . . . did endeavour to subvert and extirpate the Protestant religion and the laws and liberties of this kingdom. . . .

And whereas the said late king James the Second having abdicated the government and the throne being thereby vacant, His Highness the prince of Orange . . . did (by the advice of the lords spiritual and temporal and divers principal persons of the commons) cause letters to be written to the lords spiritual and temporal, being Protestants; and other letters to the several counties, cities, universities, boroughs and Cinque ports for the choosing of such persons to represent them, as were of right to be sent to parliament, . . . in order to such an establishment as that their religion, laws and liberties might not again be in danger of being subverted . . .

And thereupon the said lords spiritual and temporal and commons . . . being now assembled in a full and free representative of this nation, taking into their most serious consideration the best means for attaining the ends aforesaid, do in the first place (as their ancestors in like case have usually done) for the vindicating and asserting their ancient rights and liberties, declare:

That the pretended power of suspending of laws or the execution of laws by regal authority without consent of parliament is illegal.

That the pretended power of dispensing with laws or the execution of laws by regal authority as it hath been assumed and exercised of late is illegal.

That the commission for erecting the late court of commissioners for ecclesiastical causes and all other commissions and courts of like nature are illegal and pernicious.

That the levying money for or to the use of the crown by pretence of prerogative without grant of parliament for a longer time or in other manner than the same is or shall be granted is illegal.

That it is the right of the subjects to petition the king and all commitments and prosecutions for such petitioning are illegal.

That the raising or keeping a standing army within the kingdom in time of peace unless it be with consent of parliament is against law.

That the subjects which are Protestants may have arms for their defence suitable to their conditions and as allowed by law.

That election of members of parliament ought to be free.

That the freedom of speech and debates or proceedings in parliament ought not to be impeached or questioned in any court or place out of parliament.

That excessive bail ought not to be required nor excessive fines imposed nor cruel and unusual punishments inflicted.

That jurors ought to be duly impanelled and returned and jurors which pass upon men in trials for high treason ought to be freeholders.

That all grants and promises of fines and forfeitures of particular persons before conviction are illegal and void.

And that for redress of all grievances and for the amending, strengthening and preserving of the laws parliaments ought to be held frequently.

And they do claim, demand and insist upon all and singular the premises as their undoubted rights and liberties and that no declarations, judgments, doings or proceedings to the prejudice of the people in any of the said premises ought in any wise to be drawn hereafter into consequence or example. To which demand of their rights they are particularly encouraged by the declaration of His Highness the prince of Orange as being the only means for obtaining a full redress and remedy therein. Having therefore an entire confidence that His said Highness the prince of Orange will perfect the deliverance so far advanced by him, and will still preserve them from the violation of their rights, which they have here asserted, and from all other attempts upon their religion, rights and liberties, the said lords spiritual and temporal and commons assembled at Westminster do resolve, that William and Mary, prince and princess of Orange, be and be declared king and queen of England, France and Ireland and the dominions thereunto belonging . . .

Upon which Their said Majesties did accept the crown and royal dignity of the kingdoms of England, France and Ireland and the dominions thereunto belonging, according to the resolution and desire of the said lords and commons, contained in the said declaration. And thereupon Their Majesties were pleased, that the said lords spiritual and temporal and commons being the two houses of parliament should continue to sit, and with Their Majesties' royal concurrence make effectual provision for the settlement of the religion, laws and liberties of this kingdom . . . Now in pursuance of the premises, the lords spiritual and temporal and commons in parliament assembled . . . do pray that . . . all and singular the rights and liberties asserted and claimed in the said declaration are the true, ancient and indubitable rights and liberties of the people of this kingdom, and . . . shall be firmly and strictly holden and observed . . . ; and all officers and ministers whatsoever shall serve Their Majesties and their successors according to the same in all times to come. . . .

II. And be it further declared and enacted by the authority aforesaid, that, from and after this present session of parliament, no dispensation by *non obstante* of or to any statute or any part thereof shall be allowed, but that the same shall be held void and of no effect, except a dispensation be allowed of in such statute, and except in such case as shall be specially provided for by one or more bill or bills to be passed during this present session of parliament.

5. THE ACT OF SETTLEMENT, 1701

. . . We Your Majesty's most dutiful and loyal subjects, the lords spiritual and temporal and commons in this present parliament assembled, do beseech Your Majesty that it may be enacted and declared, and be it enacted and declared by the king's most excellent Majesty by and with the advice and consent of the lords spiritual and temporal and commons in this present parliament assembled, and by the authority of the same, that the most excellent princess Sophia . . . be and is hereby declared to be the next in succession in the Protestant line to the imperial crown and dignity of the . . . realms of England, France and Ireland, with the dominions and territories thereunto belonging . . . ; and that from and after the deceases of His said Majesty our now sovereign lord and of Her Royal Highness the princess Anne of Denmark, and for default of issue of the said princess Anne and of His Majesty respectively, the crown and regal government of the said kingdoms of England, France and Ireland and of the dominions thereunto belonging, with the royal state and dignity of the said realms . . . shall be, remain and continue to the said most excellent princess Sophia and the heirs of her body, being Protestants; and thereunto the said lords spiritual and temporal and commons shall and will, in the name of all the people of this realm, most humbly and faithfully submit themselves, their heirs and posterities, and do faithfully promise that after the deceases of His Majesty and Her Royal Highness, and the failure of the heirs of their respective bodies, to stand to, maintain and defend the said princess Sophia and the heirs of her body, being Protestants, according to the limitation and succession of the crown in this act specified and contained, to the utmost of their powers, with their lives and estates, against all persons whatsoever that shall attempt anything to the contrary. . . .

III. Be it enacted by the king's most excellent Majesty, by and with the advice and consent of the lords spiritual and temporal and commons in parliament assembled, and by the authority of the same:

That whosoever shall hereafter come to the possession of this crown shall join in communion with the Church of England as by laws established.

That in case the crown and imperial dignity of this realm shall hereafter come to any person, not being a native of this kingdom of England, this nation be not obliged to engage in any war for the defence of any dominions or territories which do not belong to the crown of England, without consent of parliament.

That no person who shall hereafter come to the possession of this crown shall go out of the dominions of England, Scotland or Ireland, without consent of parliament.

That from and after the time that the further limitation by this act shall take effect, all matters and things relating to the well governing of this kingdom, which are properly cognizable in the privy council by the laws and customs of this realm, shall be transacted there; and all resolutions taken thereupon shall be signed by such of the privy council as shall advise and consent to the same.

That after the said limitation shall take effect as aforesaid, no person born out of the kingdoms of England, Scotland or Ireland or the dominions thereunto belonging (although he be naturalized or made a denizen, except such as are born of English parents) shall be capable to be of the privy council, or a member of either house of parliament, or to enjoy any office or place of trust, either civil or military, or to have any grant of lands, tenements or hereditaments from the crown to himself or to any other or others in trust for him.

That no person who has an office or place of profit under the king or receives a pension from the crown shall be capable of serving as a member of the house of commons.

That after the said limitation shall take effect as aforesaid, judges commissions be made *quam diu se bene gesserint,* and their salaries ascertained and established, but upon the address of both houses of parliament it may be lawful to remove them.

That no pardon under the great seal of England be pleadable to an impeachment by the commons in parliament.

IV. And whereas the laws of England are the birthright of the people thereof, and all the kings and queens who shall ascend the throne of this realm ought to administer the government of the same according to the said laws, and all their officers and ministers ought to serve them respectively according to the same; the said lords spiritual and temporal and commons do therefore further humbly pray, that all the laws and statutes of this realm for securing the established religion and the rights and liberties of the people thereof, and all other laws and statutes of the same now in force, may be ratified and confirmed, and the same are by His Majesty, by and with the advice and consent of the said lords spiritual and temporal and commons, and by authority of the same, ratified and confirmed accordingly.

6. THE ACT OF UNION WITH SCOTLAND, 1707

Most gracious sovereign, . . .

ART. I. The two kingdoms of England and Scotland shall upon the first day of May which shall be in the year one thousand seven hundred and seven, and forever after, be united into one kingdom by the name of Great Britain; and that the ensigns armorial of the said United Kingdom be such as Her Majesty shall appoint, and the crosses of St. George and St. Andrew be conjoined in such manners as Her Majesty shall think fit, and used in all flags, banners, standards and ensigns, both at sea and land.

ART. II. That the succession to the monarchy of the United Kingdom of Great Britain and of the dominions thereto belonging after Her most sacred Majesty and in default of issue of Her Majesty be, remain and continue to the most excellent princess Sophia, electress and duchess dowager of Hanover, and the heirs of her body, being Protestants, upon whom the crown of England is settled by . . . [The Act of Settlement, 1701].

ART. III. That the United Kingdom of Great Britain be represented by one and the same parliament to be styled the Parliament of Great Britain.

ART. IV. That all the subjects of the United Kingdom of Great Britain shall from and after the union have full freedom and intercourse of trade and navigation to and from any port or place within the said United Kingdom and the dominions and plantations thereunto belonging; and that there be a communication of all other rights, privileges and advantages, which do or may belong to the subjects of either kingdom, except where it is otherwise expressly agreed in these articles . . .

ART. XVIII. That the laws concerning regulation of trade, customs and such excises, to which Scotland is by virtue of this treaty to be liable, be the same in Scotland from and after the union as in England; and that all other laws in use within the kingdom of Scotland do after the union and notwithstanding thereof remain in the same force as before, (except such as are contrary to or inconsistent with this treaty), but alterable by the parliament of Great Britain; with this difference betwixt the laws concerning public right, policy and civil government and those which concern private right, that laws which concern public right, policy, and civil government may be made the same throughout the whole United Kingdom, but that no alteration be made in laws which concern private right, except for evident utility of the subjects within Scotland.

ART. XIX. That the Court of Session or College of Justice do after the union, and notwithstanding thereof, remain in all time coming within Scotland, as it is now constituted by the laws of that kingdom, . . . and that all inferior courts within the said limits do remain subordinate, as they are now, to the supreme courts of justice within the same, in all time coming; and that no causes in Scotland be cognizable by the courts of chancery, queen's bench, common pleas, or any other court in Westminster Hall; . . .

ART. XII. That by virtue of this treaty, of the peers of Scotland at the time of the union sixteen shall be the number to sit and vote in the house of lords, and forty-five the number of representatives of Scotland in the house of commons of the parliament of Great Britain . . .

And further Her Majesty with advice aforesaid expressly declares and statutes, that none of the subjects of this kingdom shall be liable to, but all and every one of them forever free of any oath, test or subscription within this kingdom, contrary to or inconsistent with the foresaid true Protestant religion and Presbyterian church government, worship and discipline, as above established; and that the same within the bounds of this church and kingdom shall never be imposed upon or required of them in any sort; and lastly, that after the decease of Her present Majesty (whom God long preserve) the sovereign succeeding to her in the royal government of the kingdom of Great Britain shall in all time coming,

at his or her accession to the crown, swear and sub-
scribe, that they shall inviolably maintain and preserve
the foresaid settlement of the true Protestant religion,
with the government, worship, discipline, right and privileges of this church, as above established by the laws of
this kingdom, in prosecution of the Claim of Right. . . .

7. PARLIAMENT ACT, 1911

(As Amended in 1949)

Whereas it is expedient that provision should be made
for regulating the relations between the two Houses of
Parliament:

And whereas it is intended to substitute for the House
of Lords as it at present exists a Second Chamber constituted on a popular instead of hereditary basis, but
such substitution cannot be immediately brought into
operation:

And whereas provision will require hereafter to be
made by Parliament in a measure effecting such substitution for limiting and defining the powers of the new Second Chamber, but it is expedient to make such provision
as in this Act appears for restricting the existing powers
of the House of Lords:

Be it therefore enacted . . .

I.—(1) If a Money Bill, having been passed by the
House of Commons, and sent up to the House of Lords
at least one month before the end of the session, is not
passed by the House of Lords without amendment within
one month after it is so sent up to that House, the Bill
shall, unless the House of Commons direct to the contrary, be presented to His Majesty and become an Act
of Parliament on the Royal Assent being signified, notwithstanding that the House of Lords have not consented to the Bill.

(2) A Money Bill means a Public Bill which in the
opinion of the Speaker of the House of Commons contains only provisions dealing with all or any of the following subjects, namely, the imposition, repeal, remis-
sion, alteration, or regulation of taxation; the imposition for the payment of debt or other financial purposes
of charges on the Consolidated Fund, or on money pro-

vided by Parliament, or the variation or repeal of any
such charges; supply; the appropriation, receipt, custody, issue or audit of accounts of public money; the
raising or guarantee of any loan or the repayment
thereof; or subordinate matters incidental to those subjects or any of them . . .

(3) There shall be endorsed on every Money
Bill when it is sent up to the House of Lords and when it
is presented to His Majesty for assent the certificate of
the Speaker of the House of Commons signed by him
that it is a Money Bill. Before giving his certificate, the
Speaker shall consult, if practicable, two members to be
appointed from the Chairman's Panel at the beginning
of each Session by the Committee of Selection.

2.—(1) If any Public Bill (other than a Money Bill
or a Bill containing any provision to extend the maximum duration of Parliament beyond five years) is
passed by the House of Commons in two successive sessions (whether of the same Parliament or not), and, having been sent up to the House of Lords at least one
month before the end of the session, is rejected by the
House of Lords in each of those sessions, that Bill shall,
on its rejection for the second time by the House of
Lords, unless the House of Commons direct to the contrary, be presented to His Majesty and become an Act
of Parliament on the Royal Assent being signified
thereto, notwithstanding that the House of Lords have
not consented to the Bill: Provided that this provision
shall not take effect unless one year has elapsed between
the date of the second reading in the first of those sessions of the Bill in the House of Commons and the date
on which it passes the House of Commons in the second
of those sessions . . .

(3) A Bill shall be deemed to be rejected by the
House of Lords if it is not passed by the House of Lords
either without amendment or with such amendments
only as may be agreed to by both Houses.

(4) A Bill shall be deemed to be the same Bill as a
former Bill sent up to the House of Lords in the preceding session if, when it is sent up to the House of
Lords, it is identical with the former Bill or contains
only such alterations as are certified by the Speaker of

the House of Commons to be necessary owing to the time which has elapsed since the date of the former Bill, or to represent any amendments which have been made by the House of Lords in the former Bill in the preceding session, and any amendments which are certified by the Speaker to have been made by the House of Lords in the second session and agreed to by the House of Commons shall be inserted in the Bill as presented for Royal Assent in pursuance of this section:

Provided that the House of Commons may, if they think fit, on the passage of such a Bill through the House in the second session, suggest any further amendments without inserting the amendments in the Bill, and any such suggested amendments shall be considered by the House of Lords, and, if agreed to by that House, shall be treated as amendments made by the House of Lords and agreed to by the House of Commons; but the exercise of this power by the House of Commons shall not affect the operation of this section in the event of the Bill being rejected by the House of Lords.

3. Any certificate of the Speaker of the House of Commons given under this Act shall be conclusive for all purposes, and shall not be questioned in any court of law.

5. In this Act the expression "Public Bill" does not include any Bill for confirming a Provisional Order.

6. Nothing in this Act shall diminish or qualify the existing rights and privileges of the House of Commons.

7. Five years shall be substituted for seven years as the time fixed for the maximum duration of Parliament under the Septennial Act, 1715.

8. RE-ELECTION OF MINISTERS ACT, 1919

1.—(1) Notwithstanding anything in any Act, a member of the Commons House of Parliament shall not vacate his seat by reason only of his acceptance of an office of profit if that office is an office the holder of which is capable of being elected to, or sitting or voting in, that House, and if such acceptance has taken place within nine months after the issue of a proclamation summoning a new Parliament:

Provided that this section shall not . . . affect the

provisions of any Act imposing a limit on the number of Secretaries or Under Secretaries of State who may sit and vote in the Commons House of Parliament.

(2) Where by virtue of this section a member of the Commons House of Parliament does not vacate his seat by reason of his acceptance of any of the offices mentioned in Schedule H. of the Representation of the People Act, 1867, and Schedule H. of the Representation of the People (Scotland) Act, 1868, and Schedule E. of the Representation of the People (Ireland) Act, 1868, as amended by any subsequent enactment, he shall, for the purposes of section fifty-two, section fifty-one, and section eleven of those Acts, respectively, be treated as if he had been returned as a member to serve in Parliament since the acceptance by him of such office. . . .

2.—Where, before or after the passing of this Act, a member of His Majesty's Privy Council has been or is appointed to be a Minister of the Crown at a salary, without any other office being assigned to him, he shall not by reason thereof be deemed to have been or to be incapable of being elected to or of sitting or voting in the Commons House of Parliament, and the office of such Minister shall be deemed to be an office included in the above-mentioned schedules:

Provided that not more than three Ministers to whom this section applies shall sit as members of that House at the same time. . . .

9. MINISTERS OF THE CROWN ACT, 1937

1.—(1) The annual salaries payable—

(a) to each of the Ministers of the Crown named in Part I of the First Schedule to this Act, shall . . . be five thousand pounds;

(b) to each of the Ministers of the Crown named in Part II of the said Schedule, shall be three thousand pounds;

(c) to the Minister of the Crown named in Part III of the said Schedule, shall be two thousand pounds.

(2) . . . the annual salaries payable to the Parliamentary Under-Secretaries to the Departments of State shall—

(a) in the case of the Parliamentary Secretary to the

Treasury, be three thousand pounds, and in the case of the Financial Secretary to the Treasury, be two thousand pounds;

(b) in the case of the Secretary for Mines and of the Secretary of the Department of Overseas Trade, be two thousand pounds each;

(c) in the case of each of the Parliamentary Under-Secretaries to the Departments of State specified in the Second Schedule to this Act, other than the Parliamentary Secretaries mentioned in the last foregoing paragraph, be fifteen hundred pounds:

(d) in the case of the Assistant Postmaster-General, be twelve hundred pounds:

(3) Subject to the provisions of this Act as to number, the annual salaries payable to each of the Junior Lords of the Treasury shall be one thousand pounds.

2.—(1) The number of persons holding office as Secretary of State to whom salaries may be paid under this Act shall not exceed eight.

(2) The number of Parliamentary Under-Secretaries to the Departments of State to whom salaries may be paid under this Act shall—

(a) in the case of the Treasury, not exceed two;

(b) in the case of the Board of Trade, not exceed three, including the Secretary for Mines and the Secretary of the Department of Overseas Trade;

(c) in the case of the Foreign Office, of the War Office, and of the Admiralty, not exceed two;

(d) in the case of any other Department of State mentioned in the Second Schedule to this Act, and in the case of the Post Office, not exceed one.

(3) The number of the Junior Lords of the Treasury to whom salaries may be paid under this Act shall not exceed five.

3.—(1) If and so long as any Minister of the Crown to whom this section applies is a member of the Cabinet, there shall be paid to him an additional salary of such amount as together with the salary payable to him in respect of the office held by him will amount to five thousand pounds a year.

(3) This section applies to any Minister of the Crown named in Part II of the First Schedule to this Act . . .

4.—(1) There shall be paid to the person who is Prime Minister and First Lord of the Treasury an annual salary of ten thousand pounds.

(2) Any person who, . . . has been Prime Minister . . . shall be entitled to a pension of two thousand pounds a year . . .

5.—There shall be paid to the Leader of the Opposition an annual salary of two thousand pounds . . .

6.—(1) Subject to the provisions of this Act as to the payment of additional salaries to certain Cabinet Ministers, a person to whom any salary is payable under this Act, shall be entitled to receive only one such salary . . .

(2) No person in receipt of a salary or pension under this Act shall be entitled to receive any . . . salary or allowance in respect of his membership of the House of Commons.

7.—(1) The salaries payable under this Act, except that payable to the Leader of the Opposition, shall be paid out of moneys provided by Parliament.

(2) The salary payable under this Act to the Leader of the Opposition, and any pension payable under this Act to a person who has been Prime Minister and First Lord of the Treasury, shall be . . . payable out of the Consolidated Fund of the United Kingdom . . .

8.—The amount specified in this Act as being the amount of any salary payable thereunder out of moneys provided by Parliament shall be taken to be the maximum amount so payable and accordingly . . . any . . . salary . . . may be of a less amount than that so specified.

9.—(1) . . . no person to whom a salary is payable under this Act shall by reason of his being the holder of the office or place in respect of which such a salary is payable, be rendered incapable of being elected, or of sitting and voting, as a member of the House of Commons:

Provided that—

(a) the number of persons entitled to sit and vote in that House while they are Ministers of the Crown named in Part I of the First Schedule to this Act shall not exceed fifteen;

(b) the number of persons entitled to sit and vote in

that House while they are Ministers of the Crown named in Part II of the said Schedule shall not exceed three; and

(c) the number of persons entitled to sit and vote in that House while they are Parliamentary Under-Secretaries shall not exceed twenty.

(2) If at any time the number of persons who are members of the House of Commons while they are Ministers of the Crown . . . or . . . Parliamentary Under-Secretaries, exceeds the number respectively entitled under this section to sit and vote in that House, the election of those members shall not be invalidated by reason of the excess, but of the number none except any who held his office and was a member of that House before the excess occurred, shall sit or vote therein until the number of Ministers of the Crown . . . or of Parliamentary Under-Secretaries, as the case may be, who are members of the House of Commons has been reduced, by death, resignation or otherwise, to the number entitled under this section to sit and vote in that House.

(3) If any Minister of the Crown . . . or any Parliamentary Under-Secretary sits or votes in the House of Commons at a time when he is not entitled to do so by virtue of this section he shall be liable to a penalty not exceeding five hundred pounds for each day on which he so sits or votes.

10.—(1) In this Act unless the context otherwise requires the following expressions have the meanings hereby respectively assigned to them, that is to say:—

"Junior Lords of the Treasury" means the Lords Commissioners of the Treasury other than the First Lord and the Chancellor of the Exchequer;

"Leader of the Opposition" means that member of the House of Commons who is for the time being the Leader in that House of the party in opposition to His Majesty's Government having the greatest numerical strength in that House;

"Parliamentary Under-Secretary" means the Parliamentary Secretary and the Financial Secretary to the Treasury, any Parliamentary Under-Secretary of State, the Parliamentary and Financial Secretary to the Admiralty, the Financial Secretary of the War Office, the Civil Lord of the Admiralty, the Parliamentary Secretaries to the Departments of State . . . and the Assistant Postmaster-General; but does not include any Parliamentary Secretary to whom no salary is payable.

(2) For the purposes of this Act, the Secretary of the Department of Overseas Trade shall be deemed to be a Parliamentary Secretary to the Board of Trade, . . .

(3) If any doubt arises as to which is or was at any material time the party in opposition to His Majesty's Government having the greatest numerical strength in the House of Commons, or as to who is or was at any material time the leader in that House of such a party, the question shall be decided for the purposes of this Act by the Speaker of the House of Commons, and his decision, certified in writing under his hand, shall be final and conclusive . . .

Part I. Chancellor of the Exchequer, Secretaries of State, First Lord of the Admiralty, President of the Board of Trade, Minister of Agriculture and Fisheries, President of the Board of Education, Minister of Health, Minister of Labour, Minister of Transport, Minister for the Co-ordination of Defence.

Part II. Lord President of the Council, Lord Privy Seal, Postmaster-General, First Commissioner of Works.

Part III. Minister of Pensions.

10. EMERGENCY POWERS (DEFENCE) ACT, 1939

1.—(1) Subject to the provisions of this section, His Majesty may by Order in Council make such Regulations (in this Act referred to as "Defence Regulations") as appear to him to be necessary or expedient for securing the public safely, the defence of the realm, the maintenance of public order and the efficient prosecution of any war in which His Majesty may be engaged, and for maintaining supplies and services essential to the life of the community.

(2) Without prejudice to the generality of the powers conferred by the preceding subsection, Defence Regulations may, so far as appears to His Majesty in Council to be necessary or expedient for any of the purposes mentioned in that subsection,—

(a) make provision for the apprehension, trial and punishment of persons offending against the Regulations, and for the detention of persons whose detention appears to the Secretary of State to be expedient in the interests of the public safety or the defence of the realm;

(b) authorise—

(i) the taking of possession or control, on behalf of His Majesty, of any property or undertaking;

(ii) the acquisition, on behalf of His Majesty, of any property other than land;

(c) authorise the entering and search of any premises; and

(d) provide for amending any enactment, for suspending the operation of any enactment, and for applying any enactment with or without modification.

(3) Defence Regulations may provide for empowering such authorities, persons or classes of persons as may be specified in the Regulations to make orders, rules and byelaws for any of the purposes for which such Regulations are authorised by this Act to be made, and may contain such incidental and supplementary provisions as appear to His Majesty in Council to be necessary or expedient for the purposes of the Regulations.

(4) A Defence Regulation, and any order, rule or byelaw duly made in pursuance of such a Regulation, shall have effect notwithstanding anything inconsistent therewith contained in any enactment other than this Act or in any instrument having effect by virtue of any enactment other than this Act.

(5) Nothing in this section shall authorise the imposition of any form of compulsory naval, military or air force service or any form of industrial conscription, or the making of provision for the trial by courts martial of persons not being persons subject to the Naval Discipline Act, to military law or to the Air Force Act . . .

2.—(1) The Treasury may by order provide for imposing and recovering, in connection with any scheme of control contained in or authorised by Defence Regulations, such charges as may be specified in the order; and any such order may be varied or revoked by a subsequent order of the Treasury . . .

(3) Any such order as aforesaid shall be laid before the Common House of Parliament as soon as may be after it is made . . .

(4) Any such order as aforesaid imposing or increasing a charge shall cease to have effect on the expiration of the period of twenty-eight days beginning with the day on which the order is made, unless at some time before the expiration of that period it has been approved by a resolution of the Commons House of Parliament, without prejudice, however, to the validity of anything previously done under the order or to the making of a new order.

In reckoning any period of twenty-eight days for the purposes of this subsection, no account shall be taken of any time during which Parliament is dissolved or prorogued, or during which the Commons House is adjourned for more than four days. . . .

6.—(1) If, as respects any proceedings before a court (whether instituted before or after the commencement of this Act), the court is satisfied that it is expedient, in the interests of the public safety or the defence of the realm so to do, the court—

(a) may give directions that, throughout, or during any part of, the proceedings, such persons or classes of persons as the court may determine shall be excluded;

(b) may give directions prohibiting or restricting the disclosure of information with respect to the proceedings . . .

8.—(1) Every Order in Council containing Defence Regulations shall be laid before Parliament as soon as may be after it is made . . .

(2) If either House of Parliament, within the next twenty-eight days on which that House has sat after such an Order in Council as aforesaid is laid before it, resolves that the Order be annulled, the Order shall thereupon cease to have effect except as respects things previously done or omitted to be done, without prejudice, however, to the making of a new Order.

(3) Any power conferred by the preceding provisions

of this Act to make an Order in Council shall be construed as including a power to vary or revoke the Order.

9.—The powers conferred by or under this Act shall be in addition to, and not in derogation of, the powers exercisable by virtue of the prerogative of the Crown. . . .

11.—(1) Subject to the provisions of this section, this Act shall continue in force for the period of two years beginning with the date of the passing of this Act, and shall then expire:

Provided that, if at any time while this Act is in force, an address is presented to His Majesty by each House of Parliament praying that this Act should be continued in force for a further period of one year from the time at which it would otherwise expire, His Majesty may by Order in Council direct that this Act shall continue in force for that further period.

(2) Notwithstanding anything in the preceding subsection, if His Majesty by Order in Council declares that the emergency that was the occasion of the passing of this Act has come to an end, this Act shall expire at the end of the day on which the Order is expressed to come into operation.

(3) The expiry of this Act shall not affect the operation thereof as respects things previously done or omitted to be done. . . .

1940 AMENDMENT

1.—(1) The powers conferred on His Majesty by the Emergency Powers (Defence) Act, 1939, . . . shall, notwithstanding anything in that Act, include power by Order in Council to make such Defence Regulations making provision for requiring persons to place themselves, their services, and their property at the disposal of His Majesty, as appear to him to be necessary or expedient for securing the public safety, the defence of the Realm, the maintenance of public order, or the efficient prosecution of any war in which His Majesty may be engaged, or for maintaining supplies or services essential to the life of the community.

11. STATUTORY INSTRUMENTS ACT, 1946

1.—(1) Where by this Act or any Act passed after the

commencement of this Act power to make, confirm or approve orders, rules, regulations or other subordinate legislation is conferred on His Majesty in Council or on any Minister of the Crown then, if the power is expressed—

(a) in the case of a power conferred on His Majesty, to be exercisable by Order in Council;

(b) in the case of a power conferred on a Minister of the Crown, to be exercisable by statutory instrument, any document by which that power is exercised shall be known as a "statutory instrument" and the provisions of this Act shall apply thereto accordingly.

(2) Where by any Act passed before the commencement of this Act power to make statutory rules within the meaning of the Rules Publication Act, 1893, was conferred on any rule-making authority within the meaning of that Act, any document by which that power is exercised after the commencement of this Act shall, save as is otherwise provided by regulations made under this Act, be known as a "statutory instrument" and the provisions of this Act shall apply thereto accordingly.

2.—(1) Immediately after the making of any statutory instrument, it shall be sent to the King's printer of Acts of Parliament and numbered in accordance with regulations made under this Act, and except in such cases as may be provided by any Act passed after the commencement of this Act or prescribed by regulations made under this Act, copies thereof shall as soon as possible be printed and sold by the King's printer of Acts of Parliament. . . .

4.—(1) Where by this Act or any Act passed after the commencement of this Act any statutory instrument is required to be laid before Parliament after being made, a copy of the instrument shall be laid before each House of Parliament and, subject as hereinafter provided, shall be so laid before the instrument comes into operation:

Provided that if it is essential that any such instrument should come into operation before copies thereof can be so laid as aforesaid, the instrument may be made so as to come into operation before it has been so laid; and where any statutory instrument comes into operation before it is laid before Parliament, notification shall forthwith be sent to the Lord Chancellor and to the Speaker of the House of Commons drawing attention to the fact that copies of the instrument have yet to be laid before Parliament and explaining why such copies were not so laid before the instrument came into operation. . . .

5.—(1) Where by this Act or any Act passed after the commencement of this Act, it is provided that any statutory instrument hall be subject to annulment in pursuance of resolution of either House of Parliament, the instrument shall be laid before Parliament after being made . . . and if either House, within the period of forty days beginning with the day on which a copy thereof is laid before it, resolves that an Address be presented to His Majesty praying that the instrument be annulled, no further proceedings shall be taken thereunder after the date of the resolution, and His Majesty may by Order in Council revoke the instrument, so however, that any such resolution and revocation shall be without prejudice to the validity of anything previously done under the instrument or to the making of a new statutory instrument.

(2) Where any Act passed before the date of the commencement of this Act contains provisions requiring that any Order in Council or other document made in exercise of any power conferred by that or any other Act shall be laid before Parliament after being made and shall cease to be in force or may be annulled, as the case may be, if within a specified period either House presents an address to His Majesty or passes a resolution to that effect, then, subject to the provisions of any Order in Council made under this Act, any statutory instrument made in exercise of the said power shall by virtue of this Act be subject to annulment in pursuance of a resolution of either House of Parliament and the provisions of the last foregoing subsection shall apply thereto accordingly in substitution for any such provisions as aforesaid contained in the Act passed before the said date.

6.—(1) Where by this Act or any Act passed after the commencement of this Act it is provided that a draft of any statutory instrument shall be laid before Parliament, but the Act does not prohibit the making of the instrument without the approval of Parliament, then, in the case of an Order in Council the draft shall not be submitted to His Majesty in Council, and in any other case the statutory instrument shall not be made, until after the expiration of a period of forty days beginning with the day on which a copy of the draft is laid before each House of Parliament, or, if such copies are laid on different days, with the later of the two days, and if within that period either House resolves that the draft be not submitted to His Majesty or that the statutory instrument be not made, as the case may be, no further proceedings shall be taken thereon, but without prejudice to the laying before Parliament of a new draft.

(2) Where any Act passed before the date of the commencement of this Act contains provisions requiring that a draft of any Order in Council or other document to be made in exercise of any power conferred by that or any other Act shall be laid before Parliament before being submitted to His Majesty, or before being made, as the case may be, and that it shall not be so submitted or made if within a specified period either House presents an address to His Majesty or passes a resolution to that effect, then, subject to the provisions of any Order in Council made under this Act, a draft of any statutory instrument made in exercise of the said power shall by virtue of this Act be laid before Parliament and the provisions of the last foregoing subsection shall apply thereto accordingly in substitution for any such provisions as aforesaid contained in the Act passed before the said date.

7.—(1) In reckoning for the purposes of either of the last two foregoing sections any period of forty days, no account shall be taken of any time during which Parliament is dissolved or prorogued or during which both Houses are adjourned for more than four days.

(2) In relation to any instrument required by any Act, whether passed before or after the commencement of this Act, to be laid before the House of Commons only, the provisions of the last three foregoing sections shall have effect as if references to that House

were therein substituted for references to Parliament and for references to either House and each House thereof.

(3) The provisions of sections four and five of this Act shall not apply to any statutory instrument being an order which is subject to special Parliamentary procedure, or to any other instrument which is required to be laid before Parliament, or before the House of Commons, for any period before it comes into operation.

8.—(1) The Treasury may, with the concurrence of the Lord Chancellor and the Speaker of the House of Commons, by statutory instrument make regulations for the purposes of this Act, and such regulations may, in particular:—

(a) provide for the different treatment of instruments which are of the nature of a public Act, and of those which are of the nature of a local and personal or private Act;

(b) make provision as to the numbering, printing, and publication of statutory instruments including provision for postponing the numbering of any such instrument which does not take effect until it has been approved by Parliament, or by the House of Commons, until the instrument has been so approved;

(c) provide with respect to any classes or descriptions of statutory instrument that they shall be exempt, either altogether or to such extent as may be determined by or under the regulations, from the requirement of being printed and of being sold by the King's printer of Acts of Parliament, or from either of those requirements;

(d) determine the classes of cases in which the exercise of a statutory instrument by any rule-making authority constitutes or does not constitute the making of such a statutory rule as is referred to in subsection (2) of section one of this Act, and provide for the exclusion from that subsection of any such classes;

(e) provide for the determination by a person or persons nominated by the Lord Chancellor and the Speaker of the House of Commons of any question—

(i) as to the numbering, printing, or publication of any statutory instrument or class or description of such instruments:

(ii) whether or to what extent any statutory instrument or class or description of such instruments is, under the regulations, exempt from any such requirement as is mentioned in paragraph (c) of this subsection:

(iii) whether any statutory instrument or class or description of such instruments is in the nature of a public Act or of a local and personal or private Act:

(iv) whether the exercise of any power conferred by an Act passed before the commencement of this Act is or is not the exercise of a power to make a statutory rule.

(2) Every statutory instrument made under this section shall be subject to annulment in pursuance of a resolution of either House of Parliament.

9.—(1) If with respect to any power to confirm or approve orders, rules, regulations or other subordinate legislation conferred on a Minister of the Crown by any Act passed before the commencement of this Act, it appears to His Majesty in Council that, notwithstanding that the exercise of that power did not constitute the making of a statutory rule within the meaning of the Rules Publication Act, 1893, it is expedient that the provisions of this Act should apply to documents by which that power is exercised, His Majesty may by Order in Council direct that any document by which that power is exercised after such date as may be specified in the Order shall be known as a "statutory instrument" and the provisions of this Act shall apply thereto accordingly.

(2) If with respect to any Act passed before the commencement of this Act it appears to His Majesty in Council that by reason of the exceptional nature of any provisions of that Act the application of subsection (2) of section five or subsection (2) of section six of this Act to statutory instruments made under any provisions of that Act would be inexpedient, His Majesty may by Order in Council direct that those subsections shall not apply to statutory instruments made under those provisions, or shall apply thereto subject to such modifications as may be specified in the Order.

(3) A draft of any Order in Council proposed to be

made under this section shall be laid before Parliament. . . .

11.—(1) For the purposes of this Act, any power to make, confirm or approve orders, rules, regulations or other subordinate legislation conferred on the Treasury, the Admiralty, the Board of Trade or any other government department shall be deemed to be conferred on the Minister of the Crown in charge of that department.

(2) If any question arises whether any board, commissioners or other body on whom any such power as aforesaid is conferred are a government department within the meaning of this section, or what Minister of the Crown is in charge of them, that question shall be referred to and determined by the Treasury.

12.—(1) The Rules Publication Act, 1893, is hereby repealed.

REPRESENTATION OF THE PEOPLE ACT, 1948

1.—(1) Subject to any Order in Council hereafter made under the House of Commons (Redistribution of Seats) Act, 1944, there shall for the purpose of parliamentary elections be the county and borough constituencies, each returning a single member, which are described in the First Schedule to this Act, and no other constituencies.

(2) The persons entitled to vote as electors at a parliamentary election in any constituency shall be those resident there on the qualifying date who, on that date and on the date of the poll, are British subjects of full age and not subject to any legal incapacity to vote:

Provided that a person shall not be entitled to vote as an elector in any constituency unless registered there in the register of parliamentary electors to be used at the election nor, at a general election, to vote as an elector in more than one constituency.

(3) The qualifying date for parliamentary elections shall be determined by reference to the date fixed for the poll as follows:—

(a) in Great Britain—

(i) where the date fixed for the poll is between the fifteenth day of March and the second day of October in any year, the qualifying date shall be, in England and Wales, the twentieth day of the preceding November and, in Scotland, the first day of the preceding December;

(ii) where the date fixed for the poll is between the first day of October in any year and the sixteenth day of the following March, the qualifying date shall in all parts of Great Britain be the fifteenth day of the preceding June;

(b) in Northern Ireland (subject to the following provisions of this Act)—

(i) where the date fixed for the poll is between the first day of April and the second day of October in any year, the qualifying date shall be the thirty-first day of October in the preceding year;

(ii) where the date fixed for the poll is between the first day of October in any year and the second day of the following April, the qualifying date shall be the thirtieth day of the preceding April. . . .

[Paragraphs 2 through 13 deal with details of residence requirements, registration, absentee voting, etc.]

14.—(1) Where, after the counting of the votes by the returning officer (including any re-count) is completed, an equality of votes is found to exist between any candidates at a parliamentary election in any constituency, and the addition of a vote would entitle any of those candidates to be declared elected, the returning officer shall not be entitled to a casting vote but shall forthwith decide between those candidates by lot and proceed as if the candidate on whom the lot falls had received an additional vote. [Paragraphs 15 through 20 deal with electoral deposits, election officers, etc. Part II contains general provisions for local government elections, Part III regulates the conduct of elections and election campaigns, Parts IV and V contain special provisions for local government elections, and Part VI contains supplemental provisions.]

LIFE PEERAGES ACT, 1958

Be it enacted by the Queen's most Excellent Majesty, by and with the advice and consent of the Lords Spiritual and Temporal, and Commons, in this present Parliament assembled, and by the authority of the same, as follows:—

1.—(1) Without prejudice to Her Majesty's powers as to the appointment of Lords of Appeal in Ordinary, Her Majesty shall have power by letters patent to confer on any person a peerage for life having the incidents specified in subsection (2) of this section.

(2) A peerage conferred under this section shall, during the life of the person on whom it is conferred, entitle him—

      (a) to rank as a baron under such style as may be appointed by the letters patent; and

      (b) subject to subsection (4) of this section, to receive writs of summons to attend the House of Lords and sit and vote therein accordingly,

and shall expire on his death.

(3) A life peerage may be conferred under this section on a woman.

(4) Nothing in this section shall enable any person to receive a writ of summons to attend the House of Lords, or to sit and vote in that House, at any time when disqualified therefor by law . . .

— 4 —

FRANCE

A. French Constitutionalism

Since 1789 France has developed a very keen sensitivity to the need for proscription of governmental power. There have been significant periods of time, such as the two Napoleonic empires and the Vichy interlude of World War II, when the proscriptions were conspicuously violated by the authorities. Nevertheless, the close circumscription of the power of the State has been considered legitimate and natural by the French for well over a century and a half. In fact, this aspect of constitutionalism has become more widely accepted and highly developed in France than in perhaps any other western constitutional state. The attitude that the State is the enemy of the individual citizen and is to be thwarted and its power evaded in almost any manner short of armed force is deeply implanted in the French national character. This has contributed to the growth of France as a stronghold of personal liberty. It has also produced ill-disciplined civic behavior that has made the French one of the least governable of Western nations. This was particularly evident during the Third and Fourth Republic, but Petain's Vichy and de Gaulle's Fifth Republic have been able to impose little more than a veneer of authority over a basically unchanged population.

Both the Vichy State and the de Gaulle Republic framed constitutional documents to legitimize the concentration of effective authority in the hands of one man. Both originally included provisions in the documents for some dispersion of this power. The former failed to promulgate the promised Constitution that would have accomplished this. In the latter, the restraining pro-

visions of the Constitution have been consistently ignored or subverted when it has suited General de
Gaulle's purposes. Legitimacy resides in the person of
Charles de Gaulle. He has been clothed in the garments of
constitutionalism, but it is he who gives form and vitality
to them. The substance of his authority does not emanate
from them. A close reading of the Constitution will
make clear how the clothes have been cut to de Gaulle's
measure. For instance, Article 16 places in his hands virtually unlimited power over the fundamental liberties of
Frenchmen if he chooses to exercise it. The provisions
regulating the conduct of parliamentary business and
the relations between legislature and executive give to
him precisely those powers he wishes to wield. He has
been compelled by circumstances, especially the Algerian problem, to exceed them, but this has not been his
desire. He would have preferred to be a national arbiter;
he was forced to become the prime mover of public policy and action.

The evolution of the Fifth Republic illustrates the
fallacy of imputing vitality to Constitutions. It is likely
that de Gaulle could have acted with as great authority
under the Constitutions of either the Third or the Fourth
Republics, for the legitimacy of his action derives from
his personal prestige and not from its conformity either
to the spirit or to the letter of the document he created.
Despite the concentration of governmental power in his
hands, however, this power has not noticeably expanded
at the expense of private liberty. Whatever increase there
has been in infringements of traditional civil liberties
under the Fifth Republic was almost entirely the result
of the violence of rightwing resistance to de Gaulle's
Algerian policy. Otherwise, the proscription-of-power aspect of French constitutionalism has retained its force.

On the other hand, the obvious disregard for
procedural norms in the Fifth Republic is evidence of
the failure of this side of constitutionalism to take root
in France. The variety of constitutional systems with
which France has experimented since 1789, and the
seemingly inexorable tendency of all of them to become
metamorphosed within their own skins, attest to the
absence of any enduring consensus on legitimate procedure for the exercise of governmental power. It also

shows the lack of concern of the French for such procedural regularity. In the text below, this phenomenon
is highlighted by the tendency to avoid confronting
the more taxing questions of procedure through the expedient of stipulating that they shall be dealt with later
in "organic laws".

B. FRENCH CONSTITUTIONAL DOCUMENTS

1. DECLARATION OF THE RIGHTS OF MAN AND OF THE CITIZEN, 1789

The representatives of the French people, organized
in National Assembly, believing that ignorance, forget-
fulness, or contempt of the rights of man are the sole
causes of the public miseries and of the corruption of
governments, have resolved to set forth in a solemn declaration the natural, inalienable, and sacred rights of
man, in order that this declaration, being ever present
to all the members of the social body, may unceasingly
remind them of their rights and their duties; in order
that the acts of the legislative power and those of the
executive power may be each moment compared with
the aim of every political institution and thereby may be
more respected; and in order that the demands of the
citizens, grounded henceforth upon simple and incon-
testable principles, may always take the direction of
maintaining the constitution and the welfare of all.

In consequence, the National Assembly recognizes and declares, in the presence and under the aus-
pices of the Supreme Being, the following rights of man
and citizen.

1. Men are born and remain free and equal in rights.
Social distinctions can be based only upon public utility.

2. The aim of every political association is the preservation of the natural and imprescriptible rights of man.
These rights are liberty, property, security, and resistance
to oppression.

3. The source of all sovereignty is essentially in the
nation; no body, no individual can exercise authority
that does not proceed from it in plain terms.

4. Liberty consists in the power to do anything that

does not injure others; accordingly, the exercise of the natural rights of each man has no limits except those that secure to the other members of society the enjoyment of these same rights. These limits can be determined only by law.

5. The law has the right to forbid only such actions as are injurious to society. Nothing can be forbidden that is not interdicted by the law, and no one can be constrained to do that which it does not order.

6. Law is the expression of the general will. All citizens have the right to take part personally, or by their representatives, in its formation. It must be the same for all, whether it protects or punishes. All citizens, being equal in its eyes, are equally eligible to all public dignities, places and employments, according to their capacities, and without other distinction than that of their virtues and their talents.

7. No man can be accused, arrested, or detained, except in the cases determined by the law and according to the forms that it has prescribed. Those who procure, expedite, execute, or cause to be executed arbitrary orders ought to be punished: but every citizen summoned or seized by virtue of the law ought to render instant obedience; he makes himself guilty by resistance.

8. The law ought to establish only penalties that are strictly and obviously necessary, and no one can be punished except by virtue of a law established and promulgated prior to the offense and legally applied.

9. Every man being presumed innocent until he has been pronounced guilty, if it is thought indispensable to arrest him, all severity that may not be necessary to secure his person ought to be strictly suppressed by law.

10. No one should be disturbed on account of his opinions, even religious, provided their manifestation does not disturb the public order established by law.

11. The free communication of ideas and opinions is one of the most precious of the rights of man; every citizen then can freely speak, write, and print, subject to responsibility for the abuse of this freedom in cases determined by law.

12. The guarantee of the rights of man and citizen

requires a public force; this force is instituted for the advantage of all and not for the personal benefit of those to whom it is entrusted.

13. For the maintenance of the public force and for the expenses of administration a general tax is indispensable; it ought to be equally apportioned among all the citizens according to their names.

14. All the citizens have the right to ascertain, by themselves or by their representatives, the necessity of the public tax, to consent to it freely, to follow the employment of it, and to determine the quota, the assessment, the collection, and the duration of it.

15. Society has the right to call for an account of his administration from every public agent.

16. Any society in which the guarantee of the rights is not secured, or the separation of powers not determined, has no constitution at all.

17. Property being a sacred and inviolable right, no one can be deprived of it, unless a legally established public necessity obviously requires it, under the condition of a just and prior indemnity.

2. PREAMBLE TO THE CONSTITUTION OF THE FOURTH FRENCH REPUBLIC, 1946

On the morrow of the victory of the free peoples over the regimes that attempted to enslave and degrade the human person, the French people proclaims once more that every human being, without distinction of race, religion or belief, possesses inalienable and sacred rights. It solemnly reaffirms the rights and freedoms of man and of the citizen consecrated by the Declaration of Rights of 1789 and the fundamental principles recognized by the laws of the Republic.

It further proclaims as most vital in our time the following political, economic and social principles:

The law guarantees to women equal rights with men in all domains.

Anyone persecuted because of his activities in the cause of freedom has the right of asylum within the territories of the Republic.

Everyone has the duty to work and the right to obtain employment. No one may suffer in his work or his employment because of his origin, his opinions or his beliefs.

Everyone may defend his rights and interests by trade-union action and may join the union of his choice.

The right to strike may be exercised within the framework of the laws that govern it.

Every worker through his delegates may participate in collective bargaining to determine working conditions, as well as in the management of business.

All property and all enterprises that now have or subsequently shall have the character of a national public service or a monopoly in fact must become the property of the community.

The nation ensures to the individual and the family the conditions necessary to their development.

It guarantees to all, and notably to the child, the mother and the aged worker, protection of health, material security, rest and leisure. Every human being who, because of his age, his physical or mental condition, or because of the economic situation, finds himself unable to work, has the right to obtain from the community the means to lead a decent existence.

The nation proclaims the solidarity and equality of all Frenchmen with regard to the burdens resulting from national disasters.

The nation guarantees equal access of children and adults to education, professional training and culture. The establishment of free, secular, public education on all levels is a duty of the State.

The French Republic, faithful to its traditions, abides by the rules of international public law. It will not undertake wars of conquest and will never use its arms against the freedom of any people.

On condition of reciprocity, France accepts the limitations of sovereignty necessary to the organization and defense of peace.

France forms with the people of its overseas territories a Union based upon equality of rights and duties without distinction of race or religion.

The French Union is composed of nations and peoples who wish to place in common or coordinate their resources and their efforts in order to develop their civilization, increase their well-being and ensure their security.

Faithful to her traditional mission, France proposes to guide the peoples for whom she has assumed responsibility toward freedom to govern themselves and democratically to manage their own affairs; putting aside any system of colonization based upon arbitrary power, she guarantees to all equal access to public office and the ininindividual or collective exercise of the rights and liberties proclaimed or confirmed above.

3. CONSTITUTION OF THE FIFTH FRENCH REPUBLIC, 1958*

PREAMBLE

The French people solemnly proclaim their attachment to the Rights of Man and to the principles of national sovereignty as defined by the Declaration of 1789, confirmed and completed by the preamble of the Constitution of 1946.

In accordance with those principles and with that of the free determination of peoples, The Republic offers to those Overseas Territories which express a desire for membership in them new institutions based on the common ideal of liberty, equality, and fraternity and conceived with a view to their democratic evolution.

ART. 1. The Republic and those peoples who, by an act of free decision, adopt the present Constitution, establish a Community.

The Community shall be based on the equality and solidarity of the people composing it.

TITLE I—SOVEREIGNTY

ART. 2. France is an indivisible, secular, democratic and social Republic. It shall insure equality before the law for all citizens without distinction of origin, race, or religion. It shall respect all beliefs.

The national emblem shall be the blue, white, and red tricolor flag.

* Translated by the editor. As amended through June 15, 1968.

The national anthem is the "Marseillaise."

The motto of the Republic is "Liberty, Equality, Fraternity."

Its principle is: government of the people, by the people, and for the people.

ART. 3. National sovereignty belongs to the people who shall exercise it through their representatives and by way of referendum.

Neither any section of the people nor any individual may claim to exercise it.

Suffrage may be direct or indirect in the conditions provided for by the Constitution. It shall in all cases be universal, equal, and secret.

All French nationals of both sexes who have attained their majority and are in possession of their civil and political rights shall be eligible to vote in accordance with conditions determined by law.

ART. 4. Political parties and groups shall participate in the exercise of the suffrage. They may form and engage in their activities freely. They must respect the principles of national sovereignty and democracy.

TITLE II—THE PRESIDENT OF THE REPUBLIC

ART. 5. The President of the Republic shall take care to see that the Constitution is respected. He shall assure, by his arbitration, the regular functioning of the political organs of government as well as the continuity of the State.

He shall be the protector of the independence of the nation, of its territorial integrity, of respect for treaties and Community Agreements.

ART. 6.* The President of the Republic shall be elected for seven years by *universal, direct suffrage.*

* As amended by popular referendum, October 28, 1962. The revised portion is italicized. Previously, the President was elective by a college of some 80,000 "grand electors" that included members of parliament, departmental and municipal councillors, and supplementary delegates from the larger municipal councils. Representation in the college was roughly proportionate to population, but the smaller, rural communes were overrepresented.

The means for implementing the present article shall be determined by organic law.

ART. 7.* Election of the President of the Republic shall be by absolute majority *of the valid ballots.* If this majority is not attained *on the first round of balloting, two Sundays later there shall be held a second round. Only those two candidates may present themselves for it who, after withdrawals, if any, of better-placed candidates, are found to have received the largest number of votes on the first round.*

Balloting shall begin at the summons of the Government.

The election of the new President shall take place not less than twenty days nor more than thirty-five days before the expiration of the term of the President in office.

In case the Presidency of the Republic falls vacant, for any reason, or the Constitutional Council, ruling on petition of the Government and by an absolute majority of its members, certifies the incapacity of the President, the functions of the President of the Republic, except those conferred in Articles 11 and 12 below, shall be temporarily performed by the President of the Senate *and, if the latter is, in his turn, prevented from performing those functions, by the Government.* In case of vacancy or if the incapacity is declared by the Constitutional Council to be permanent, balloting for the election of the new president shall take place, except in the event of *force majeure* certified by the Constitutional Council, no less than twenty days nor more than *thirty-five* days after the vacancy occurs or the permanent character of the incapacity is declared.

Neither Articles 49 and 50 nor Article 89 of the Constitution may be applied during the vacancy of the Presidency of the Republic or during the period that elapses between the declaration of the permanent character of

---

* As amended by popular referendum, October 28, 1962. The revised portion is italicized. Previously, the election was "by absolute majority on the first ballot" or by a plurality on the second. *"Thirty-five"* replaced "fifty" in both instances. The words *"and, if the latter, . . ."* and the final paragraph were added.

*the incapacity of the President of the Republic and the
election of his successor.*

ART. 8. The President of the Republic shall appoint
the Prime Minister. He shall terminate the appointment
on presentation by the latter of the resignation of the
Government.

On the proposal of the Prime Minister, he shall appoint and dismiss the other members of the Government.

ART. 9. The President of the Republic shall preside
over the Council of Ministers.

ART. 10. The President of the Republic shall promulgate laws within two weeks of the transmittal to the
Government of the law finally adopted.

He may, before this period expires, request Parliament to reconsider the law or certain of its articles. This
reconsideration cannot be refused.

ART. 11. The President of the Republic, at the request of the Government while Parliament is in session
or on joint petition of the two Assemblies, published in
the *Journal Officiel,* may submit to referendum any Government bill dealing with the organization of the political
branches of government, approving a Community agreement, or authorizing ratification of a treaty which, although not contrary to the Constitution, would affect the
functioning of the organs of government.

If the referendum favors adoption of the bill, the
President of the Republic shall promulgate it within the
time limit stipulated in the preceding article.

ART. 12. The President of the Republic can, after
consulting the Prime Minister and the Presidents of the
Assemblies, announce the dissolution of the National
Assembly.

A general election shall take place not less than
twenty days nor more than forty days after the dissolution.

The National Assembly shall meet by right the second
Thursday after its election. If this meeting takes place
outside the periods fixed for the regular sessions, a session shall be opened by right for a period of two weeks.

No new dissolution may be announced during the
year following these elections.

ART. 13. The President of the Republic shall sign the ordinances and decrees that have been considered in the Council of Ministers.

He shall make appointments to the civil and military posts of the State.

Councillors of State, the Grand Chancellor of the Legion of Honor, Ambassadors and Envoys Extraordinary, Master Councillor of the Court of Accounts, prefects, Government representatives in the Overseas Territories, general officers, rectors of academies,* and directors of central departments shall be appointed in the Council of Ministers.

An organic law shall determine the other appointments to be made in the Council of Ministers as well as the conditions in which the appointment power of the President of the Republic may be delegated by him to be exercised in his name.

ART. 14. The President of the Republic shall accredit Ambassadors and Envoys Extraordinary to foreign powers; foreign Ambassadors and Envoys Extraordinary shall be accredited to him.

ART. 15. The President of the Republic shall be the commander-in-chief of the armed forces. He shall preside over the higher councils and committees of the defense establishment.

ART. 16. When the institutions of the Republic, the independence of the Nation, the integrity of its territory, or the execution of its international commitments are endangered in a grave and immediate manner and the regular functioning of the constitutional organs of government is interrupted, the President of the Republic shall take the measures required by these circumstances, after official consultation with the Prime Minister, the Presidents of the Chambers, and the Constitutional Council.

He shall inform the nation of these by a message.

These measures must be inspired by a desire to assure to the constitutional organs of government, in the least possible time, the means to accomplish their mission.

---

* The seventeen administrative regions of the public educational system.—*Ed.'s note.*

The Constitutional Council shall be consulted about them.

Parliament shall meet by right.

The National Assembly may not be dissolved while the emergency powers are being exercised.

ART. 17. The President of the Republic shall have the right of pardon.

ART. 18. The President of the Republic shall communicate with the two parliamentary assemblies by means of messages which shall be read for him and shall not lead to a debate.

If not in session, Parliament shall be summoned specially for this purpose.

ART. 19. The acts of the President of the Republic, except those provided for in Articles 8 (paragraph 1), 11, 12, 16, 18, 54, 56, and 61, shall be countersigned by the Prime Minister and, when appropriate, by the responsible ministers.

TITLE III—THE GOVERNMENT*

ART. 20. The Government shall determine and direct national policy.

It shall have at its disposal the administration and the armed forces.

It shall be responsible to Parliament in the conditions and according to the procedures stipulated in Articles 49 and 50.

ART. 21. The Prime Minister shall direct the action of the Government. He shall be responsible for national defense. He shall ensure that the laws are executed. Except as stipulated in Article 13, he shall exercise the rule-making power** and make appointments to civil and military posts.

He may delegate certain of his powers to the ministers.

He shall preside over the councils and committees provided for in Article 15 in place of the President of the Republic when the occasion arises.

* *"Le Gouvernement"* is used here in the narrow, Continental sense of the responsible ministry, the cabinet.—*Ed.'s note.*

** The authority of the executive to legislate in respect to certain matters.

He may, in exceptional circumstances, take his place as Chairman of a meeting of the Council of Ministers by virtue of an express delegation of authority and for a specific agenda.

ART. 22. The acts of the Prime Minister shall be countersigned, when appropriate, by the ministers responsible for their execution.

ART. 23. Membership in the Government shall be incompatible with the exercise of any parliamentary mandate, with the performance of any national function in a trade or professional organization, with public employment, or with any professional activity.

An organic law shall determine the conditions in which the holders of such mandates, functions, or employment shall be replaced.

Members of parliament shall be replaced in a manner conforming to the provisions of Article 25.

TITLE IV—PARLIAMENT

ART. 24. Parliament shall be composed of the National Assembly and the Senate.

Deputies shall be elected to the National Assembly by direct suffrage.

The Senate shall be elected by indirect suffrage. It shall assure representation of the territorial entities of the Republic. Frenchmen residing outside France shall be represented in the Senate.

ART. 25. An organic law shall determine the duration of each Assembly, the number of its members, their compensation, the conditions for eligibility and the system of ineligibilities and incompatibilities.

It shall also determine the conditions for the election, in case of vacancy, of replacements for deputies or senators until a general or partial election of the assembly in which the vacancy occurs.

ART. 26. No member of Parliament may be prosecuted, sought out, arrested, detained, or tried on account of opinions expressed or votes cast by him in the performance of his functions.

No member of Parliament may be prosecuted or arrested on criminal or misdemeanor charges during parliamentary sessions without the authorization of the Assembly of which he is a member, except in case of *flagrante delicto*.

No member of Parliament may be arrested when Parliament is not in session without the authorization of the *bureau** of the Assembly of which he is a member, except in case of *flagrante delicto*, of prosecutions [already] authorized, or for final sentencing.

The detention or prosecution of a member of Parliament shall be suspended if the Assembly of which he is a member so demands.

ART. 27. Imperative mandates† shall be null and void.

The voting rights of members of Parliament shall be personal.

Organic law may, in exceptional circumstances, authorize proxy voting. In that case no one may exercise more than one proxy.

ART. 28.‡ Parliament shall assemble by right for two regular sessions each year.

The first session shall begin *October 2; it shall last eighty days.*

The second session shall open *on April 2;* its duration may not exceed *ninety days.*

ART. 29. Parliament shall assemble in extraordinary session at the request of the Prime Minister or of the majority of the members composing the National Assembly, for a specific agenda.

When the extraordinary session is held at the request of members of the National Assembly, the closure decree shall take effect as soon as Parliament has completed the agenda for which it was convened and no later than twelve days after it assembled.

Only the Prime Minister may ask for a new session before the end of the month following the decree of closure.

ART. 30. Except when Parliament meets by right, the extraordinary sessions shall be opened and closed by decree of the President of the Republic.

* The steering committee of the Assembly.—*Ed.'s note.*
† Compulsory voting instructions to members of parliament, usually issued by a political party.—*Ed.'s note.*
‡ As amended by parliament, December 30, 1963. Italics represent amendment.—*Ed.'s note.*

ART. 31. The members of the Government shall have access to the two assemblies. They shall be heard when they so request.

They may be assisted by Government commissioners.

ART. 32. The President of the National Assembly shall be elected for the duration of the legislature. The President of the Senate shall be elected after each partial renewal.

ART. 33. The sittings of the two Houses shall be public. A complete account of the debates shall be published in the *Journal Officiel*.

Each House may meet in secret session at the request of the Prime Minister or of one tenth of its members.

TITLE V—RELATIONS BETWEEN PARLIAMENT AND THE GOVERNMENT

ART. 34. Laws shall be voted by Parliament.

Laws shall determine the rules concerning:

—Civic rights and the fundamental guarantees accorded to citizens for the exercise of civil liberties; the obligations imposed for national defense on the persons and property of citizens;

—Nationality, status, and legal capacity of persons; marriage agreements; inheritance and gifts;

—The definition of crimes and misdemeanors as well as the penalties applicable to them; criminal procedure; amnesty; the creation of new types of jurisdiction and the status of the judiciary;

—The basis, rate, and methods of collecting taxes of all kinds; the currency system.

Laws shall also determine the rules concerning:

—The electoral systems for the Houses of Parliament and the local assemblies;

—The creation of categories of public corporations;

—The fundamental guarantees accorded to the civil and military personnel of the State;

—The nationalization of enterprises and the transfer of the property of enterprises from the public to the private sector.

Laws shall also determine the fundamental principles:

—of the general organization of the national defense;

—of the free administration of local entities, of their

powers and of their resources;

—of education;

—of the law of property, of real estate rights, and of civil and commercial obligations;

—of labor law, trade union law, and social security.

Finance laws shall determine the revenues and expenditures of the State in the conditions and with the reservations to be prescribed by an organic law.

Program-laws* shall determine the objectives of the economic and social action of the State.

The provisions of the present article may be elaborated and completed by an organic law.

ART. 35. Declarations of war shall be authorized by Parliament.

ART. 36. States of siege shall be decreed in the Council of Ministers.

Their prolongation beyond twelve days can be authorized only by Parliament.

ART. 37. Matters other than those which are in the domain of law shall be subject to the rule-making power.

Documents in the form of laws intruding on these matters may be modified by decrees issued after consultation with the Council of State. Such of these documents as come into existence after the present Constitution comes into force may be modified by decree only if the Constitutional Council has declared that they are in the rule-making sphere as defined in the preceding paragraph.

ART. 38. The Government may, in order to implement its program, request of Parliament authorization to take by ordinance, during a limited period of time, measures which are normally in the domain of law.

Ordinances shall be enacted in the Council of Ministers after consultation with the Council of State. They shall take effect upon publication but shall become null and void if the Government bill for ratification is not submitted to Parliament before the date set by the enabling act.

After the period of time mentioned in the first paragraph of the present article, ordinances may be modi-

* Laws authorizing long term projects for which funds may be required from revenues of future years.—*Ed.'s note.*

fied only by law in regard to matters in the legislative domain.

Art. 39. Legislative initiative shall be exercised concurrently by the Prime Minister and by the members of Parliament.

Government bills shall be considered in the Council of Ministers after consultation with the Council of State and shall be laid before one of the two houses. Government finance bills shall be submitted first to the National Assembly.

Art. 40. Bills and amendments drafted by members of Parliament shall be out of order if their adoption would result in a reduction in public revenues or the creation or increase of public expenditures.

Art. 41. If it appears in the course of the legislative process that a private member's bill, resolution, or amendment is not within the domain of law or is contrary to a delegation of authority made in accordance with Article 38, the Government may request that it be ruled out of order.

In case of disagreement between the Government and the President of the house concerned, the Constitutional Council, at the request of either, shall make a ruling within one week.

Art. 42. The text as presented by the Government shall be the basis for the discussion of Government bills in the first House to which they are submitted.

A House considering a bill passed by the other House shall discuss the text transmitted to it.

Art. 43. Bills shall be sent for study to *ad hoc* committees at the request of the Government or of the House considering them.

Bills for which no such request has been made shall be sent to one of the standing committees the number of which shall be limited to six in each House.

Art. 44. Members of Parliament and the Government shall have the right of amendment.

After the opening of debate, the Government may object to the consideration of any amendment which has not previously been submitted to the committee.

If the Government so requests, the House concerned shall decide by a single ballot on all or part of the bill under discussion including only the amendments proposed or accepted by the Government.

Art. 45. Every bill shall be examined successively by the two Houses with a view to the adoption of identical versions.

When, as a result of disagreement between the two Houses, a bill has not been adopted after two readings in each House, or, if the Government has declared the bill urgent, after a single reading by each of them, the Prime Minister shall be entitled to call a meeting of a joint committee, composed of an equal number of members of both Houses, assigned the task of proposing a text for the provisions on which disagreement remains.

The version prepared by the joint committee may be submitted by the Government for approval by the two Houses. No amendments shall be in order without the Government's agreement.

If the joint committee does not adopt a joint version or if this version is not adopted as provided for in the preceding paragraph, the Government may, after a new reading by the National Assembly and by the Senate, ask the National Assembly to rule definitively. In that case, the National Assembly may take either the version prepared by the joint committee, or the last version passed by the Assembly, modified as appropriate by one or more of the amendments adopted by the Senate.

Art. 46. The laws on which the Constitution confers the status of organic laws shall be passed and amended in accordance with the following conditions:

The bill shall not be debated and voted on by the first House to which it is submitted until two weeks after its introduction.

The procedure of Article 45 shall be applicable. However, failing agreement between the two Houses, the text may be adopted by the National Assembly on final reading only by an absolute majority of its members.

Organic laws relating to the Senate must be passed in the same terms by both Houses.

Organic laws may be promulgated only after being declared by the Constitutional Council to be in conformity with the Constitution.

ART. 47. Parliament shall pass Government finance bills in the manner to be prescribed by an organic law.

If the National Assembly has not voted on first reading within forty days after the introduction of a Government bill, the Government shall refer it to the Senate which must decide within two weeks. The procedure set forth in Article 45 shall then be followed.

If Parliament has not reached a decision within seventy days, the provisions of the bill may be put into effect by ordinance.

If the finance bill determining the revenues and expenditures for a fiscal year has not been submitted in time to be promulgated before the beginning of that fiscal year, the Government shall urgently request Parliament for authorization to levy the taxes and shall allocate by decree the funds needed for services [already] approved.

The time limits provided for in the present article shall be suspended when Parliament is not in session.

The Court of Accounts shall assist Parliament and the Government in supervising the execution of the finance laws.

ART. 48. The agenda of the Houses shall give priority in the order determined by the Government to discussion of the bills submitted by the Government and private members' bills accepted by it.

One sitting each week shall be reserved by priority for questions from the members of Parliament and replies by the Government.

ART. 49. The Prime Minister after discussion by the Council of Ministers shall* commit the Government before the National Assembly to responsibility for its program or, possibly, for a general policy declaration.

The National Assembly shall call into question the responsibility of the Government by passing a motion of censure. Such a motion is in order only if it has been signed by at least one-tenth of the members of the National Assembly. The vote may not take place for forty-

* The use of "shall" rather than "may" here and three lines below may have been a drafting error, for common sense and practice lead one to believe that no obligations were intended.—*Ed.'s note.*

eight hours after its introduction. Only those votes shall be counted that are favorable to the motion which shall be considered adopted only if supported by a majority of the members of the Assembly. If the motion is rejected, its signers may not propose another one during the same session, except as provided in the paragraph below.

The Prime Minister may, after discussion in the Council of Ministers, commit the Government before the National Assembly to responsibility for passage of all or part of a bill or motion. In that case, it shall be considered passed unless a motion of censure, introduced within the following twenty-four hours, is passed in the manner prescribed by the preceding paragraph.

The Prime Minister shall be entitled to request the Senate to approve a declaration of general policy.

ART. 50. When the National Assembly passes a motion of censure or rejects the program or a general policy declaration of the Government, the Prime Minister must submit to the President of the Republic the resignation of the Government.

ART. 51. The closure of regular or extraordinary sessions is automatically deferred, if necessary, to permit the application of the provisions of Article 49.

TITLE VI—TREATIES AND INTERNATIONAL AGREEMENTS

ART. 52. The President of the Republic shall negotiate and ratify treaties.

He shall be informed of any negotiation for the conclusion of an international agreement not requiring ratification.

ART. 53. Peace treaties, commercial treaties, treaties or agreements concerning international organization, those which entail financial obligations by the State, those which modify legislative provisions, those relating to personal status, those which entail the cession, exchange, or annexation of territory, may be ratified or approved only by virtue of a law.

They shall come into force only after having been ratified or approved.

No cession, no exchange, no annexation of territory shall be valid without the consent of the populations concerned.

ART. 54. If the Constitutional Council on petition of the President of the Republic, of the Prime Minister, or of the President of either House of Parliament, declares that an international commitment contains a clause contrary to the Constitution, authorization to ratify it or approve it may be accorded only after revision of the Constitution.

ART. 55. Regularly ratified or approved treaties or agreements shall have, upon publication, authority superior to that of laws, provided that, in the case of each agreement or treaty, it is implemented by the other party.

TITLE VII—THE CONSTITUTIONAL COUNCIL

ART. 56. The Constitutional Council shall contain nine members whose appointment shall be for nine years and is not renewable. The Constitutional Council shall be renewed by thirds every three years. Three of the members shall be appointed by the President of the Republic, three by the President of the National Assembly, three by the President of the Senate.

In addition to the nine members provided for above, former Presidents of the Republic shall be ex officio members of the Constitutional Council for life.

The President shall be appointed by the President of the Republic. His vote shall be deciding in case of a tie.

ART. 57. The functions of member of the Constitutional Council shall be incompatible with those of minister or member of Parliament. Other incompatibilities shall be determined by an organic law.

ART. 58. The Constitutional Council shall supervise the election of the President of the Republic with a view to ensuring its regularity.

It shall investigate protests and proclaim the election results.

ART. 59. The Constitutional Council shall rule in case of disputed results, on the regularity of the election of deputies and senators.

ART. 60. The Constitutional Council shall supervise the conduct of referenda and proclaim the results.

ART. 61. Organic laws, before their promulgation, and the rules of procedure of the Houses of Parliament, before their implementation, must be submitted to the Constitutional Council which shall decide on their conformity with the Constitution.

For the same purpose, laws may be referred to the Constitutional Council, before their promulgation, by the President of the Republic, the Prime Minister, or the President of either House of Parliament.

In the cases covered by the two preceding paragraphs, the Constitutional Council must rule within one month. However, at the request of the Government, in case of urgency, this period shall be reduced to one week.

In the same cases, submittal to the Constitutional Council shall suspend the time limit for promulgation.

ART. 62. A provision declared to be unconstitutional may not be promulgated nor implemented.

Decisions of the Constitutional Council shall be subject to no appeal. They shall be binding on the executive and parliament and on all administrative and judicial authorities.

ART. 63. An organic law shall determine the rules of organization and operation of the Constitutional Council, the procedure which shall be followed before it and especially the time limits within which disputes may be laid before it.

TITLE VIII—THE JUDICIAL AUTHORITY

ART. 64. The President of the Republic shall be the protector for the independence of the judicial authority.

He shall be assisted by the Superior Council of the Judiciary.

An organic law shall treat the status of the magistrates.

Judges shall be irremovable.

ART. 65. The Superior Council of the Judiciary shall be presided over by the President of the Republic. The Minister of Justice is, ex officio, vice-president. He may preside in place of the President of the Republic.

The Superior Council shall include, in addition, nine members appointed by the President of the Republic in conditions to be determined by an organic law.

The Superior Council of the Judiciary shall submit nominations for appointments to the Court of Cassation* and for those of first President of the Court of Appeals. It shall render its opinion in conditions to be determined by organic law on proposals of the Minister of Justice relating to other judges. It shall be consulted on pardons and reprieves in conditions to be determined by an organic law.

The Superior Council of the Judiciary shall act as disciplinary council for the judges. As such it shall be presided over by the First President of the Court of Cassation.

ART. 66. No person may be detained arbitrarily.

The judicial authority, guardian of individual liberty, shall assure respect for this principle in conditions to be determined by law.

TITLE IX—THE HIGH COURT OF JUSTICE

ART. 67. A High Court of Justice shall be established.

It shall be composed of members elected, from their own membership and in equal numbers, by the National Assembly and by the Senate after each general or partial election of those Houses. It shall elect its president from among its members.

An organic law shall determine the composition of the High Court, the rules of its operation, and the rules of procedure applicable before it.

ART. 68. The President of the Republic shall be responsible for acts committed in performing the functions of his office only in the case of high treason. He may be indicted only by identical motions passed in both Houses by open ballot and by absolute majorities of their members; he shall be tried by the High Court of Justice.

The members of the Government shall be penally responsible for acts committed in performing their functions and designated as crimes or misdemeanors at the time of their commission. The procedure defined above shall be applicable to them and to their accomplices in

* The highest court of appeal.—*Ed.'s note.*

the case of conspiracy against the security of the State. In the cases covered by the present paragraph, the High Court shall be bound by the definitions of the crimes and misdemeanors and by the rules as to penalties prescribed in the penal laws in force when the acts were committed.

TITLE X—THE ECONOMIC AND SOCIAL COUNCIL

ART. 69. The Economic and Social Council, at the request of the Government, shall render opinions on such Government bills, draft ordinances, or draft decrees, and on such private members' bills as are submitted to it.

A member of the Economic and Social Council may be designated by it to present before the Houses of Parliament the opinions of the Council on the bills which have been submitted to it.

ART. 70. The Economic and Social Council may also be consulted by the Government on any problem of an economic or social nature concerning the Republic or the Community. All plans or programmatic Government bills of an economic or social nature shall be submitted to it for an opinion.

ART. 71. The composition of the Economic and Social Council and its rules of procedure shall be determined by an organic law.

TITLE XI—TERRITORIAL UNITS

ART. 72. The territorial units of the Republic shall be the communes, the *départements,* the Overseas Territories. Any other territorial units shall be created by law.

These units shall be administered freely by elected councils and in conditions laid down by law.

In the *départements* and the territories, the Government delegate shall be responsible for the national interests, for supervising administration, and for ensuring that the laws are respected.

ART. 73. The legal status and administrative organization of the Overseas *départements* may be modified by adaptive measures necessitated by the local situation.

ART. 74. The Overseas Territories of the Republic shall have a special organization that takes into account their own interests in the context of the interests of the Republic. This organization shall be laid out and altered by law after consultation with the territorial assembly concerned.

ART. 75. Citizens of the Republic who do not have common law civil status, the only status covered by Article 34, shall retain their personal status as long as they do not renounce it.

ART. 76. The Overseas Territories may retain their status within the Republic.

If they demonstrate such a desire through deliberation in their territorial assembly within the time limit prescribed in the first paragraph of Article 91, they shall become either Overseas *départements* of the Republic or whether grouped together or not, member States of the Community.

TITLE XII—THE COMMUNITY

ART. 77. In the Community established by the present Constitution, the States shall enjoy autonomy; they shall administer themselves and conduct their own affairs freely and democratically.

There shall be only one citizenship in the Community.

All citizens shall be equal before the law whatever may be their origin, their race, or their religion. They shall have the same duties.

ART. 78. The area of competence of the Community shall include foreign policy, defense, currency, common economic and financial policies, as well as policies regarding strategic raw materials.

In addition, it shall include, in the absence of a special agreement, control of the judicial system, higher education, the general organization of external and common transport and of telecommunications.

Special agreements may create other areas of common jurisdiction or provide for any transfer of competence from the Community to one of its members.

ART. 79. Member States shall benefit from the provisions of Article 77 as soon as they have made the choice provided for in Article 76.

Until the measures necessary for the implementation of the present title enter into force, questions in the area of common competence shall be handled by the Republic.

ART. 80. The President of the Republic shall preside over and represent the Community.

The latter's organs shall be an Executive Council, a Senate, and a Court of Arbitration.

ART. 81. The member States of the Community shall participate in the election of the President in the conditions prescribed in Article 6.

The President of the Republic, in his capacity of President of the Community, shall be represented in each State of the Community.

ART. 82. The President of the Community shall preside over the Executive Council of the Community. It shall be composed of the Prime Minister of the Republic, the heads of Government of each of the member States of the Community, and the ministers responsible, on behalf of the Community, for common affairs.

The Executive Council shall organize the cooperation on the governmental and administrative level of the members of the Community.

The organization and the operation of the Executive Council shall be determined by an organic law.

ART. 83. The Senate of the Community shall be composed of delegates that the Parliament of the Republic and the legislative assemblies of the other members of the Community shall choose from among their members. In determining the number of delegates from each State its population and the responsibilities it assumes in the Community shall be taken into account.

It shall hold two sessions annually which shall be opened and closed by the President of the Community and neither of which may exceed one month in duration.

At the request of the President of the Community, it shall debate common economic and financial policies before laws concerning these matters are voted upon by the Parliament of the Republic and, when appropriate, the legislative assemblies of the other members of the Community.

The Senate of the Community shall consider the acts and international treaties and agreements provided for in

Articles 35 and 53 and which entail commitments by the Community.

It shall take binding decisions in the areas in which it has been delegated authority by the legislative assemblies of the members of the Community. These decisions shall be promulgated on the territory of all of the States concerned in the same form as law.

An organic law shall determine its composition and rules of procedure.

ART. 84. A Court of Arbitration of the Community shall adjudge disputes arising among the members of the Community.

Its composition and competence shall be determined by an organic law.

ART. 85.* As an exception to the procedure prescribed in Article 89, the provisions of the present title which concern the functioning of the common institutions may be amended by laws framed in identical terms and passed by the Parliament of the Republic and by the Senate of the Community.

The provisions of the present title can alo be revised by agreements concluded among all the States of the Community; the new provisions shall be implemented in accordance with the requirements of the Constitution of each State.

ART. 86.** The transformation of the status of a member State of the Community may be requested either by the Republic or by a resolution passed by the legislative assembly of the State concerned and ratified by a local referendum organized and supervised by the institutions of the Community. The arrangements for this transformation shall be determined by an agreement approved by the Parliament of the Republic and the legislative assembly concerned.

Under the same conditions, a member State of the

---

* As amended June 4, 1960, by Parliament. Italicized lines were added.
** As amended June 4, 1960, by Parliament. Italicized lines were added.

Community may become independent. It shall thereby cease to belong to the Community.

A member State of the Community can also, by means of agreements, become independent without ceasing for that reason to belong to the Community.

An independent State, not a member of the Community, can, by means of agreements, join the Community without ceasing to be independent.

The status of these States within the Community shall be determined by the agreements concluded to this effect, especially the agreements provided for in the preceding clauses, as well as the agreements provided for in the second clause of Article 85, where appropriate.

ART. 87. The special agreements concluded for the implementation of the present titles shall be approved by the Parliament of the Republic and the legislative assembly concerned.

TITLE XIII—AGREEMENTS OF ASSOCIATION

ART. 88. The Republic or the Community may conclude agreements with States desiring to associate with either in order to develop their civilizations.

TITLE XIV—AMENDMENT

ART. 89. The right of initiative for the revision of the Constitution shall be held concurrently by the President of the Republic on the proposal of the Prime Minister and by the members of Parliament.

The proposed amendment must be passed by both Houses in identical terms. It shall become effective after approval by a referendum.

However, it shall not be submitted to a referendum if the President of the Republic decides to submit it to Parliament convened in Congress;* in this case, the proposed amendment shall not stand approved unless it receives a three-fifths majority of the votes cast. The *bureau* of the Congress shall be that of the National Assembly.

The amendment procedure may not be initiated or

* That is, a joint meeting of the two Houses.—*Ed.'s note.*

pursued when the integrity of the territory is in jeopardy.

The republican form of government is not subject to amendment.

TITLE XV—TRANSITIONAL PROVISIONS

ART. 90. The regular session of Parliament shall be suspended. The terms of office of the members of the present National Assembly shall expire on the day that the Assembly elected under this Constitution assembles.

Until that meeting, only the Government shall have authority to convene Parliament.

The terms of office of the members of the Assembly of the French Union shall expire at the same time as the terms of office of the members of the National Assembly in office at present.

ART. 91. The institutions of the Republic provided for by the present Constitution will be set up within four months after its promulgation.

This period shall be extended to six months for the institutions of the Community.

The powers of the President of the Republic now in office will expire only with the proclamation of the results of the election provided for by Articles 6 and 7 of the present Constitution.

The member States of the Community will participate in this first election under conditions deriving from their status on the date of the promulgation of the Constitution.

The incumbent authorities will continue to perform their functions in the States in conformity with the laws and regulations applicable at the time of the entry into force of the Constitution until the authorities provided for by their new regimes take office.

Until its constitution is finally determined, the Senate shall be formed of the present members of the Council of the Republic. The organic laws which will determine the ultimate constitution of the Senate must come into existence before July 31, 1959.

The powers conferred on the Constitutional Council by Articles 58 and 59 of the Constitution will be exercised, until the Council takes office, by a Commission composed of the vice-president of the Council of State as presiding member, of the First President of the Court of Cassation, and of the First President of the Court of Accounts.

The peoples of the member States of the Community shall continue to be represented in Parliament until the entry into force of the necessary measures for the implementation of Title XII.

ART. 92. The legislative measures necessary to install the institutions and, until this installation, for the functioning of the political branches of government will be taken in the Council of Ministers, with the advice of the Council of State, by ordinances having the force of law.

During the period provided for in paragraph 1 of Article 91, the Government shall have the authority to determine by ordinances having the force of law and drafted in the same form the electoral systems for the assemblies provided for in the Constitution.

During the same period and in the same conditions, the Government may also take for all matters the measures it considers necessary for the life of the Nation, the protection of its citizens, or the preservation of liberty.

GERMANY

— 5 —

GERMANY

A. German Constitutionalism

Whereas the French have marked clearly the boundary between public and private power while regarding procedural regularity rather casually, the Germans historically have assumed a nearly opposite attitude. They have tended, as a nation, to develop such high respect for authority that they have, on occasion, freely permitted its almost unrestricted command. This was particularly evident under Hitler; it was also a feature of Bismarck's empire, and it is clearly present in a much less virulent form in the Bonn Republic. It is notable, in this regard, that de Gaulle's authority derives primarily from the prestige he had before taking office, but Adenauer had relatively little stature with the average German before becoming chancellor. Although his unbending determination enabled him to capitalize his opportunities, his authority derived, in the first instance, from his position. Germany's postwar international position and her internal prosperity have not created the conditions for a test of the present foundation of the proscriptions on power that are contained in the Basic Law. The unanticipated use to which Article 48 of the ill-fated Weimar Constitution was put even before the advent of Hitler shows of what little avail were documentary restraints at that time when confronted by harsh social, economic, and political realities.

But if the Germans have a spotty record of respect for constitutional limits on power, they have taken quite a different course in regard to procedures. Even Hitler's rise to power was accomplished in strict conformity to the procedural requirements of the Constitution. And during Adenauer's reign, when authority was highly concentrated in the hands of the chancellor, there was virtually no suggestion that serious violations of procedural regularity occurred. Adenauer was criticized for allegedly impeding the growth of a genuinely democratic ethos in Germany through his authoritarian manner, but he was not seriously accused of failing to adhere to procedural constitutionalism. This was not the case during the Fourth Republic in France and is even less so under the Fifth. It should not be forgotten, as the text below will remind us, that the German system is not and was not intended to be, strictly speaking, a parliamentary regime. For one thing, collective cabinet responsibility was not envisaged and does not exist. On the other hand, if we are to believe its founders, the Fifth French Republic was intended to be parliamentary—however great were to be the reforms of Fourth Republic practices—but has been so even less than the Bonn regime, especially since Adenauer's resignation.

Procedural constitutionalism in Germany has been marred, however, by an instability of regimes as great as that of France. Since 1870 both countries have lived under four different constitutional systems. The fact that the expectation of procedural regularity has survived despite this instability indicates the extent to which attitudes of procedural constitutionalism have become engrained in the Germans.

B. Basic Law of the Federal Republic of Germany, 1949 *

* Official translation supplied by the Press and Information Office, German Embassy, Washington. As amended through April 15, 1968. For later amendments, see Addenda.

PREAMBLE—The German People in the *Laender* of Baden, Bavaria, Bremen, Hamburg, Hesse, Lower Saxony, North-Rhine-Westphalia, Rhineland-Palatinate, Schleswig-Holstein, Wuerttemberg-Baden and Wuerttemberg-Hohenzollern, conscious of its responsibility before God and men, animated by the resolve to preserve its national and political unity and to serve the peace of the world as an equal partner in a united Europe, desiring to give a new order to political life for a transitional period, has enacted, by virtue of its constituent power, this Basic Law of the Federal Republic of Germany. It has also acted on behalf of those Germans to whom participation was denied. The entire German people is called on to achieve by free self-determination the unity and freedom of Germany.

TITLE I. BASIC RIGHTS

ART. 1—(1) The dignity of man is inviolable. To respect and protect it is the duty of all state authority.

(2) The German people therefore acknowledge inviolable and inalienable human rights as the basis of every community, of peace and of justice in the world.

(3) The following basic rights bind the legislature, the executive and the judiciary as directly enforceable law.

ART. 2—(1) Everyone has the right to the free development of his personality insofar as he does not violate the rights of others or offend against the constitutional order or the moral code.

(2) Everyone has the right to life and to inviolability of his person. The freedom of the individual is inviolable. These rights may only be encroached upon pursuant to a law.

ART. 3—(1) All persons are equal before the law.

(2) Men and women have equal rights.

(3) No one may be prejudiced or favored because of his sex, his parentage, his race, his language, his homeland and origin, his faith or his religious or political opinions.

ART. 4—(1) Freedom of faith and of conscience,

and freedom of creed, religious or ideological, are inviolable.

(2) The undisturbed practice of religion is guaranteed.

(3) No one may be compelled against his conscience to render war service as an armed combatant. Details will be regulated by a Federal Law.

ART. 5—(1) Everyone has the right freely to express and to disseminate his opinion by speech, writing and pictures and freely to inform himself from generally accessible sources. Freedom of the press and freedom of reporting by radio and motion pictures are guaranteed. There shall be no censorship.

(2) These rights are limited by the provisions of the general laws, the provisions of law for the protection of youth and by the right to inviolability of personal honor.

(3) Art and science, research and teaching are free. Freedom of teaching does not absolve from loyalty to the constitution.

ART. 6—(1) Marriage and family enjoy special protection by the state.

(2) Care and upbringing of children are the natural right of the parents and a duty primarily incumbent on them. The state watches over the performance of this duty.

(3) Separation of children from the family against the will of the persons entitled to bring them up may take place only pursuant to a law, if those so entitled fail in their duty or if the children are otherwise threatened with neglect.

(4) Every mother is entitled to the protection and care of the community.

(5) Illegitimate children shall be provided by legislation with the same opportunities for their physical and spiritual development and their position in society as are enjoyed by legitimate children.

ART. 7—(1) The entire educational system is under the supervision of the state.

(2) The persons entitled to bring up a child have the right to decide whether it shall receive religious instruction.

(3) Religious instruction forms part of the ordinary curriculum in state and municipal schools, except in secular schools. Without prejudice to the state's right of supervision, religious instruction is given in accordance with the tenets of the religious communities. No teacher may be obliged against his will to give religious instruction.

(4) The right to establish private schools is guaranteed. Private schools, as a substitute for state or municipal schools, require the approval of the state and are subject to the laws of the *Laender*. This approval must be given if private schools are not inferior to the state or municipal schools in their educational aims, their facilities and the professional training of their teaching staff, and if a segregation of the pupils according to the means of the parents is not promoted. This approval must be withheld if the economic and legal position of the teaching staff is not sufficiently assured.

(5) A private elementary school shall be admitted only if the educational authority finds that it serves a special pedagogic interest or if, on the application of persons entitled to bring up children, it is to be established as an inter-denominational or denominational or ideological school and a state or municipal elementary school of this type does not exist in the community.

(6) Preparatory schools remain abolished.

ART. 8—(1) All Germans have the right to assemble peacefully and unarmed without prior notification or permission.

(2) With regard to open-air meetings this right may be restricted by or pursuant to a law.

ART. 9—(1) All Germans have the right to form associations and societies.

(2) Associations, the objects or activities of which conflict with the criminal laws or which are directed against the constitutional order or the concept of international understanding, are prohibited.

(3) The right to form associations to safeguard and improve working and economic conditions is guaranteed to everyone and to all trades and professions. Agreements which restrict or seek to hinder this right are null

and void; measures directed to this end are illegal.

ART. 10—Secrecy of the mail and secrecy of posts and telecommunications are inviolable. Restrictions may be ordered only pursuant to a law.

ART. 11—(1) All Germans enjoy freedom of movement throughout the Federal territory.

(2) This right may be restricted only by a law and only in cases in which an adequate basis of existence is lacking and special burdens would arise to the community as a result thereof or in which the restriction is necessary for the protection of youth against neglect, for combatting the danger of epidemics or for the prevention of crime.

ART. 12—* (1) All Germans have the right freely to choose their trade or profession, their place of work and their place of training. The practice of trades and professions may be regulated by law.

(2) No one may be compelled to perform a particular work except within the framework of a traditional compulsory public service which applies generally and equally to all. Anyone who refuses on conscientious grounds to render war service involving the use of arms, may be required to render an alternative service. The duration of this alternative service shall not exceed the duration of military service. Details shall be regulated by a law which shall not prejudice freedom of conscience and shall provide also for the possibility of an alternative service having no connection with any unit of the Armed Forces.

(3) Women shall not be required by law to render service in any unit of the Armed Forces. On no account shall they be employed in any service involving the use of arms.

(4) Forced labor may be imposed only in the event that a person is deprived of his freedom by the sentence of a court.

ART. 13—(1) The home is inviolable.

(2) Searches may be ordered only by a judge or, in the event of danger in delay, by other organs as pro-

* As amended March 19, 1956.

vided by law and may be carried out only in the form prescribed by law.

(3) Otherwise, this inviolability may be encroached upon or restricted only to avert a common danger or a mortal danger to individuals, or, pursuant to a law, to prevent imminent danger to public security and order, especially to alleviate the housing shortage, to combat the danger of epidemics or to protect endangered juveniles.

Art. 14—(1) Property and the rights of inheritance are guaranteed. Their content and limits are determined by the laws.

(2) Property imposes duties. Its use should also serve the public weal.

(3) Expropriation is permitted only in the public weal. It may take place only by or pursuant to a law which provides for kind and extent of the compensation. The compensation shall be determined upon just consideration of the public interest and of the interests of the persons affected. In case of dispute regarding the amount of compensation, recourse may be had to the ordinary courts.

Art. 15—Land, natural resources and means of production may for the purpose of socialization be transferred into public ownership or other forms of publicly controlled economy by a law which provides for kind and extent of the compensation. With respect to such compensation Article 14, paragraph 3, sentences 3 and 4, apply *mutatis mutandis*.

Art. 16—(1) No one may be deprived of his German citizenship. Loss of citizenship may arise only pursuant to a law, and against the will of the person affected it may arise only if such person does not thereby become stateless.

(2) No German may be extradited to a foreign country. Persons persecuted for political reasons enjoy the right of asylum.

Art. 17—Everyone has the right individually or jointly with others to address written requests or complaints to the competent authorities and to the representative assemblies.

ART. 17a—* (1) Laws concerning military service and alternative service may, by provisions applying to members of the Armed Forces and of alternative Services during their period of military or alternative service, restrict the basic right freely to express and to disseminate opinions by speech, writing, and pictures (Article 5 paragraph (1) first half-sentence), the basic right of assembly (Article 8), and the right of petition (Article 17) in so far as it permits to address requests or complaints jointly with others.

(2) Laws for defense purposes, including the protection of the civilian population, may provide for the restriction of the basic rights of freedom of movement (Article 11) and inviolability of the home (Article 13).

ART. 18—Whoever abuses freedom of expression of opinion, in particular freedom of the press (Article 5, paragraph 1), freedom of teaching (Article 5, paragraph 3), freedom of assembly (Article 8), freedom of association (Article 9), the secrecy of mail, posts and telecommunications (Article 10), property (Article 14), or the right of asylum (Article 16, paragraph 2) in order to attack the free democratic basic order, forfeits these basic rights. The forfeiture and its extent are pronounced by the Federal Constitutional Court.

ART. 19—(1) Insofar as under this Basic Law a basic right may be restricted by or pursuant to a law, the law must apply generally and not solely to an individual case. Furthermore, the law must name the basic right, indicating the Article.

(2) In no case may a basic right be infringed upon in its essential content.

(3) The basic rights apply also to corporations established under German Public Law to the extent that the nature of such rights permits.

(4) Should any person's right be violated by public authority, recourse to the court shall be open to him. If no other court has jurisdiction, recourse shall be to the ordinary courts.

* As amended March 19, 1956.

TITLE II. THE FEDERATION AND
THE LAENDER

Art. 20—(1) The Federal Republic of Germany is a democratic and social federal state.

(2) All state authority emanates from the people. It is exercised by the people by means of elections and voting and by separate legislative, executive and judicial organs.

(3) Legislation is subject to the constitutional order; the executive and the judiciary are bound by the law.

Art. 21—(1) The political parties participate in the forming of the political will of the people. They may be freely formed. Their internal organization must conform to democratic principles. They must publicly account for the sources of their funds.

(2) Parties which, by reason of their aims or the behavior of their adherents, seek to impair or destroy the free democratic basic order or to endanger the existence of the Federal Republic of Germany are unconstitutional. The Federal Constitutional Court decides on the question of unconstitutionality.

(3) Details will be regulated by Federal legislation.

Art. 22—The Federal flag is black-red-gold.

Art. 23—For the time being, this Basic Law applies in the territory of the *Laender* of Baden, Bavaria, Bremen, Greater Berlin, Hamburg, Hesse, Lower-Saxony, North-Rhine-Westphalia, Rhineland-Palatinate, Schleswig-Holstein, Wuerttemberg-Baden and Wuerttemberg-Hohenzollern. In other parts of Germany it shall be put into force on their accession.

Art. 24—(1) The Federation may, by legislation, transfer sovereign powers to international institutions.

(2) For the maintenance of peace, the Federation may join a system of mutual collective security; in doing so it will consent to such limitations upon its sovereign powers as will bring about and secure a peaceful and lasting order in Europe and among the nations of the world.

(3) For the settlement of disputes between nations, the Federation will accede to agreements concerning a

general, comprehensive and obligatory system of international arbitration.

ART. 25—The general rules of public international law form part of the federal law. They take precedence over the laws and directly create rights and duties for the inhabitants of the Federal territory.

ART. 26—(1) Activities tending and undertaken with the intent to disturb peaceful relations between nations, especially to prepare for aggressive war, are unconstitutional. They shall be made a punishable offense.

(2) Weapons designed for warfare may be manufactured, transported or marketed only with the permission of the Federal Government. Details will be regulated by a federal law.

ART. 27—All German merchant vessels form one merchant fleet.

ART. 28—(1) The constitutional order in the *Laender* must conform to the principles of republican, democratic and social government based on the rule of law, within the meaning of this Basic Law. In each of the *Laender,* counties and communities, the people must be represented by a body chosen in universal, direct, free, equal and secret elections. In the communities the assembly of the community may take the place of an elected body.

(2) The communities must be guaranteed the right to regulate on their own responsibility all the affairs of the local community within the limits set by law. The associations of communities also have the right of self-government in accordance with the law within the limits of the functions given them by law.

(3) The Federation guarantees that the constitutional order of the *Laender* conforms to the basic rights and to the provisions of paragraphs (1) and (2).

ART. 29—(1) The Federal territory shall be reorganized by a Federal law with due regard to regional ties, historical and cultural connections, economic expediency and social structure. Such reorganization should create *Laender* which by their size and capacity are able effectively to fulfill the functions incumbent upon them.

(2) In areas which upon the reorganization of the

Laender after May 8, 1945, became, without plebiscite, part of another *Land,* a specific change in the decision then taken regarding the *Land* boundaries may be demanded by popular initiative within a year from the coming into force of the Basic Law. The popular initiative requires the assent of one-tenth of the population entitled to vote in *Landtag* elections. If the popular initiative receives such assent, the Federal Government must include in the draft of the reorganization law a provision determining to which *Land* the area shall belong.

(3) After the law has been passed, such part of the law as provides for the transfer of an area from one *Land* to another must be submitted to a referendum in that area. If a popular initiative received the assent required under paragraph 2, a referendum must in any event be held in the area concerned.

(4) Insofar as the law is rejected in at least one area, it must be reintroduced into the Bundestag. After it has been passed again, it requires to that extent acceptance by a referendum in the entire federal territory.

(5) In a referendum the majority of the votes cast decides.

(6) The procedure shall be established by a Federal law. The reorganization should be concluded before the expiration of three years after promulgation of the Basic Law and, should it become necessary as a result of the accession of another part of Germany, within two years after such accession.

(7) The procedure regarding any other change in the territory of the *Laender* shall be established by a Federal law which requires the consent of the Bundesrat and of the majority of the members of the Bundestag.

ART. 30—The exercise of governmental powers and the discharge of governmental functions is incumbent on the *Laender* insofar as this Basic Law does not otherwise prescribe or permit.

ART. 31—Federal law overrides *Land* law.

ART. 32—(1) The conduct of relations with foreign states is the concern of the Federation.

(2) Before the conclusion of a treaty affecting the

special interests of a *Land,* this *Land* must be consulted in sufficient time.

(3) Insofar as the *Laender* have power to legislate, they may, with the consent of the Federal Government, conclude treaties with foreign states.

ART. 33—(1) Every German has in every *Land* the same civic rights and duties.

(2) Every German is equally eligible for any public office according to his aptitude, qualifications and professional achievements.

(3) Enjoyment of civil and civic rights, eligibility for public office, and rights acquired in the public service are independent of religious denomination. No one may suffer disadvantage by reason of his adherence or non-adherence to a denomination or ideology.

(4) The exercise of state authority as a permanent function shall as a rule be entrusted to members of the public service whose status, service and loyalty are governed by public law.

(5) The law of the public service shall be regulated with due regard to the traditional principles of the permanent civil service.

ART. 34—If any person, in the exercise of a public office entrusted to him, violates his official obligations to a third party, liability rests in principle on the state or the public authority which employs him. In the case of willful intent or gross carelessness the right of recourse is reserved. With respect to the claim for compensation or the right of recourse, the jurisdiction of the ordinary courts must not be excluded.

ART. 35—All Federal and *Land* authorities render each other mutual legal and administrative assistance.

ART. 36—* (1) Civil servants employed in the highest Federal authorities shall be drawn from all *Laender* in appropriate proportion. Persons employed in other Federal authorities should, as a rule, be drawn from the *Land* in which they serve.

(2) Military laws shall take into account the division of the Federation into *Laender* and the latter's particular ethnic conditions.

* As amended March 19, 1956.

ART. 37—(1) If a *Land* fails to comply with its obligations of a Federal character imposed by the Basic Law or another Federal law, the Federal Government may, with the consent of the Bundesrat, take the necessary measures to enforce such compliance by the *Land* by way of Federal compulsion.

(2) To carry out such Federal compulsion the Federal Government or its commissioner has the right to give instructions to all *Laender* and their authorities.

TITLE III. THE LOWER HOUSE OF PARLIAMENT (BUNDESTAG)

ART. 38—(1) The deputies to the German Bundestag are elected in universal, direct, free, equal and secret elections. They are representatives of the whole people, are not bound by orders and instructions and are subject only to their conscience.

(2) Anyone who has attained the age of twenty-one is entitled to vote; anyone who has attained the age of twenty-five is eligible for election.

(3) Details will be regulated by a Federal law.

ART. 39—(1) The Bundestag is elected for a four-year term. Its legislative term ends four years after its first meeting or on its dissolution. The new election takes place during the last three months of the term or within sixty days after dissolution.

(2) The Bundestag assembles within thirty days after the election, but not before the end of the term of the previous Bundestag.

(3) The Bundestag determines the termination and resumption of its meetings. The President of the Bundestag may convene it at an earlier date. He must do so if one-third of the members, the Federal President or the Federal Chancellor so demand.

ART. 40—(1) The Bundestag elects its President, Vice-presidents and Secretaries. It draws up its rules of procedure.

(2) The President exercises the proprietary and police powers in the Bundestag building. No search or seizure may take place in the premises of the Bundestag without his permission.

ART. 41—(1) The scrutiny of elections is the responsibility of the Bundestag. It also decides whether a deputy has lost his seat in the Bundestag.

(2) Against the decision of the Bundestag an appeal can be made to the Federal Constitutional Court.

(3) Details will be regulated by a Federal law.

ART. 42—(1) The meetings of the Bundestag are public. Upon a motion of one-tenth of its members, or upon a motion of the Federal Government, the public may, by a two-thirds majority vote, be excluded. The decision on the motion is taken at a meeting not open to the public.

(2) Decisions of the Bundestag require a majority of votes cast unless this Basic Law provides otherwise. For the elections to be made by the Bundestag the rules of procedure may provide exceptions.

(3) True and accurate reports of the public meetings of the Bundestag and of its committees shall not give rise to any liability.

ART. 43—(1) The Bundestag and its committees may demand the presence of any member of the Federal Government.

(2) The members of the Bundesrat and of the Federal Government as well as persons commissioned by them have access to all meetings of the Bundestag and its committees. They must be heard at any time.

ART. 44—(1) The Bundestag has the right, and upon the motion of one-fourth of its members the duty, to set up a committee of investigation which shall take the requisite evidence at public hearings. The public may be excluded.

(2) The rules of criminal procedure shall apply *mutatis mutandis* to the taking of evidence. The secrecy of the mail, posts and telecommunications remains unaffected.

(3) Courts and administrative authorities are bound to render legal and administrative assistance.

(4) The decisions of the committees of investigations are not subject to judicial consideration. The courts are free to evaluate and judge the facts on which the investigation is based.

ART. 45—(1) The Bundestag appoints a Standing Committee which shall safeguard the rights of the Bundestag as against the Federal Government in the interval between two legislative terms. The Standing Committee has also the powers of a committee of investigation.

(2) Wider powers, such as the right to legislate, to elect the Federal Chancellor, and to impeach the Federal President, are not within the province of the Standing Committee.

ART. 45a—* (1) The Bundestag shall appoint a Committee on Foreign Affairs and a Committee on Defense. Both committees shall function also in the intervals between any two legislative terms.

(2) The Committee on Defense shall also have the rights of a committee of investigation. Upon the motion of one-fourth of its members it shall have the duty to make a specific matter the subject of investigation.

(3) Article 44 paragraph (1) shall not be applied in matters of defense.

ART. 45b—** A Defense Commissioner of the Bundestag shall be appointed to safeguard the basic rights and to assist the Bundestag in exercising parliamentary control. Details shall be regulated by a Federal law.

ART. 46—(1) A deputy may not at any time be prosecuted in the courts or subjected to disciplinary action or otherwise called to account outside the Bundestag on account of a vote cast or an utterance made by him in the Bundestag or one of its committees. This does not apply to defamatory insults.

(2) A deputy may be called to account or arrested for a punishable offense only by permission of the Bundestag, unless he is apprehended in the commission of the offense or during the course of the following day.

(3) The permission of the Bundestag is also necessary for any other restriction of the personal freedom of a deputy or for the initiation of proceedings against a deputy under Article 18.

(4) Any criminal proceedings and any proceedings under Article 18 against a deputy, any detention and any other restriction of his personal freedom shall be suspended upon the request of the Bundestag.

* Added March 19, 1956.
** Added March 19, 1956.

ART. 47—Deputies may refuse to give evidence concerning persons who have confided facts to them in their capacity as deputies or to whom they have confided facts in such capacity, as well as concerning these facts themselves. To the extent that this right to refuse to give evidence exists, no seizure of documents may take place.

ART. 48—(1) Any person seeking election to the Bundestag is entitled to the leave necessary for his election campaign.

(2) No one may be prevented from accepting and exercising the office of deputy. He may not be dismissed from employment, with or without notice, on this ground.

(3) Deputies are entitled to compensation adequate to ensure their independence. They are entitled to the free use of all state-owned transport. Details will be regulated by a Federal law.

ART. 49—* In respect of the members of the Presidency, the Standing Committee, the Committee on Foreign Affairs and the Committee on Defense, as well as their principal substitutes, Articles 46, 47 and paragraphs (2) and (3) of Article 48 shall apply also in the intervals between any two legislative terms.

TITLE IV. THE UPPER HOUSE OF PARLIAMENT (BUNDESRAT)

ART. 50—The *Laender* participate through the Bundesrat in the legislation and administration of the Federation.

ART. 51—(1) The Bundesrat consists of members of the *Laender* governments which appoint and recall them. Other members of such governments may act as substitutes.

(2) Each *Land* has at least three votes; *Laender* with more than two million inhabitants have four, *Laender* with more than six million inhabitants, five votes.

(3) Each *Land* may delegate as many members as it has votes. The votes of each *Land* may be cast only as

* As amended March 19, 1956.

a block vote and only by members present or their substitutes.

Art. 52—(1) The Bundesrat elects its President for one year.

(2) The President convenes the Bundesrat. He must convene it if the members for at least two *Laender* or the Federal Government so demand.

(3) The Bundesrat takes its decisions by at least a majority of its votes. It draws up its rules of procedure. Its meetings are public. The public may be excluded.

(4) Other members of, or persons commissioned by, *Laender* governments may serve on the committees of the Bundesrat.

Art. 53—The members of the Federal Government have the right, and on demand the duty, to take part in the debates of the Bundesrat and of its committees. They must be heard at any time. The Bundesrat must be currently kept informed by the Federal Government of the conduct of affairs.

TITLE V. THE FEDERAL PRESIDENT

Art. 54—(1) The Federal President is elected, without debate, by the Federal Convention. Every German is eligible who is entitled to vote for the Bundestag and who has attained the age of forty.

(2) The term of office of the Federal President is five years. Re-election for a consecutive term is permitted only once.

(3) The Federal Convention consists of the members of the Bundestag and an equal number of members elected by the representative assemblies of the *Laender* according to the rules of proportional representation.

(4) The Federal Convention meets not later than thirty days before the expiration of the term of office of the Federal President or, in the case of premature termination, not later than thirty days after this date. It is convened by the President of the Bundestag.

(5) After expiration of the legislative term, the period specified in paragraph 4, first sentence, begins with the first meeting of the Bundestag.

(6) The person receiving the votes of the majority of the members of the Federal Convention is elected. If

such majority is not obtained by any candidate in two ballots, the candidate who receives the largest number of votes in a further ballot is elected.

(7) Details will be regulated by a Federal law.

ART. 55—(1) The Federal President may not be a member of the Government or of a legislative body of the Federation or of a *Land*.

(2) The Federal President may not hold any other salaried office, nor engage in a trade, nor practice a profession, nor belong to the management or the board of directors of an enterprise carried on for profit.

ART. 56—On assuming his office the Federal President takes the following oath before the assembled members of the Bundestag and the Bundesrat.

> "I swear that I will dedicate my efforts to the well-being of the German people, enhance its benefits, ward harm from it, uphold and defend the Basic Law and the laws of the Federation, fulfill my duties conscientiously, and do justice to all. So help me God."

The oath may also be taken without religious affirmation.

ART. 57—If the Federal President is prevented from exercising his powers, or if his office falls prematurely vacant, his powers will be exercised by the President of the Bundesrat.

ART. 58—Orders and decrees of the Federal President require for their validity the countersignature of the Federal Chancellor or the appropriate Federal Minister. This does not apply to the appointment and dismissal of the Federal Chancellor, the dissolution of the Bundestag under Article 63 and the request under Article 69, paragraph 3.

ART. 59—(1) The Federal President represents the Federation in its international relations. He concludes treaties with foreign states on behalf of the Federation. He accredits and receives envoys.

(2) Treaties which regulate the political relations of the Federation or relate to matters of Federal legislation require the consent or participation, in the form of

a Federal law, of the bodies competent in any specific case for such Federal legislation. For administrative agreements the provisions concerning the Federal administration apply *mutatis mutandis*.

ART. 59a—* (1) The Bundestag shall determine when a case of defense has occurred. Its decision shall be promulgated by the Federal President.

(2) If insurmountable difficulties prevent the Bundestag from assembling, the Federal President may, when there is danger in delay, make and promulgate this determination, subject to countersignature by the Federal Chancellor. The Federal President should previously consult the Presidents of the Bundestag and the Bundesrat.

(3) Statements concerning the existence of a case of defense which involve international relations shall not be issued by the Federal President until after such promulgation.

(4) Any decision on the conclusion of peace shall be taken by means of a Federal law.

ART. 60—** (1) The Federal President appoints and dismisses the Federal judges, the Federal civil servants, the officers and non-commissioned officers, unless otherwise provided for by law.

(2) He exercises the power of pardon on behalf of the Federation in individual cases.

(3) He may delegate these powers to other authorities.

(4) Paragraphs 2 to 4 of Article 46 apply *mutatis mutandis* to the Federal President.

ART. 61—(1) The Bundestag or the Bundesrat may impeach the Federal President before the Federal Constitutional Court for willful violation of the Basic Law or any other Federal law. The motion for impeachment must be brought forward by at least one-fourth of the members of the Bundestag or one-fourth of the votes of the Bundesrat. The decision to impeach requires a majority of two-thirds of the members of the Bundestag or of two-thirds of the votes of the Bundesrat. The pros-

* Added March 19, 1956.
** As amended March 19, 1956.

ecution is conducted by a person commissioned by the impeaching body.

(2) If the Federal Constitutional Court finds the Federal President guilty of a willful violation of the Basic Law or of another Federal law, it may declare him to have forfeited his office. After impeachment, it may issue an interim order preventing the Federal President from exercising the powers of his office.

TITLE VI. THE FEDERAL GOVERNMENT

ART. 62—The Federal Government consists of the Federal Chancellor and the Federal Ministers.

ART. 63—(1) The Federal Chancellor is elected, without debate, by the Bundestag on the proposal of the Federal President.

(2) The person obtaining the votes of the majority of the members of the Bundestag is elected. The person elected must be appointed by the Federal President.

(3) If the person proposed is not elected, the Bundestag may elect within fourteen days of the ballot a Federal Chancellor by more than one-half of its members.

(4) If there is no election within this period, a new ballot shall take place without delay, in which the person obtaining the largest number of votes is elected. If the person elected obtained the votes of the majority of the members of the Bundestag, the Federal President must appoint him within seven days of the election. If the person elected did not receive this majority, the Federal President must within seven days either appoint him or dissolve the Bundestag.

ART. 64—(1) The Federal Ministers are appointed and dismissed by the Federal President upon the proposal of the Federal Chancellor.

(2) The Federal Chancellor and the Federal Ministers, on assuming office, take before the Bundestag the oath provided in Article 56.

ART. 65—The Federal Chancellor determines, and is responsible for, general policy. Within the limits of this general policy, each Federal Minister conducts the business of his department autonomously and on his own responsibility. The Federal Government decides on differences of opinion between the Federal Ministers. The

Federal Chancellor conducts the business of the Federal Government in accordance with rules of procedure adopted by it and approved by the Federal President.

ART. 65a—* (1) Power of command in respect of the Armed Forces shall be vested in the Federal Minister of Defense.

(2) Upon promulgation of the determination concerning the case of defense, the power of command shall devolve on the Federal Chancellor.

ART. 66—The Federal Chancellor and the Federal Ministers may not hold any other salaried office, nor engage in a trade, nor practice a profession, nor belong to the management or, without the consent of the Bundestag, to the board of directors of an enterprise carried on for profit.

ART. 67—(1) The Bundestag can express its lack of confidence in the Federal Chancellor only by electing a successor by the majority of its members and by requesting the Federal President to dismiss the Federal Chancellor. The Federal President must comply with the request and appoint the person elected.

(2) Forty-eight hours must elapse between the motion and the election.

ART. 68—(1) If a motion of the Federal Chancellor for a vote of confidence is not assented to by the majority of the members of the Bundestag, the Federal President may, upon the proposal of the Federal Chancellor, dissolve the Bundestag within twenty-one days. The right to dissolve lapses as soon as the Bundestag by the majority of its members elects another Federal Chancellor.

(2) Forty-eight hours must elapse between the motion and the vote thereon.

ART. 69—(1) The Federal Chancellor appoints a Federal Minister as his deputy.

(2) The tenure of office of the Federal Chancellor or a Federal Minister ends in any event on the first meeting of a new Bundestag; the tenure of office of a Federal Minister ends also on any other termination of the tenure of office of the Federal Chancellor.

(3) At the request of the Federal President, the Federal Chancellor, or at the request of the Federal Chan-

* Added March 19, 1956.

cellor or of the Federal President, a Federal Minister is bound to continue to transact the business of his office until the appointment of a successor.

TITLE VII. LEGISLATIVE POWERS OF THE FEDERATION

ART. 70—(1) The *Laender* have the power to legislate insofar as this Basic Law does not confer legislative powers on the Federation.

(2) The division of competence between the Federation and the *Laender* is determined by the provisions of this Basic Law concerning exclusive and concurrent legislative powers.

ART. 71—On matters within the exclusive legislative powers of the Federation the *Laender* have authority to legislate only if, and to the extent that, a Federal law explicitly so authorizes them.

ART. 72—(1) On matters within the concurrent legislative powers the *Laender* have authority to legislate as long as, and to the extent that, the Federation does not use its legislative power.

(2) The Federation has the right to legislate on these matters to the extent that a need for a Federal rule exists because

1. a matter cannot be effectively dealt with by the legislation of individual *Laender*, or
2. dealing with a matter by *Land* law might prejudice the interests of other *Laender* or of the entire community, or
3. the maintenance of legal or economic unity, especially the maintenance of uniformity of living conditions beyond the territory of a *Land*, necessitates it.

ART. 73—* The Federation has the exclusive power to legislate on:—

1. Foreign affairs as well as defense, including both military service for males over 18 years and the protection of the civilian population.
2. citizenship in the Federation;
3. freedom of movement, passports, immigration and emigration, and extradition;

* As amended March 27, 1954.

4. currency, money and coinage, weights and measures, as well as computation of time;
5. the unity of the customs and commercial territory, commercial and navigation agreements, the freedom of movement of goods, and the exchanges of goods and payments with foreign countries, including customs and frontier protection;
6. Federal railroads and air traffic;
7. postal and telecommunication services;
8. the legal status of persons employed by the Federation and by Federal bodies-corporate under public law;
9. industrial property rights, copyrights and publication rights;
10. cooperation of the Federation and the *Laender* in matters of criminal police and of protection of the Constitution, establishment of a Federal office of the criminal police, as well as international control of crime;
11. statistics for Federal purposes.

ART. 74—Concurrent legislative powers extend to the following matters:—

1. civil law, criminal law and execution of sentences, the system of judicature, the procedure of the courts, the legal profession, notaries and legal advice;
2. registration of births, deaths, and marriages;
3. the law of association and assembly;
4. the law relating to residence and establishment of aliens;
5. the protection of German cultural treasures against removal abroad;
6. the affairs of refugees and expellees;
7. public welfare;
8. citizenship in the *Laender;*
9. war damage and reparations;
10.* benefits to war-disabled persons and to dependents of those killed in the war, *and* assistance to former prisoners of war;
10a.* *war graves of other victims of the war and of victims of despotism;*

* Amendment by parliament, June 16, 1965.—*Ed.'s note.*

11. the law relating to economic matters (mining, industry, supply of power, crafts, trades, commerce, banking and stock exchanges, private insurance);

11a.* The production and utilization of nuclear energy for peaceful purposes, the construction and operation of installations serving these purposes, protection against dangers arising from the release of nuclear energy or from ionizing rays, and removal of radioactive material;

12. labor law, including the legal organization of enterprises; protection of workers, employment exchanges and agencies, as well as social insurance, including unemployment insurance;

13. the promotion of scientific research;

14. the law regarding expropriation, to the extent that matters enumerated in Articles 73 and 74 are concerned;

15. transfer of land, natural resources and means of production into public ownership or other forms of publicly controlled economy;

16. prevention of the abuse of economic power;

17. promotion of agricultural and forest production, safeguarding of the supply of food, the import and export of agricultural and forest products, deep sea and coastal fishing, and preservation of the coasts;

18. dealings in real estate, land law and matters concerning agricultural leases, housing, settlements and homesteads;

19. measures against epidemic and infectious diseases of humans and animals, admission to medical and other professions and practices in the field of healing, traffic in drugs, medicines, narcotics, and poisons;

20. protection with regard to traffic in food and stimulants as well as in necessities of life, in fodder, in agricultural and forest seeds and seedlings, and protection of trees and plants against diseases and pests;

* Added December 23, 1959.

21. ocean and coastal shipping as well as aids to navigation, inland shipping, meteorological services, sea waterways and inland waterways used for general traffic;

22. road traffic, motor transport, and construction and maintenance of long distance highways;

23. railroads other than Federal railroads, except mountain railroads.

ART. 75—Subject to the conditions of Article 72 the Federation has the right to enact general rules concerning:

1. the legal status of persons in the public service of the *Laender,* communities and other bodies-corporate of public law;

2. the general rules of law concerning the status of the press and motion pictures;

3. hunting, protection of nature and care of the countryside;

4. land distribution, regional planning and water conservation;

5. matters relating to registration and identity cards.

ART. 76—(1) Bills are introduced in the Bundestag by the Federal Government, by members of the Bundestag or by the Bundesrat.

(2) Bills of the Federal Government shall be submitted first to the Bundesrat. The Bundesrat is entitled to state its position on these bills within three weeks.

(3) Bills of the Bundesrat shall be submitted to the Bundestag by the Federal Government. In doing so the Federal Government must state its own views.

ART. 77—(1) Federal laws are adopted by the Bundestag. Upon their adoption, they shall, without delay, be transmitted to the Bundesrat by the President of the Bundestag.

(2) The Bundesrat may, within two weeks of the receipt of the adopted bill, demand that a committee for joint consideration of bills, composed of members of the Bundestag and the Bundesrat, be convened. The composition and the procedure of this committee are regulated by rules of procedure adopted by the Bundestag and requiring the consent of the Bundesrat. The members of the Bundesrat on this committee are not bound

by instructions. If the consent of the Bundesrat is required for a law, the demand for convening this committee may also be made by the Bundestag or the Federal Government. Should the committee propose any amendment to the adopted bill, the Bundestag must again vote on the bill.

(3) Insofar as the consent of the Bundesrat is not required for a law, the Bundesrat may, if the proceedings under paragraph 2 are completed, enter a protest within one week against a law adopted by the Bundestag. This period begins, in the case of paragraph 2, last sentence, on the receipt of the bill as re-adopted by the Bundestag, in all other cases on the conclusion of the proceedings of the committee provided for in paragraph 2.

(4) If the protest is adopted by a majority of the votes of the Bundesrat; it can be rejected by a decision of the majority of the members of the Bundestag. If the Bundesrat adopted the protest by a majority of at least two-thirds of its votes, the rejection by the Bundestag requires a majority of two-thirds, including at least the majority of the members of the Bundestag.

ART. 78—A law adopted by the Bundestag is deemed to have been passed if the Bundesrat consents to it, does not make a demand pursuant to Article 77, paragraph 2, does not enter a protest within the time limited by Article 77, paragraph 3, or withdraws such protest, or if the protest is overridden by the Bundestag.

ART. 79—* (1) The Basic Law can be amended only by a law which expressly amends or supplements the text thereof.

With respect to international treaties the subject of which is a peace settlement, the preparation of a peace settlement or the abolition of an occupation regime, or which are designed to serve the defense of the Federal Republic, it shall be sufficient, for the purpose of a clarifying interpretation to the effect that the provisions of the Basic Law are not contrary to the conclusion and entry into force of such treaties, to effect a supplementation of the text of the Basic Law confined to this clarifying interpretation.

* As amended March 27, 1954.

(2) Such a law requires the affirmative vote of two-thirds of the members of the Bundestag and two-thirds of the votes of the Bundesrat.

(3) An amendment of this Basic Law affecting the division of the Federation into *Laender,* the participation in principle of the *Laender* in legislation, or the basic principles laid down in Articles 1 and 20, is inadmissible.

ART. 80—(1) The Federal Government, a Federal Minister or the *Land* Governments may be authorized by a law to issue ordinances having the force of law. The content, purpose and scope of the powers conferred must be set forth in the law. The legal basis must be stated in the ordinance. If a law provides that a power may be further delegated, an ordinance having the force of law is necessary in order to delegate the power.

(2) The consent of the Bundesrat is required, unless otherwise provided by federal legislation, for ordinances having the force of law issued by the Federal Government or a Federal Minister concerning basic rules for the use of facilities of the Federal railroads and of postal and telecommunication services, or charges therefor, or concerning the construction and operation of railroads, as well as for ordinances having the force of law issued on the basis of federal laws that require the consent of the Bundesrat or that are executed by the *Laender* as agents of the Federation or as matters of their own concern.

ART. 81—(1) Should in the circumstances of Article 68 the Bundestag not be dissolved, the Federal President may, at the request of the Federal Government and with the consent of the Bundesrat, declare a state of legislative emergency with respect to a bill, if the Bundestag rejects the bill although the Federal Government has declared it to be urgent. The same applies if a bill has been rejected although the Federal Chancellor had combined with it the motion under Article 68.

(2) If, after a state of legislative emergency has been declared, the Bundestag again rejects the bill or adopts it in a version declared to be unacceptable to the Federal Government, the bill is deemed to have been passed insofar as the Bundesrat consents to it. The same applies

if the bill is not adopted by the Bundestag within four weeks of its reintroduction.

(3) During the term of office of a Federal Chancellor, any other bill rejected by the Bundestag may be passed in accordance with paragraphs 1 and 2 within a period of six months after the first declaration of a state of legislative emergency. After expiration of this period, a further declaration of a state of legislative emergency is inadmissible during the term of office of the same Federal Chancellor.

(4) The Basic Law may not be amended nor be repealed nor suspended in whole or in part by a law passed pursuant to paragraph 2.

ART. 82—(1) Laws passed in accordance with the provisions of this Basic Law will, after countersignature, be signed by the Federal President and promulgated in the Federal Gazette. Ordinances having the force of law will be signed by the agency which issues them, and unless otherwise provided by law, will be promulgated in the Federal Gazette.

(2) Every law and every ordinance having the force of law should specify its effective date. In the absence of such a provision, it becomes effective on the fourteenth day after the end of the day on which the Federal Gazette was published.

TITLE VIII. THE EXECUTION OF FEDERAL LAWS AND THE FEDERAL ADMINISTRATION

ART. 83—The *Laender* execute Federal laws as matters of their own concern insofar as this Basic Law does not otherwise provide or permit.

ART. 84—(1) If the *Laender* execute Federal laws as matters of their own concern, they provide for the establishment of authorities and the regulation of administrative procedures insofar as Federal laws consented to by the Bundesrat do not otherwise provide.

(2) The Federal Government may, with the consent of the Bundesrat, issue general administrative rules.

(3) The Federal Government exercises supervision to ensure that the *Laender* execute Federal laws in accordance with applicable law. For this purpose the Federal Government may send commissioners to the highest *Land*

authorities and, with their consent or, if this consent is refused, with the consent of the Bundesrat, also to subordinate authorities.

(4) Should any shortcomings which the Federal Government has found to exist in the execution of Federal laws in the *Laender* not be corrected, the Bundesrat decides, on the application of the Federal Government or the *Land,* whether the *Land* has acted unlawfully. The decision of the Bundesrat may be challenged in the Federal Constitutional Court.

(5) For the execution of Federal laws, the Federal Government may, by Federal law requiring the consent of the Bundesrat, be authorized to issue individual instructions for particular cases. They must be addressed to the highest *Land* authorities unless the Federal Government considers the matter urgent.

ART. 85—(1) Where the *Laender* execute Federal laws as agents of the Federation, the establishment of the authorities remains the concern of the *Laender* insofar as Federal laws consented to by the Bundesrat do not otherwise provide.

(2) The Federal Government may, with the consent of the Bundesrat, issue general administrative rules. It may regulate the uniform training of civil servants and salaried government employees. The heads of authorities at intermediate level shall be appointed with its agreement.

(3) The *Land* authorities are subject to the instructions of the appropriate highest Federal authorities. The instructions shall be addressed to the highest *Land* authorities unless the Federal Government considers the matter urgent. Execution of the instructions shall be ensured by the highest *Land* authorities.

(4) Federal supervision extends to the conformity with law and appropriateness of the execution. The Federal Government may, for this purpose, require the submission of reports and documents and send commissioners to all authorities.

ART. 86—Where the Federation executes laws by Federal administrative agencies or by Federal bodies-corporate or institutions under public law, the Federal

Government issues, insofar as the law contains no special provision, the general administrative rules. It provides for the establishment of authorities insofar as the law does not otherwise provide.

ART. 87—(1) The foreign service, the Federal finance administration, the Federal railroads, the Federal postal service and, in accordance with the provisions of Article 89, the administration of the Federal waterways and of shipping are conducted as matters of Federal administration with their own subordinate administrative structure. Federal frontier protection authorities and central offices for police information and communications, for the compilation of data for the purpose of protecting the Constitution and for the criminal police may be established by Federal legislation.

(2) Social insurance institutions whose sphere of competence extends beyond the territory of one *Land* are conducted as Federal bodies-corporate under public law.

(3) In addition, independent Federal higher authorities and Federal bodies-corporate and institutions under public law may be established by Federal law for matters on which the Federation has the power to legislate. If new functions arise for the Federation in matters on which it has the power to legislate, Federal authorities at intermediate and lower level may be established, in case of urgent need, with the consent of the Bundesrat and of the majority of the members of the Bundestag.

ART. 87a—* The numerical strength and general organizational structure of the Armed Forces raised for defense by the Federation shall be shown in the budget.

ART. 87b—** (1) The administration of the Federal Defense Forces shall be conducted as a Federal administration with its own administrative substructure. Its function shall be to administer matters pertaining to personnel and to the immediate supply of the material requirements of the Armed Forces. Tasks connected with benefits to invalids or construction work shall not be as-

* Added March 19, 1956.
** Added March 19, 1956.

signed to the administration of the Federal Defense Forces except by Federal legislation which shall require the consent of the Bundesrat. Such consent shall also be required for any legislative provisions empowering the administration of the Federal Defense Forces to interfere with rights of third parties; this shall, however, not apply in the case of laws concerning personnel.

(2) Moreover, Federal laws concerning defense including recruitment for military service and protection of the civilian population may, with the consent of the Bundesrat, stipulate that they shall be carried out, wholly or in part, either under Federal administration with its own administrative substructure or by the *Laender* acting as agents of the Federation. If such laws are executed by the *Laender* acting as agents of the Federation, they may, with the consent of the Bundesrat, stipulate that the powers vested by virtue of Article 85 in the Federal Government and appropriate highest Federal authorities shall be transferred wholly or partly to higher Federal authorities; in such an event it may be enacted that these authorities shall not require the consent of the Bundesrat in issuing general administrative rules as referred to in Article 85 paragraph (2) first sentence.

ART. 87c—* Laws enacted under item 11a of Art. 74 may, with the consent of the Bundesrat, stipulate that they shall be executed by the *Laender* acting as agent of the Federation.

ART. 87d—** (1) The administration of air transportation shall be conducted as a Federal administration with its own administrative substructure.

(2) Through Federal legislation which shall require the consent of the Bundesrat matters concerning the administration of air transportation may be transferred to the *Laender* as agents.

ART. 88—The Federation establishes a note-issuing and currency bank as the Federal bank.

ART. 89—(1) The Federation is the owner of the former *Reich* waterways.

* Added December 23, 1959.
** Added February 6, 1961.

(2) The Federation administers the Federal waterways through its own authorities. It exercises the public
functions relating to inland shipping which extend beyond the territory of one *Land* and those relating to
maritime shipping which are conferred on it by law.
Upon request, the Federation may transfer the administration of Federal waterways, insofar as they lie within
the territory of one *Land,* to this *Land* as an agent. If a
waterway touches the territories of several *Laender* the
Federation may designate as its agent one *Land* if so requested by the *Laender* concerned.

(3) In the administration, development and new
construction of waterways the needs of soil cultivation
and of regulating water supply shall be safeguarded in
agreement with the *Laender*.

ART. 90—(1) The Federation is the owner of the
former *Reich* motor roads and *Reich* highways.

(2) The *Laender,* or such self-governing bodies-corporate as are competent under *Land* law, administer as
agents of the Federation the Federal motor roads and
other Federal highways used for long-distance traffic.

(3) At the request of a *Land,* the Federation may
take under direct Federal administration Federal motor
roads and other Federal highways used for long-distance
traffic, insofar as they lie within the territory of that
Land.

ART. 91—(1) In order to avert any imminent danger to the existence or to the free democratic basic order of the Federation or of a *Land,* a *Land* may request the services of the police forces of other *Laender*.

(2) If the *Land* in which the danger is imminent is
not itself willing or able to fight the danger, the Federal
Government may place the police in that *Land* and the
police forces of other *Laender* under its own instructions. The order for this shall be rescinded after the danger is past, or else at any time on the demand of the
Bundesrat.

TITLE IX. THE ADMINISTRATION OF JUSTICE

ART. 92—The judicial authority is vested in the
judges; it is exercised by the Federal Constitutional

Court, by the Supreme Federal Court, by the Federal courts provided for in this Basic Law and by the courts of the *Laender.*

ART. 93—(1) The Federal Constitutional Court decides:—

1. on the interpretation of this Basic Law in the event of disputes concerning the extent of the rights and duties of a supreme Federal organ or of other parties concerned who have been endowed with independent rights by this Basic Law or by rules of procedure of a supreme Federal organ;

2. in case of differences of opinion or doubts on the formal and material compatibility of Federal law or *Land* law with this Basic Law, or on the compatibility of *Land* law with other Federal law, at the request of the Federal Government, of a *Land* government or of one-third of the Bundestag members;

3. in case of differences of opinion on the rights and duties of the Federation and the *Laender,* particularly in the execution of Federal law by the *Laender* and in the exercise of Federal supervision;

4. on other disputes of public law between the Federation and the *Laender,* between different *Laender* or within a *Land,* unless recourse to another court exists;

5. in the other cases provided for in this Basic Law.

(2) The Federal Constitutional Court shall also act in such cases as are otherwise assigned to it by Federal law.

ART. 94—(1) The Federal Constitutional Court consists of Federal judges and other members. Half of the members of the Federal Constitutional Court are elected by the Bundestag and half by the Bundesrat. They may not belong to the Bundestag, the Bundesrat, the Federal Government or the corresponding organs of a *Land.*

(2) Its constitution and procedure will be regulated by a Federal law, which will specify in what cases its decisions shall have the force of law.

ART. 95—(1) To preserve the uniformity of application of Federal law a Supreme Federal Court will be established.

(2) The Supreme Federal Court decides cases in which the decision is of fundamental importance for the uniformity of the administration of justice by the higher Federal courts.

(3) The judges of the Supreme Federal Court are selected jointly by the Federal Minister of Justice and a committee for the selection of judges consisting of the *Land* Ministers of Justice and an equal number of members elected by the Bundestag.

(4) In other respects, the constitution of the Supreme Federal Court and its procedure will be regulated by Federal legislation.

ART. 96—* (1) Higher Federal courts shall be established for the fields of ordinary, administrative, finance, labor and social jurisdiction.

(2) Article 95, paragraph 3, applies to the judges of the higher Federal courts, provided that the Ministers competent for the particular matter take the place of the Federal Minister of Justice and the *Land* Ministers of Justice. The terms of service of these judges shall be regulated by special Federal legislation.

ART. 96a—** (1) The Federation may establish a Federal court for the protection of industrial rights.

(2) The Federation may establish military criminal courts for the armed forces as Federal courts. They may exercise criminal jurisdiction only in case of defense or over members of the armed forces serving abroad or on board warships. Details shall be regulated by a Federal law. These courts shall be within the sphere of business of the Federal Minister of Justice. Their full-time judges must be professional judges.

(3) The Federal Supreme Court shall be the superior Federal court for the courts named in paragraph 1 and 2.

ART. 97—(1) The judges are independent and subject only to the law.

(2) Judges appointed permanently on a full time basis to an established post can, against their will, be dismissed, or permanently or temporarily suspended from office, or transferred to another post, or retired before

* As amended March 19, 1956.
** Added March 19, 1956, and revised February 6, 1961.

expiration of their term of office only under authority of a judicial decision and only on grounds and in the form provided for by law. Legislation may set age limits for the retirement of judges appointed for life. In the event of changes in the structure of the courts or their areas of jurisdiction, judges may be transferred to another court or removed from their office, provided they retain their full salary.

ART. 98—(1) The legal status of the Federal judges shall be regulated by a special Federal law.

(2) If a Federal judge, in his official capacity or unofficially, infringes upon the principles of the Basic Law or the constitutional order of a *Land,* the Federal Constitutional Court may decide by a two-thirds majority, upon the request of the Bundestag, that the judge be transferred to another office or placed on the retired list. In a case of an intentional infringement, his dismissal may be ordered.

(3) The legal status of the judges in the *Laender* shall be regulated by special *Land* laws. The Federation may enact general rules.

(4) The *Laender* may provide that the *Land* Minister of Justice together with a committee for the selection of judges shall decide on the appointment of judges in the *Laender.*

(5) The *Laender* may, with respect to *Land* judges, enact provisions corresponding with paragraph 2. Existing *Land* constitutional law remains unaffected. The decision in a case of impeachment of a judge rests with the Federal Constitutional Court.

ART. 99—The decision on constitutional disputes within a *Land* may be assigned by a *Land* law to the Federal Constitutional Court, and the decision of last instance in matters involving the application of *Land* law, to the higher Federal courts.

ART. 100—(1) If a court considers a law unconstitutional, the validity of which is relevant to its decision, the proceedings shall be stayed, and a decision shall be obtained from the *Land* court competent for constitutional disputes if the matter concerns the violation of the constitution of a *Land,* or from the Federal Constitutional Court if the matter concerns a violation of the

Basic Law. This also applies if the matter concerns the violation of this Basic Law by *Land* law or the incompatibility of a *Land* law with a Federal law.

(2) If, in the course of litigation, doubt exists whether a rule of public international law forms part of the Federal law and whether such rule directly creates rights and duties for the individual (Article 25), the court shall obtain the decision of the Federal Constitutional Court.

(3) If the constitutional court of a *Land*, in interpreting the Basic Law, intends to deviate from a decision of the Federal Constitutional Court or of the constitutional court of another *Land*, it must obtain the decision of the Federal Constitutional Court; if, in interpreting other Federal law, it intends to deviate from the decision of the Supreme Federal Court or a higher Federal court, it must obtain the decision of the Supreme Federal Court.

ART. 101—(1) Extraordinary courts are inadmissible. No one may be removed from the jurisdiction of his lawful judge.

(2) Courts for special fields may be established only by a law.

ART. 102—Capital punishment is abolished.

ART. 103—(1) In the courts everyone is entitled to a hearing in accordance with the law.

(2) An act can be punished only if it was a punishable offense by law before the act was committed.

(3) No one may be punished for the same act more than once in pursuance of general penal legislation.

ART. 104—(1) The freedom of the individual may be restricted only on the basis of a formal law and only with due regard to the forms prescribed therein. Detained persons may be subjected neither to mental nor to physical ill-treatment.

(2) Only judges may decide on admissibility or extension of a deprivation of liberty. Where such deprivation is not based on the order of a judge, a judicial decision must be obtained without delay. The police may hold no one on their own authority in their own custody longer than the end of the day after the arrest. Details shall be regulated by legislation.

(3) Any person provisionally detained on suspicion of having committed a punishable offense must be brought before a judge at the latest on the day following the arrest; the judge shall inform him of the reasons for the detention, examine him and give him an opportunity to raise objections. The judge must, without delay, either issue a warrant of arrest setting forth the reasons therefor or order the release from detention.

(4) A relative of the person detained or a person enjoying his confidence must be notified without delay of any judicial decision ordering or extending a deprivation of liberty.

TITLE X. FINANCE

ART. 105—(1) The Federation has the exclusive power to legislate on customs and fiscal monopolies.

(2) The Federation has concurrent power to legislate on:

1. excise taxes and taxes on transactions, with the exception of taxes with localized application, in particular of the taxes on the acquisition of real estate, on increments in value, and for fire protection;
2. taxes on income, on property, on inheritances and on donations;
3. taxes on real estate and businesses, with the exception of the fixing of the tax rates,

if it claims the taxes in whole or in part to cover Federal expenditure or if the conditions laid down in Article 72, paragraph 2, exist.

(3) Federal laws relating to taxes the yield of which accrues in whole or in part to the *Laender* or the communities (community associations) require the consent of the Bundesrat.

ART. 106—* (1) The yield of fiscal monopolies and receipts from the following taxes shall accrue to the Federation:

1. customs duties,
2. such excise taxes as do not accrue to the *Laender* in accordance with paragraph (2),

* As amended December 23, 1955 and December 24, 1956.

3. turnover tax,
4. transportation tax,
5. non-recurrent capital levies, and equalization taxes imposed for the purpose of implementing the equalization of burdens legislation,
6. Berlin emergency aid tax,
7. supplementary levies on income and corporation taxes.

(2) Receipts from the following taxes shall accrue to the *Laender*

1. property tax,
2. inheritance tax,
3. motor-vehicle tax,
4. such taxes on transactions as do not accrue to the Federation in accordance with paragraph (1),
5. beer tax,
6. levies on gambling establishments,
7. taxes on real estate and businesses,
8. taxes with localized application.

(3) Receipts from income tax and corporation tax shall accrue: until 31 March 1958, to the Federation and the *Laender* in a ratio of 33⅓ per cent to 66⅔ per cent, and from 1 April 1958, to the Federation and the *Laender* in a ratio of 35 per cent to 65 per cent.

(4) The ratio of apportionment of the income and corporation taxes paragraph (3) should be modified by a Federal law requiring the consent of the Bundesrat whenever the development of the relation of revenues to expenditures in the Federation differs from that in the *Laender* and whenever the budgetary needs of the Federation or those of the *Laender* exceed the estimated revenues by a margin substantial enough to call for a corresponding adjustment of the ratio of apportionment in favor of either the Federation or the *Laender*. Any such adjustment shall be based on the following principles:

1. The Federation and the *Laender* shall each bear the expenditures resulting from the administration

of their respective tasks; Article 120 paragraph (1) shall not be affected;

2. there shall be equality of rank between the claim of the Federation and the claim of the *Laender* to have their respective necessary expenditures covered from ordinary revenues;

3. the requirements of the Federation and of the *Laender* in respect of budget coverage shall be coordinated in such a way that a fair equalization is achieved, any overburdening of taxpayers precluded, and uniformity of living standards in the Federal territory ensured.

The ratio of apportionment may be modified for the first time with effect from 1 April 1958, and subsequently at intervals of not less than two years after the entry into force of any law determining such ratio; provided that this stipulation shall not affect any modification of such ratio effected in accordance with paragraph (5).

(5) If a Federal law imposes additional expenditures on, or withdraws revenues from, the *Laender,* the ratio of apportionment of the income and corporation taxes shall be modified in favor of the *Laender,* provided that conditions as envisaged in paragraph (4) have developed. If the additional burden placed upon the *Laender* is limited to a period of short duration, such burden may be compensated by grants from the Federation under a Federal law requiring the consent of the Bundesrat and which shall lay down the principles for assessing the amounts of such grants and for distributing them among the *Laender*.

(6) Receipts from taxes on real estate and businesses shall accrue to the communes. In case there are no communes in a *Land* the receipts shall accrue to the *Land*. In accordance with *Land* legislation, taxes on real estate and businesses may be used to ascertain assessments and surtaxes. The receipts of the *Laender* from income tax and corporation tax shall accrue to the communes and associations of communes in a percentage to be determined by *Land* legislation. Furthermore, the *Land* legislation shall determine whether and how much of the receipts of the *Land* taxes shall accrue to the communes (associations of communes).

(7) If the Federation establishes special institutions in the *Laender* or communes (associations of communes) which cause immediate higher expenditures or lower receipts to those *Laender* or communes (associations of communes), the Federation shall grant the necessary financial equalization, if and insofar as it is anticipated that the *Laender* or communes (associations of communes) are unable to bear these special burdens. Compensation by a third party and financial advantages which accrue to these *Laender* or communes (associations of communes) as a consequence of these institutions shall be considered in such equalization.

(8) For the purposes of the present Article, revenues and expenditures of communes (associations of communes) shall be deemed to be *Land* revenues and expenditures.

ART. 107—* (1) Receipts from *Land* taxes shall accrue to the individual *Laender* to the extent that such taxes are collected by revenue authorities within their respective territories (local receipts). Federal legislation requiring the consent of the Bundesrat may provide in detail for the determination and allotment of local receipts from specific taxes (tax shares).

(2) A Federal law requiring the consent of the Bundesrat shall ensure a reasonable financial equalization between financially strong *Laender* and financially weak *Laender,* due account being taken of the financial capacity and requirements of communes (associations of communes). Such law shall provide for equalization grants to be paid to financially weak *Laender* from equalization contributions made by financially strong *Laender;* it shall furthermore specify the conditions governing equalization claims and equalization liabilities as well as the criteria for determining the amounts of equalization payments. Such law may also provide for grants to be made by the Federation from Federal funds to financially weak *Laender* in order to complement the coverage of their general financial requirements (complemental grants).

ART. 108—(1) Customs, fiscal monopolies, the excise taxes subject to concurrent legislative powers, the

* As amended December 23, 1955.

transportation tax, the turnover tax and the non-recurrent capital levies are administered by Federal finance authorities. The organization of these authorities and the procedure to be applied by them will be regulated by Federal law. The heads of the authorities at intermediate level shall be appointed after consultation with the *Land* governments. The Federation may transfer the administration of non-recurrent capital levies to the *Land* financial authorities as its agents.

(2) If the Federation claims part of the income and corporation taxes for itself, it is entitled to administer them to that extent; it may, however, transfer the administration to the *Land* finance authorities as its agents.

(3) The remaining taxes are administered by *Land* finance authorities. The Federation may, by Federal laws which require the consent of the Bundesrat, regulate the organization of these authorities, the procedure to be applied by them and the uniform training of the civil servants. The heads of the authorities at intermediate level shall be appointed in agreement with the Federal Government. The administration of the taxes accruing to the communities (community associations) may be transferred by the *Laender* in whole or in part to the communities (community associations).

(4) Insofar as taxes accrue to the Federation, the *Land* finance authorities act as agents of the Federation. The *Laender* are liable to the extent of their revenues for an orderly administration of such taxes; the Federal Minister of Finance may supervise the orderly administration, acting through authorized Federal agents who have a right to give instructions to the authorities at intermediate and lower levels.

(5) The jurisdiction of finance courts will be uniformly regulated by Federal law.

(6) The general administrative rules will be issued by the Federal Government and, insofar as the administration is incumbent upon the *Land* finance authorities, will require the consent of the Bundesrat.

ART. 109*—(1) The Federation and the *Laender* are

---

* As amended by parliament, June 8, 1967, to add the italicized clauses.—*Ed.'s note.*

autonomous and independent of each other as regards their budgets.

(2) *The Federation and the* Laender *must use their budgets to maintain general economic stability.*

(3) *Federal legislation, with the consent of the Bundesrat, may lay down principles for counter-cyclical budgeting and for long-term financial planning.*

(4) *To prevent a disruption of general economic stability, Federal legislation, with the consent of the Bundesrat, may issue regulations concerning*

1. *Maximum amounts, terms, and timing of loans made by public authorities and local administrative associations and*
2. *An obligation of the Federation and the* Laender *to maintain interest-free deposits in the German Federal Bank (reserve funds for stabilizing the economy).*

Authorization to issue decrees can be delegated only to the Federal Government [Cabinet]. The decrees require the consent of the Bundesrat. They must be rescinded at the request of the Bundestag; details will be regulated by Federal legislation.

ART. 110—(1) All revenues and expenditures of the Federation must be estimated for each fiscal year and included in the budget.

(2) The budget shall be established by a law before the beginning of the fiscal year. It must be balanced as regards revenue and expenditure. Expenditures will as a rule be authorized for one year; in special cases, they may be authorized for a longer period. Otherwise no provisions may be inserted in the Federal budget law which extend beyond the fiscal year or which do not relate to the revenues and expenditures of the Federation or its administration.

(3) The assets and liabilities shall be set forth in an appendix to the budget.

(4) In the case of commercially operated enterprises of the Federation the individual receipts and expenditures need not be included in the budget, but only the final balance.

ART. 111—(1) If, by the end of a fiscal year, the

budget for the following year has not been established by a law, the Federal Government may, until such law comes into force, make all payments which are necessary:—

(a) to maintain institutions existing by law and to carry out measures authorized by law;

(b) to meet legal obligations of the Federation;

(c) to continue building projects, procurements and other services or to continue the grant of subsidies for these purposes, provided amounts have already been authorized in the budget of a previous year.

(2) Insofar as revenues provided by special legislation and derived from taxes, levies, or other sources, or the working capital reserves, do not cover the expenditures set forth in paragraph 1, the Federal Government may borrow the funds necessary for the conduct of current operations to a maximum of one quarter of the total amount of the previous budget.

ART. 112—Expenditures in excess of budget items and extraordinary expenditures require the consent of the Federal Minister of Finance. The consent may only be given if there exists an unforeseen and compelling necessity.

ART. 113—Decisions of the Bundestag and of the Bundesrat which increase the budget expenditure proposed by the Federal Government or involve new expenditure or will cause new expenditure in the future, require the consent of the Federal Government.

ART. 114—(1) The Federal Minister of Finance must submit annually to the Bundestag and to the Bundesrat an account of all revenues and expenditures as well as assets and liabilities.

(2) This account shall be audited by an Audit Office, the members of which shall enjoy judicial independence. The general account and a summary of the assets and liabilities shall be submitted to the Bundestag and the Bundesrat in the course of the following fiscal year together with the comments of the Audit Office in order to secure a discharge for the Federal Government. The audit of accounts will be regulated by a Federal law.

ART. 115—Funds may be obtained by borrowing only in case of extraordinary need and as a rule only for expenditure for productive purposes and only pursuant to a Federal law. The granting of credits and the provision of security by the Federation the effect of which extends beyond the fiscal year may take place only pursuant to a Federal law. The amount of the credit, or the extent of the obligation for which the Federation assumes liability, must be fixed in the law.

TITLE XI. TRANSITIONAL AND CONCLUDING PROVISIONS

ART. 116—(1) Unless otherwise provided by law, a German within the meaning of this Basic Law is a person who possesses German citizenship or who has been admitted to the territory of the German *Reich*, as it existed on December 31, 1937, as a refugee or expellee of German stock or as the spouse or descendant of such person.

(2) Former German citizens who, between January 30, 1933 and May 8, 1945, were deprived of their citizenship for political, racial or religious reasons, and their descendants, shall be re-granted German citizenship on application. They are considered as not having been deprived of their German citizenship if they have established their domicile in Germany after May 8, 1945 and have not expressed a contrary intention.

ART. 117—(1) Law which conflicts with Article 3, paragraph 2, remains in force until adapted to this provision of the Basic Law, but not beyond March 31, 1953.

(2) Laws which restrict the right of freedom of movement in view of the present housing shortage remain in force until repealed by Federal legislation.

ART. 118—The reorganization of the territory comprising the *Laender* of Baden, Wuerttemberg-Baden and Wuerttemberg-Hohenzollern may be effected notwithstanding the provisions of Article 29, by agreement between the *Laender* concerned. If no agreement is reached, the reorganization will be regulated by a Federal law which must provide for a referendum.

ART. 119—In matters relating to refugees and expellees, in particular as regards their distribution among the *Laender,* the Federal Government may, with the consent of the Bundesrat, issue ordinances having the force

of law, pending settlement of the matter by Federal legislation. The Federal Government may in this matter
be authorized to issue individual instructions for particular cases. Except where there is danger in delay, the instructions shall be addressed to the highest *Land* authorities.

ART. 120—* (1) The Federation bears the expenditure
for occupation costs and the other internal and external
burdens caused as a consequence of the war, as provided
for in detail by a Federal law. *So far as these burdens were
governed up to 1 October 1965 by federal law, the expenditure shall be borne, in accordance with these federal
laws, by the Federation and the* Laender *proportionally.
So far as the* Laender, *the communes (associations of
communes) or other entities carrying out functions of the*
Laender *and the communes have borne the expenditure for
burdens caused as a consequence of the war and which
were, or are, not governed by federal law, the Federation
shall not be obliged to take over any such expenditure
even after the above date. The Federation shall bear the
subsidies toward the burdens of social insurance, including
unemployment insurance and public assistance for the
unemployed. The distribution among the Federation and*
Laender *of the burdens caused as a consequence of the
war shall not affect the statutory provisions with regard
to claims for compensation for consequences of the war.*

(2) The revenues are transferred to the Federation at
the same time as the Federation assumes responsibility
for the expenditures.

ART. 120a—** (1) Law concerning the implementation of the Equalization of Burdens may, with the consent of the Bundesrat, stipulate that in the field of equalization benefits, they shall be executed partly by the Federation and partly by the *Laender* acting as agents of the
Federation, and that the relevant powers vested in the
Federal Government and the competent highest federal
authorities by virtue of Article 85, shall be wholly or
partly delegated to the Federal Equalization Office. In
the exercise of these powers the Federal Equalization
Office shall not require the consent of the Bundesrat;

* As amended by parliament, July 30, 1965.—*Ed.'s note.*
** Added August 14, 1952.

with the exception of urgent cases, its instructions shall be given to the highest *Land* authorities (*Land* Equalization Offices).

(2) The provisions of Article 87, paragraph 3, second sentence, shall not be affected hereby.

ART. 121—Within the meaning of this Basic Law, a majority of the members of the Bundestag and of the Federal Convention is the majority of the number of their members established by law.

ART. 122—(1) From the time of the first meeting of the Bundestag, laws shall be passed exclusively by the legislative organs recognized in this Basic Law.

(2) Legislative bodies and bodies participating in legislation in an advisory capacity whose competence ends by virtue of paragraph 1, are dissolved from that date.

ART. 123—(1) Law in force before the first meeting of the Bundestag remains in force, insofar as it does not conflict with the Basic Law.

(2) Subject to all rights and objections of the interested parties, the state treaties concluded by the German *Reich* concerning matters for which, under this Basic Law, *Land* legislation is competent, remain in force, if they are and continue to be valid in accordance with general principles of law, until new state treaties are concluded by the agencies competent under this Basic Law, or until they are in any other way terminated pursuant to their provisions.

ART. 124—Law affecting matters within the exclusive power to legislate of the Federation becomes Federal law wherever it is applicable.

ART. 125—Law affecting matters within the concurrent power to legislate of the Federation becomes Federal law wherever it is applicable:—

1. insofar as it applies uniformly within one or more zones of occupation;

2. insofar as it is law by which former *Reich* law has been amended after May 8, 1945.

ART. 126—The Federal Constitutional Court decides disputes regarding the continuance of law as Federal law.

ART. 127—Within one year of the promulgation of this Basic Law the Federal Government may, with the consent of the governments of the *Laender* concerned, extend to the *Laender* of Baden, Greater Berlin, Rhineland-Palatinate and Wuerttemberg-Hohenzollern any legislation of the Bizonal Economic Administration, insofar as it continues to be in force as Federal law under Articles 124 or 125.

ART. 128—Insofar as law continuing in force provides for powers to give instructions within the meaning of Article 84, paragraph 5, these powers remain in existence until otherwise provided by law.

ART. 129—(1) Insofar as legal provisions which continue in force as Federal law contain an authorization to issue ordinances having the force of law or general administrative rules or to perform administrative acts, the authorization passes to the agencies henceforth competent in the matter. In cases of doubt, the Federal Government will decide in agreement with the Bundesrat; the decision must be published.

(2) Insofar as legal provisions which continue in force as *Land* law contain such an authorization, it will be exercised by the agencies competent under *Land* law.

(3) Insofar as legal provisions within the meaning of paragraphs 1 and 2 authorize their amendment or supplementation or the issue of legal provisions in place of laws, these authorizations have expired.

(4) The provisions of paragraphs 1 and 2 apply *mutatis mutandis* whenever legal provisions refer to regulations no longer valid or to institutions no longer in existence.

ART. 130—(1) Administrative agencies and other institutions which serve the public administration or the administration of justice and are not based on *Land* law or treaties between *Laender,* as well as the Association of Management of Southwest German Railroads and the Administrative Council for the Postal Services and Telecommunications of the French Zone of Occupation are placed under the Federal Government. The Federal Government provides with the consent of the Bundesrat for their transfer, dissolution or liquidation.

(2) The highest disciplinary superior of the personnel of these administrations and institutions is the appropriate Federal Minister.

(3) Bodies-corporate and institutions of public law not directly under a *Land*, and not based on treaties between *Laender*, are under the supervision of the appropriate highest Federal authority.

ART. 131—Federal legislation shall regulate the legal status of persons, including refugees and expellees, who, on May 8, 1945, were employed in the public service, have left the service for reasons other than those arising from civil service regulations or collective agreement rules, and have not until now been employed or are employed in a position not corresponding to their former one. The same applies *mutatis mutandis* to persons, including refugees and expellees, who, on May 8, 1945, were entitled to a pension or other assistance and who no longer receive any assistance or any commensurate assistance for reasons other than those arising from civil service regulations or collective agreement rules. Until the Federal law comes into force, no legal claims can be made, unless otherwise provided by *Land* legislation.

ART. 132—(1) Civil servants and judges who, when the Basic Law comes into force, are appointed for life, may, within six months after the first meeting of the Bundestag, be placed on the retired list or waiting list or be transferred to another office with lower remuneration, if they lack the personal or professional aptitude for their office. This provision applies *mutatis mutandis* also to salaried employees whose service cannot be terminated by notice. In the case of salaried employees whose service can be terminated by notice, periods of notice in excess of the periods fixed by collective agreement rules may be cancelled within the same period.

(2) This provision does not apply to members of the public service who are not affected by the provisions regarding the liberation from National Socialism and militarism or who are recognized victims of National Socialism, unless there exists an important reason with respect to their personality.

(3) Those affected may have recourse to the courts in accordance with Article 19, paragraph 4.

(4) Details will be regulated by an ordinance of the

Federal Government which requires the consent of the Bundesrat.

ART. 133—The Federation succeeds to the rights and obligations of the Bizonal Economic Administration.

ART. 134—(1) *Reich* property becomes in principle Federal property.

(2) Insofar as the property was originally intended to be used predominantly for administrative tasks which, under this Basic Law, are not administrative tasks of the Federation, it shall be transferred without compensation to the authorities now charged with such tasks, and to the *Laender* insofar as it is being used at present, and not merely temporarily, for administrative tasks which under the Basic Law are now within the administrative functions of the *Laender*. The Federation may also transfer other property to the *Laender*.

(3) Property which was placed at the disposal of the *Reich* by the *Laender* and communities (associations of communities) without compensation shall again become the property of the *Laender* and communities (community associations), insofar as it is not required by the Federation for its own administrative tasks.

(4) Details will be regulated by a Federal law which requires the consent of the Bundesrat.

ART. 135—(1) If after May 8, 1945, and before the coming into force of this Basic Law an area has passed from one *Land* to another, the *Land* to which the area now belongs is entitled to the property located therein of the *Land* to which it formerly belonged.

(2) Property of *Laender* and other bodies-corporate and institutions under public law, which no longer exist, passes insofar as it was originally intended to be used predominantly for administrative tasks or is being used at present, and not merely temporarily, predominantly for administrative tasks, to the *Land* or the body-corporate or institution under public law which now discharges these tasks.

(3) Real estate of *Laender* which no longer exist, including appurtenances, passes to the *Land* within which it is located insofar as it is not included among property within the meaning of paragraph 1.

(4) If an overriding interest of the Federation or the

particular interest of an area so requires, a settlement deviating from paragraphs 1 to 3 may be effected by Federal law.

(5) For the rest, the succession in law and the settlement of the property, insofar as it has not been effected before January 1, 1952, by agreement between the *Laender* or bodies-corporate or institutions under public law concerned, will be regulated by a Federal law which requires the consent of the Bundesrat.

(6) Interests of the former *Land* of Prussia in enterprises under private law pass to the Federation. A Federal law, which may also deviate from this provision, will regulate details.

(7) Insofar as, on the coming into force of the Basic Law, property which would fall to a *Land* or a body-corporate or institution under public law pursuant to paragraphs 1 to 3 had been disposed of through or under authority of a *Land* law or in any other manner by the party thus entitled, the passing of the property is deemed to have taken place before such disposition.

ART. 135a—* The legislation reserved to the Federation in Art. 134, para. 4, and Art. 135, para. 5, may also stipulate that the following liabilities shall not be discharged, or not to their full extent:

(1) Liabilities of the *Reich* or the former *Land* Prussia or liabilities of such other bodies-corporate and institutions under public law as no longer exist,

(2) Such liabilities of the Federation or other bodies-corporate and institutions under public law as are connected with the transfer of properties pursuant to Arts. 89, 90, 134, or 135, and such liabilities of these same as arise from measures taken by the holders of rights defined under item 1,

(3) Such liabilities of *Laender* or communes (associations of communes) as have arisen from measures taken by these holders of rights before August 1, 1945, within the sphere of administrative functions incumbent upon, or delegated by the *Reich* to comply with regulations of Occupying Powers or to remove a state of emergency due to the war.

* Added October 22, 1957.

ART. 136—(1) The Bundesrat assembles for the first time on the day of the first meeting of the Bundestag.

(2) Until the election of the first Federal President his powers will be exercised by the President of the Bundesrat. He does not have the right to dissolve the Bundestag.

ART. 137—* (1) The right of civil servants, of salaried employees of the public services, of professional soldiers, of temporary volunteer soldiers and of judges to stand for election in the Federation, in the *Laender* or in the communes may be restricted by legislation.

(2) The Electoral Law to be adopted by the Parliamentary Council applies to the election of the first Bundestag, of the first Federal Convention and of the first Federal President of the Federal Republic.

(3) The function of the Federal Constitutional Court pursuant to Article 41, paragraph 2, shall, pending its establishment, be exercised by the German High Court for the Combined Economic Area, which shall decide in accordance with its rules of procedures.

ART. 138—Changes in the rules relating to notaries as they now exist in the *Laender* of Baden, Bavaria, Wuerttemberg-Baden and Wuerttemberg-Hohenzollern, require the consent of the governments of these *Laender*.

ART. 139—The provisions of law enacted for the liberation of the German people from National Socialism and militarism are not affected by the provisions of this Basic Law.

ART. 140—The provisions of Articles 136, 137, 138, 139 and 141 of the German Constitution of August 11, 1919, are an integral part of this Basic Law.

Article 136. Civil and political rights and duties are neither dependent upon nor restricted by the practice of religious freedom.

The enjoyment of civil and political rights, as well as admission to official posts, is independent of religious creed.

No one is bound to disclose his religious convictions. The authorities have the right to make enquiries as to membership of a religious body only when rights and

* As amended March 19, 1956.

duties depend upon it, or when the collection of statistics ordered by law requires it.

No one may be compelled to take part in any ecclesiastical act or ceremony, or the use of any religious form of oath.

Article 137. There is no state church.

Freedom of association is guaranteed to religious bodies. There are no restrictions as to the union of religious bodies within the territory of the Federation.

Each religious body regulates and administers its affairs independently within the limits of general laws. It appoints its officials without the cooperation of the *Land,* or of the civil community.

Religious bodies acquire legal rights in accordance with the general regulations of the civil code.

Religious bodies remain corporations with public rights insofar as they have been so up to the present.

Equal rights shall be granted to other religious bodies upon application, if their constitution and the number of their members offer a guarantee of permanency.

When several such religious bodies holding public rights combine to form one union this union becomes a corporation of a similar class.

Religious bodies forming corporations with public rights are entitled to levy taxes on the basis of the civil tax-rolls, in accordance with the provisions of *Land* law.

Associations adopting as their work the common encouragement of a world-philosophy shall be placed upon an equal footing with religious bodies.

So far as the execution of these provisions may require further regulation, this is the duty of the *Land* Legislatures.

Article 138. Land connections with religious bodies, depending upon law, agreement or special legal titles, are dissolved by *Land* legislation. The principle for such action shall be laid down by the Federal Government.

Ownership and other rights of religious bodies and unions to their institutions, foundations and other properties devoted to purposes of public worship, education or charity, are guaranteed.

Article 139. Sundays and holidays recognized by the *Land* shall remain under legal protection as days of rest from work and for the promotion of spiritual purposes.

Article 141. Religious bodies shall have the right of entry for religious purposes into the army, hospitals, prisons, or other public institutions, so far as is necessary for the arrangement of public worship or the exercise of pastoral offices, but every form of compulsion must be avoided.

ART. 141—Article 7, paragraph 3, first sentence, has no application in a *Land* in which different provisions of *Land* law were in force on January 1, 1949.

ART. 142—Notwithstanding the provision of Article 31, such provisions of *Land* Constitution as guarantee basic rights in conformity with Articles 1 to 18 of this Basic Law also remain in force.

ART. 142a—* The provisions of this Basic Law are not contrary to the conclusion and entry into force of the treaties signed in Bonn and Paris on May 26 and 27, 1952 (Treaty on Relations between the Federal Republic of Germany and the Three Powers and Treaty establishing a European Defense Community) with their related and additional conventions, especially the Protocol of July 26, 1952.

ART. 143—** The conditions under which it will be admissible to have recourse to the Armed Forces in case of a state of internal emergency, may be regulated only by a law which fulfills the requirements of Article 79.

ART. 144—(1) This Basic Law requires ratification by the representative assemblies in two-thirds of the German *Laender* in which it is for the time being to apply.

(2) Insofar as the application of this Basic Law is subject to restrictions in any *Land* listed in Article 23 or in any part of such *Land,* the *Land* or the part thereof has the right to send representatives to the Bundestag in accordance with Article 38 and to the Bundesrat in accordance with Article 50.

ART. 145—(1) The Parliamentary Council shall note in public session, with the participation of the representatives of Greater Berlin, the ratification of this Basic Law and shall sign and promulgate it.

* Added March 27, 1954.
** As amended March 19, 1956.

(2) This Basic Law shall come into force at the end of the day of promulgation.

(3) It shall be published in the Federal Gazette.

ART. 146—This Basic Law shall cease to be in force on the day on which a constitution adopted by a free decision of the German people comes into force.

—6—

THE SOVIET UNION

A. Constitutionalism and the Soviet Union

The 1936 "Stalin" Constitution contains well-defined guarantees for the protection of civil liberties, prescribes relationships among the various governmental organs, and stipulates procedures for the formulation and implementation of public policy. In these respects, it differs little from Western democratic Constitutions. In fact, we know that constitutionalism is not practised in the Soviet Union, that the only effective limitations on the actions of the Soviet leaders are non-constitutional, and that the only meaningful procedures are quite unlike those prescribed in the document. Why, then, have the Soviet leaders persisted in emulating the "bourgeois sham democracies" by establishing a Western-type Constitution?

The answer to this is far from easy. One wonders, first, why the Soviet leaders want a Constitution at all and, second, why it has been framed on the Western parliamentary model. An answer to the first question may begin with the observation that it would be very unusual if the Soviet Union did not have a documentary Constitution. Almost all modern States have one or more documents forming their "basic law." A written Constitution is particularly desirable when a regime wishes to mark a clear break with a previous political system, as did the Soviets in 1917. There are also reasons that arise out of the peculiar, "scriptural" character of Soviet politics. The Marxist leaders of the Soviet Union are impelled by the logic of their ideology to justify their po-

152

litical actions in terms of the theories elaborated in the writings of Karl Marx, and Friederich Engels. They profess to believe that the answers to all political, social, and economic problems can be found only if the ideas and methods of those two men are followed. But most of the writings of Marx and Engels analyzed the forces and conditions that they believed would produce the proletarian revolution. Aside from rather sketchy references to the "dictatorship of the proletariat" and the "withering away of the State," neither Marx nor Engels formulated any very clear concepts of the form that would be taken by Marxist regimes. The applicability of their constitutional concepts to the Soviet situation is further limited by their assumption that Communism would come only to highly-industrialized states, whereas the principal task and leading achievement of the Soviet political system has been the industrialization of the nation.

On the one hand, then, Soviet leaders are committed to heavy reliance on documentary authority; but, on the other, they inherited no clear, usable constitutional formulas from their ideological forefathers. Consequently, they have been led to design constitutional instruments that conform to Marxian principles and thus give their authority a certain scriptural sanctity.

Stalin had additional reasons for promulgating the 1936 Constitution. For one thing, it was intended to be a landmark in the march of Soviet society from the Czarist regime to pure Communism. Specifically, it was claimed to be a reflection of the transition of the Soviet system from a dictatorship of the proletariat to a "socialist" State. Therefore, it was a symbol of progress, justifying the sacrifices being required of the Soviet people at the time. Stalin may also have regarded it— and this brings us to the question of why Western forms were copied so faithfully—as an implicit promise that the blood purges and unrestrained arbitrary rule that were so prominent a feature of Soviet life at the time were not to be regarded as permanent. The inclusion in the Constitution of civil liberties protections and of grants of territorial autonomy may well be regarded as ideals toward which the Soviet people were to believe

their system would progress. These protections would
eventually prevail over the provisions that had thus far
permitted their violation at the arbitrary will of the Soviet rulers. Another reason for the adoption of Western
forms may have been to create a façade of constitutional
legitimacy for international appearances in an age when
constitutional democracy is the norm.

In any case, we are entitled to ask if the appearance
that the Soviet Constitution adheres to Western forms
is correct and if, therefore, the arbitrariness of Soviet
practice violates its own Constitution. A careful reading
of the Constitution in the light of Marxian theory indicates that this is not the case. Although the Constitution contains numerous provisions that seem to establish
norms of power limitation and procedural regularity in
the Western tradition, it also contains Marxian "escape
clauses."

For instance, the provision in Article 125 that "the
citizens of the U.S.S.R. are guaranteed by law" broad
freedoms of expression conforms closely to Western
constitutional practice in limiting the action of the government over its citizens. But the preceding phrase stipulates that these guarantees are made "in conformity
with the interests of the working people, and in order to
strengthen the socialist system." Obviously, then, exercise of these freedoms in a manner not conforming to
the authoritative interpretation of the interests of the
working people or the socialist system is not protected
by Article 125. Furthermore, the Constitution seems to
provide no means by which a private person can initiate
proceedings to compel observance of the guarantees.

In regard to procedural constitutionalism, the Soviet
Constitution establishes most of the standard Western
parliamentary institutions and regulates their relations
in a very similar manner. But in Article 126 the Communist Party is designated "the vanguard of the working
people in the struggle to build [a] communist society
and is the leading core of all organizations, both public
and state," and Article 141 reserves to "public organizations and societies of the working people: Communist
Party organizations and cultural societies" "the right to
nominate candidates" for the Soviets. Taken together

and in the general context of Marxist ideology, these stipulations provide a constitutional foundation for subordinating the formal machinery of the State to party domination. Federalism is dealt with in the same double-handed way. The federal structure established with bold flourishes in Articles 13 through 29-a and elsewhere loses much of its meaning when clause "k" of Article 14 reserves to the central authority complete control of the public revenues of both the local units and the central government.

From this analysis the conclusion emerges that the Soviet leaders are not violating their so-called "most democratic" Constitution. Rather, the Constitution itself does not conform to the concept of constitutionalism. It channels control over public policy out of public, constitutional channels and into the "private" organization, the Communist Party of the Soviet Union (CPSU). It also defines in a broad, ambiguous manner the ends which civil liberties protections must serve and, consequently, subordinates the limitations on governmental power to the government's interpretation of the extent to which the exercise of freedom conforms to its purposes. In other words, it provides no effective limitations at all.

B. SOVIET CONSTITUTIONAL DOCUMENTS

1. CONSTITUTION OF THE UNION OF SOVIET SOCIALIST REPUBLICS, 1936*

CHAPTER I—THE SOCIAL STRUCTURE

ART. 1—The Union of Soviet Socialist Republics is a socialist state of workers and peasants.

ART. 2—The political foundation of the U.S.S.R. is the Soviets of Working People's Deputies, which grew and became strong as a result of the overthrow of the

---

* Translated by Foreign Language Publishing House, Moscow. As amended through April 15, 1968. It was announced early in 1962 that a new Soviet constitution was being prepared. By Spring of 1968 no date had yet been given for its presentation.

power of the landlords and capitalists and the conquest of the dictatorship of the proletariat.

ART. 3—All power in the U.S.S.R. belongs to the working people of town and country as represented by the Soviets of Working People's Deputies.

ART. 4—The economic foundation of the U.S.S.R. is the socialist system of economy and the socialist ownership of the instruments and means of production, firmly established as a result of the liquidation of the capitalist system of economy, the abolition of private ownership of the instruments and means of production, and the elimination of the exploitation of man by man.

ART. 5—Socialist property in the U.S.S.R. exists either in the form of state property (belonging to the whole people) or in the form of co-operative and collective-farm property (property of collective farms, property of co-operative societies).

ART. 6—The land, its mineral wealth, waters, forests, mills, factories, mines, rail, water and air transport, banks, communications, large state-organized agricultural enterprises (state farms, machine and tractor stations and the like), as well as municipal enterprises and the bulk of the dwelling-houses in the cities and industrial localities, are state property, that is, belong to the whole people.

ART. 7—The common enterprises of collective farms and co-operative organizations, with their live-stock and implements, the products of the collective farms and co-operative organizations, as well as their common buildings, constitute the common, socialist property of the collective farms and co-operative organizations.

Every household in a collective farm, in addition to its basic income from the common collective-farm enterprise, has for its personal use a small plot of household land and, as its personal property, a subsidiary husbandry on the plot, a dwelling-house, live-stock, poultry and minor agricultural implements—in accordance with the rules of the agricultural artel.

ART. 8—The land occupied by collective farms is secured to them for their use free of charge and for an unlimited time, that is, in perpetuity.

ART. 9—Alongside the socialist system of economy,

which is the predominant form of economy in the
U.S.S.R., the law permits the small private economy of
individual peasants and handicraftsmen based on their
own labor and precluding the exploitation of the labor of
others.

ART. 10—The personal property right of citizens in
their incomes and savings from work, in their dwelling-
houses and subsidiary husbandries, in articles of domestic economy and use and articles of personal use and
convenience, as well as the right of citizens to inherit
personal property, is protected by law.

ART. 11—The economic life of the U.S.S.R. is determined and directed by the state national-economic plan,
with the aim of increasing the public wealth, of steadily
raising the material and cultural standards of the working people, of consolidating the independence of the
U.S.S.R. and strengthening its defensive capacity.

ART. 12—Work in the U.S.S.R. is a duty and a matter of honor for every able-bodied citizen, in accordance
with the principle: "He who does not work, neither shall
he eat."

The principle applied in the U.S.S.R. is that of socialism: "From each according to his ability, to each according to his work."

CHAPTER II—THE STATE STRUCTURE

ART. 13—The Union of Soviet Socialist Republics is a
federal state, formed on the basis of a voluntary union
of equal Soviet Socialist Republics, namely: The Russian
Soviet Federative Socialist Republic, the Ukrainian Soviet
Socialist Republic, the Byelorussian Soviet Socialist Re-
public, the Uzbek Soviet Socialist Republic, the Kazakh
Soviet Socialist Republic, the Georgian Soviet Socialist
Republic, the Azerbaijan Soviet Socialist Republic, the
Lithuanian Soviet Socialist Republic, the Moldavian So-
viet Socialist Republic, the Latvian Soviet Socialist Re-
public, the Kirghiz Soviet Socialist Republic, the Tajik
Soviet Socialist Republic, the Armenian Soviet Socialist
Republic, the Turkmen Soviet Socialist Republic [and]
the Estonian Soviet Socialist Republic.

ART. 14—The jurisdiction of the Union of Soviet Socialist Republics, as represented by its higher organs of

state power and organs of state administration, embraces:

a) Representation of the U.S.S.R. in international relations, conclusion, ratification and denunciation of treaties of the U.S.S.R. with other states, establishment of general procedure governing the relations of Union Republics with foreign states;

b) Questions of war and peace;

c) Admission of new republics into the U.S.S.R.;

d) Control over the observance of the Constitution of the U.S.S.R., and ensuring conformity of the Constitutions of the Union Republics with the Constitution of the U.S.S.R.;

e) Confirmation of alterations of boundaries between Union Republics;

f) Confirmation of the formation of new Autonomous Republics and Autonomous Regions within Union Republics;

g) Organization of the defense of the U.S.S.R., direction of all the Armed Forces of the U.S.S.R., determination of directing principles governing the organization of the military formations of the Union Republics;

h) Foreign trade on the basis of state monopoly;

i) Safeguarding the security of the state;

j) Determination of the national-economic plans of the U.S.S.R.;

k) Approval of the consolidated state budget of the U.S.S.R. and of the report on its fulfillment; determination of the taxes and revenues which go to the Union, the Republican and the local budgets;

l) Administration of the banks, industrial and agricultural institutions and enterprises and also trading enterprises under all-Union jurisdiction; the general guidance of industry and construction under Union-Republican jurisdiction;

m) Administration of transport and communications of all-Union importance;

n) Direction of the monetary and credit system;

o) Organization of state insurance;

p) Contracting and granting of loans;

q) Determination of the basic principles of land tenure and of the use of mineral wealth, forests and waters;

r) Determination of the basic principles in the spheres of education and public health;

s) Organization of a uniform system of national-economic statistics;

t) Determination of the principles of labor legislation;

u) Determination of the principles of legislation concerning the judicial system and judicial procedure and of the principles of civil and criminal codes;

v) Legislation concerning Union citizenship; legislation concerning rights of foreigners;

w) Determination of the principles of legislation concerning marriage and the family;

x) Issuing of all-Union acts of amnesty.

ART. 15—The sovereignty of the Union Republics is limited only in the spheres defined in Article 14 of the Constitution of the U.S.S.R. Outside of these spheres each Union Republic exercises state authority independently. The U.S.S.R. protects the sovereign rights of the Union Republics.

ART. 16—Each Union Republic has its own Constitution, which takes account of the specific features of the Republic and is drawn up in full conformity with the Constitution of the U.S.S.R.

ART. 17—The right freely to secede from the U.S.S.R. is reserved to every Union Republic.

ART. 18—The territory of a Union Republic may not be altered without its consent.

ART. 18a—Each Union Republic has the right to enter into direct relations with foreign states and to conclude agreements and exchange diplomatic and consular representatives with them.

ART. 18b—Each Union Republic has its own Republican military formations.

ART. 19—The laws of the U.S.S.R. have the same force within the territory of every Union Republic.

ART. 20—In the event of divergence between a law of a Union Republic and a law of the Union, the Union law prevails.

ART. 21—Uniform Union citizenship is established for citizens of the U.S.S.R.

Every citizen of a Union Republic is a citizen of the U.S.S.R.

ART. 22—The Russian Soviet Federative Socialist Republic includes the Bashkirian, Buryat, Daghestan, Kabardinian-Balkar, Kalmyk, Karelian, Komi, Mari, Mordovian, North Ossetian, Tatar, Tuva, Udmurt, Checheno-Ingush, Chuvash and Yakut Autonomous Soviet Socialist Republics; and the Adygei, Gorny-Altai, Jewish, Karachayevo-Cherkess and Khakass Autonomous Regions.

ART. 23—Repealed.

ART. 24—The Georgian Soviet Socialist Republic includes the Nakhichevan Autonomous Soviet Socialist Republic and the Nagorny Karabakh Autonomous Region.

ART. 25—The Georgian Soviet Socialist Republic includes the Abkhazian Autonomous Soviet Socialist Republic, the Ajarian Autonomous Soviet Socialist Republic and the South Ossetian Autonomous Region.

ART. 26—The Uzbek Soviet Socialist Republic includes the Kara-Kalpak Autonomous Soviet Socialist Republic.

ART. 27—The Tajik Soviet Socialist Republic includes the Gorny Badakhshan Autonomous Region.

ART. 28—The solution of problems pertaining to the administrative-territorial structure of the region and territories of the Union Republics comes within the jurisdiction of the Union Republics.

ART. 29—Repealed.

CHAPTER III—THE HIGHER ORGANS OF STATE POWER IN THE UNION OF SOVIET SOCIALIST REPUBLICS

ART. 30—The highest organ of state power in the U.S.S.R. is the Supreme Soviet of the U.S.S.R.

ART. 31—The Supreme Soviet of the U.S.S.R. exercises all rights vested in the Union of Soviet Socialist Republics in accordance with Article 14 of the Constitution, insofar as they do not, by virtue of the Constitution, come within the jurisdiction of organs of the U.S.S.R. that are accountable to the Supreme Soviet of the U.S.S.R., that is, the Presidium of the Supreme Soviet of the U.S.S.R., the Council of Ministers of the U.S.S.R., and the Ministries of the U.S.S.R.

ART. 32—The legislative power of the U.S.S.R. is exercised exclusively by the Supreme Soviet of the U.S.S.R.

ART. 33—The Supreme Soviet of the U.S.S.R. consists of two Chambers: the Soviet of the Union and the Soviet of Nationalities.

ART. 34—The Soviet of the Union is elected by the citizens of the U.S.S.R. voting by election districts on the basis of one deputy for every 300,000 of the population.

ART. 35*—The Soviet of Nationalities is elected by the citizens of the U.S.S.R. voting by Union Republics, Autonomous Republics, Autonomous Regions, and National Areas on the basis of 32 deputies from each Union Republic, 11 deputies from each Autonomous Republic, 5 deputies from each Autonomous Region and one deputy from each National Area.

ART. 36—The Supreme Soviet of the U.S.S.R. is elected for a term of four years.

ART. 37—The two Chambers of the Supreme Soviet of the U.S.S.R., the Soviet of the Union and the Soviet of Nationalities, have equal rights.

ART. 38—The Soviet of the Union and the Soviet of Nationalities have equal powers to initiate legislation.

ART. 39—A law is considered adopted if passed by both Chambers of the Supreme Soviet of the U.S.S.R. by a simple majority vote in each.

ART. 40—Laws passed by the Supreme Soviet of the U.S.S.R. are published in the languages of the Union Republics over the signatures of the President and Secretary of the Presidium of the Supreme Soviet of the U.S.S.R.

ART. 41—Sessions of the Soviet of the Union and of the Soviet of Nationalities begin and terminate simultaneously.

ART. 42—The Soviet of the Union elects a Chairman of the Soviet of the Union and four Vice-Chairmen.

ART. 43—The Soviet of Nationalities elects a Chairman of the Soviet of Nationalities and four Vice-Chairmen.

ART. 44—The Chairmen of the Soviet of the Union and the Soviet of Nationalities preside at the sittings of the respective Chambers and have charge of the conduct of their business and proceedings.

* As amended by the Supreme Soviet, August 3, 1966, to substitute "32" for "25."—*Ed.'s note.*

ART. 45—Joint sittings of the two Chambers of the Supreme Soviet of the U.S.S.R. are presided over alternately by the Chairman of the Soviet of the Union and the Chairman of the Soviet of Nationalities.

ART. 46—Sessions of the Supreme Soviet of the U.S.S.R. are convened by the Presidium of the Supreme Soviet of the U.S.S.R. twice a year.

Extraordinary sessions are convened by the Presidium of the Supreme Soviet of the U.S.S.R. at its discretion or on the demand of one of the Union Republics.

ART. 47—In the event of disagreement between the Soviet of the Union and the Soviet of Nationalities, the question is referred for settlement to a conciliation commission formed by the Chambers on a parity basis. If the conciliation commission fails to arrive at an agreement or if its decision fails to satisfy one of the Chambers, the question is considered for a second time by the Chambers. Failing agreement between the two Chambers, the Presidium of the Supreme Soviet of the U.S.S.R. dissolves the Supreme Soviet of the U.S.S.R. and orders new elections.

ART. 48*—The Supreme Soviet of the U.S.S.R. at a joint sitting of the two Chambers elects the Presidium of the Supreme Soviet of the U.S.S.R., consisting of a President of the Presidium of the Supreme Soviet of the U.S.S.R., fifteen Vice-Presidents, one from each Union Republic, a Secretary of the Presidium and *twenty* members of the Presidium of the Supreme Soviet of the U.S.S.R.

The Presidium of the Supreme Soviet of the U.S.S.R. is accountable to the Supreme Soviet of the U.S.S.R. for all its activities.

ART. 49—The Presidium of the Supreme Soviet of the U.S.S.R.:

a) Convenes the sessions of the Supreme Soviet of the U.S.S.R.;

b) Issues decrees;

c) Gives interpretations of the laws of the U.S.S.R. in operation;

d) Dissolves the Supreme Soviet of the U.S.S.R. in conformity with Article 47 of the Constitution of the U.S.S.R. and orders new elections;

* As amended August 3, 1966.—*Ed.'s note.*

e) Conducts nation-wide polls (referendums) on its own initiative or on the demand of one of the Union Republics;

f) Annuls decisions and orders of the Council of Ministers of the U.S.S.R. and of the Councils of Ministers of the Union Republics if they do not conform to law;

g) In the intervals between sessions of the Supreme Soviet of the U.S.S.R., releases and appoints Ministers of the U.S.S.R. on the recommendation of the Chairman of the Council of Ministers of the U.S.S.R., subject to subsequent confirmation by the Supreme Soviet of the U.S.S.R.;

h) Institutes decorations (Orders and Medals) and titles of honor of the U.S.S.R.;

i) Awards Orders and Medals and confers titles of honor of the U.S.S.R.;

j) Exercises the right of pardon;

k) Institutes military titles, diplomatic ranks and other special titles;

l) Appoints and removes the high command of the Armed Forces of the U.S.S.R.;

m) In the intervals between sessions of the Supreme Soviet of the U.S.S.R., proclaims a state of war in the event of military attack on the U.S.S.R., or when necessary to fulfill international treaty obligations concerning mutual defense against aggression;

n) Orders general or partial mobilization;

o) Ratifies and denounces international treaties of the U.S.S.R.;

p) Appoints and recalls plenipotentiary representatives of the U.S.S.R. to foreign states;

q) Receives the letters of credence and recall of diplomatic representatives accredited to it by foreign states;

r) Proclaims martial law in separate localities or throughout the U.S.S.R. in the interests of the defense of the U.S.S.R. or of the maintenance of public order and the security of the state.

ART. 50—The Soviet of the Union and the Soviet of Nationalities elect Credentials Committees to verify the credentials of the members of the respective Chambers.

On the report of the Credentials Committees, the Chambers decide whether to recognize the credentials of deputies or to annul their election.

ART. 51—The Supreme Soviet of the U.S.S.R., when it deems necessary, appoints commissions of investigation and audit on any matter.

It is the duty of all institutions and officials to comply with the demands of such commissions and to submit to them all necessary materials and documents.

ART. 52—A member of the Supreme Soviet of the U.S.S.R. may not be prosecuted or arrested without the consent of the Supreme Soviet of the U.S.S.R., or, when the Supreme Soviet of the U.S.S.R. is not in session, without the consent of the Presidium of the Supreme Soviet of the U.S.S.R.

ART. 53—On the expiration of the term of office of the Supreme Soviet of the U.S.S.R., or on its dissolution prior to the expiration of its term of office, the Presidium of the Supreme Soviet of the U.S.S.R. retains its powers until the newly-elected Supreme Soviet of the U.S.S.R. shall have formed a new Presidium of the Supreme Soviet of the U.S.S.R.

ART. 54—On the expiration of the term of office of the Supreme Soviet of the U.S.S.R., or in the event of its dissolution prior to the expiration of its term of office, the Presidium of the Supreme Soviet of the U.S.S.R. orders new elections to be held within a period not exceeding two months from the date of expiration of the term of office or dissolution of the Supreme Soviet of the U.S.S.R.

ART. 55—The newly-elected Supreme Soviet of the U.S.S.R. is convened by the outgoing Presidium of the Supreme Soviet of the U.S.S.R. not later than three months after the elections.

ART. 56—The Supreme Soviet of the U.S.S.R., at a joint sitting of the two Chambers, appoints the Government of the U.S.S.R., namely, the Council of Ministers of the U.S.S.R.

CHAPTER IV—THE HIGHER ORGANS OF STATE POWER IN THE UNION REPUBLICS

ART. 57—The highest organ of state power in a Union

Republic is the Supreme Soviet of the Union Republic.

ART. 58—The Supreme Soviet of a Union Republic is elected by the citizens of the Republic for a term of four years.

The basis of representation is established by the Constitution of the Union Republic.

ART. 59—The Supreme Soviet of a Union Republic is the sole legislative organ of the Republic.

ART. 60*—The Supreme Soviet of a Union Republic:

a) Adopts the Constitution of the Republic and amends it in conformity with Article 16 of the Constitution of the U.S.S.R.;

b) Confirms the Constitutions of the Autonomous Republics forming part of it and defines the boundaries of their territories;

c) Approves the national-economic plan and the budget of the Republic;

d) Exercises the right of amnesty and pardon of citizens sentenced by the judicial organs of the Union Republic;

e) Decides questions of representation of the Union Republic in its international relations;

f) Determines the manner of organizing the Republic's military formations.

ART. 61—The Supreme Soviet of a Union Republic elects the Presidium of the Supreme Soviet of the Union Republic, consisting of a President of the Presidium of the Supreme Soviet of the Union Republic, Vice-Presidents, a Secretary of the Presidium and members of the Presidium of the Supreme Soviet of the Union Republic.

The powers of the Presidium of the Supreme Soviet of a Union Republic are defined by the Constitution of the Union Republic.

ART. 62—The Supreme Soviet of a Union Republic elects a Chairman and Vice-Chairman to conduct its sittings.

ART. 63—The Supreme Soviet of a Union Republic

* As amended by the Supreme Soviet, October 2, 1965, to delete "and constitutes the economic administrative areas" at the conclusion of c).—*Ed.'s note.*

appoints the Government of the Union Republic, namely, the Council of Ministers of the Union Republic.

CHAPTER V—THE ORGANS OF STATE ADMINISTRATION OF THE UNION OF SOVIET SOCIALIST REPUBLICS

ART. 64—The highest executive and administrative organ of the state power of the Union of Soviet Socialist Republics is the Council of Ministers of the U.S.S.R.

ART. 65—The Council of Ministers of the U.S.S.R. is responsible and accountable to the Supreme Soviet of the U.S.S.R. or, in the intervals between sessions of the Supreme Soviet, to the Presidium of the Supreme Soviet of the U.S.S.R.

ART. 66—The Council of Ministers of the U.S.S.R. issues decisions and orders on the basis and in pursuance of the laws in operation, and verifies their execution.

ART. 67—Decisions and orders of the Council of Ministers of the U.S.S.R. are binding throughout the territory of the U.S.S.R.

ART. 68*—The Council of Ministers of the U.S.S.R.:

a) Co-ordinates and directs the work of the all-Union and Union-Republican Ministries of the U.S.S.R. *and the U.S.S.R. Council of Ministers State Committees* and of other institutions under its jurisdiction;

b) Adopts measures to carry out the national-economic plan and the state budget, and to strengthen the credit and monetary system;

c) Adopts measures for the maintenance of public order, for the protection of the interests of the state, and for the safeguarding of the rights of citizens;

d) Exercises general guidance in the sphere of relations with foreign states;

* As amended by the Supreme Soviet, December 19, 1963, to add the italicized words and to delete from a) the concluding phrase, "and exercises guidance over the economic councils of the economic administrative areas through the Councils of Ministers of the Union Republics." The phrase "the U.S.S.R. Supreme Council of the National Economy of the U.S.S.R. Council of Ministers" was inserted in a) after "the work of", but was deleted by amendment of the Supreme Soviet, October 2, 1965.— *Ed.'s note.*

e) Fixes the annual contingents of citizens to be called up for military service and directs the general organization of the Armed Forces of the country;

f) Sets up *U.S.S.R. State Committees and also,* whenever necessary, special Committees and Central Administrations under the Council of Ministers of the U.S.S.R. for economic and cultural affairs and defense.

ART. 69*—The Council of Ministers of the U.S.S.R. has the right, in respect of those branches of administration and economy which come within the jurisdiction of the U.S.S.R., to suspend decisions and orders of the Councils of Ministers of the Union Republics and to annul orders and instructions of Ministers of the U.S.S.R. *as well as acts of other institutions under its jurisdiction.*

ART. 70**—The Council of Ministers of the U.S.S.R. is appointed by the U.S.S.R. Supreme Soviet and consists of: the Chairman of the Council of Ministers of the U.S.S.R.; the First Vice-Chairmen of the Council of Ministers of the U.S.S.R.; the Vice-Chairmen of the Council of Ministers of the U.S.S.R.; the Ministers of the U.S.S.R.; the Chairman of the Council of Ministers' State Planning Committee; the Chairman of the State Committee for Construction Affairs of the Council of Ministers of the U.S.S.R.; the Chairman of the State Committee for Material and Technical Supply of the Council of Ministers of the U.S.S.R.; the Chairman of the People's Control Committee of the U.S.S.R.; the Chairman of the State Committee for Questions of Labor and Wages of the Council of Ministers of the U.S.S.R.; the Chairman of the State Committee for Science and Technology of the Council of Ministers of the U.S.S.R.; the Chairman of the State Committee for Vocational-Technical Education of the Council of Ministers of the U.S.S.R.; the Chairman of the State Procurements Committee of the Council of Ministers of the U.S.S.R.; the Chairman of the State

* As amended by the Supreme Soviet, December 19, 1963, to add the italicized words and to delete the phrase "and of the economic councils of the economic administrative areas" after "Union Republics."—*Ed.'s note.*
** As amended by the Supreme Soviet December 9, 1965, and August 3, 1966, to alter the composition of the Council. —*Ed's note.*

Forestry Committee of the Council of Ministers of the U.S.S.R.; the Chairman of the State Committee for Foreign Economic Relations of the Council of Ministers of the U.S.S.R.; the Chairman of the State Security Committee under the Council of Ministers of the U.S.S.R.; the Chairman of the All-Union Farm Machinery Association of the Council of Ministers of the U.S.S.R.; the Chairman of the Board of the State Bank of the U.S.S.R.; the Director of the Central Statistical Administration under the Council of Ministers of the U.S.S.R.

The Council of Ministers of the U.S.S.R. includes the Chairmen of the Councils of Ministers of the Union Republics as ex officio members.

ART. 71—The Government of the U.S.S.R. or a Minister of the U.S.S.R. to whom a question of a member of the Supreme Soviet of the U.S.S.R. is addressed must give a verbal or written reply in the respective Chamber within a period not exceeding three days.

ART. 72—The Ministers of the U.S.S.R. direct the branches of state administration which come within the jurisdiction of the U.S.S.R.

ART. 73—The Ministers of the U.S.S.R., within the limits of the jurisdiction of their respective Ministries, issue orders and instructions on the basis and in pursuance of the laws in operation, and also of decisions and orders of the Council of Ministers of the U.S.S.R., and verify their execution.

ART. 74—The Ministries of the U.S.S.R. are either all-Union or Union-Republican Ministries.

ART. 75—Each all-Union Ministry directs the branch of state administration entrusted to it throughout the territory of the U.S.S.R. either directly or through bodies appointed by it.

ART. 76—The Union-Republican Ministries, as a rule, direct the branches of state administration entrusted to them through corresponding Ministries of the Union Republics; they administer directly only a definite and limited number of enterprises according to a list confirmed by the Presidium of the Supreme Soviet of the U.S.S.R.

ART. 77*—The following Ministries are all-Union Ministries:

The Aviation Industry; the Motor Vehicle Industry; Foreign Trade; the Gas Industry; Civil Aviation; Machine Building for Light Industry and the Food Industry and of Household Appliances; the Medical Industry; the Merchant Marine; the Defense Industry; General Machine Building; Instrument Making, Means of Automation and Control Systems; Transportation; the Radio Industry; Medium Machine Building; the Machine Tool and Tool Industry; Machine Building for Construction, Road Building and Civil Engineering; the Shipbuilding Industry; Tractor and Farm Machine Building; Transport Construction; Heavy, Power and Transport Machine Building; Chemical and Petroleum Machine Building; the Electronics Industry; the Electrical Equipment Industry.

ART. 78*—The following Ministries are Union-Republican Ministries:

Higher and Specialized Secondary Education; Geology; Public Health; Foreign Affairs; Culture; Light Industry; the Lumber, Pulp-and-Paper and Wood-Processing Industry; Land Reclamation and Water Resources; Installation and Specialized Construction Work; the Meat and Dairy Industry; the Petroleum-Extracting Industry; the Petroleum-Refining and Petrochemical Industry; Defense; Defense of Public Order; the Food Industry; the Building Industry; the Building Materials Industry; the Fishing Industry; Education; Communications; Rural Construction; Agriculture; Construction; Heavy Industry Construction; Trade; the Coal Industry; Finance; the Chemical Industry; Nonferrous Metallurgy; Ferrous Metallurgy; Power and Electrification.

CHAPTER VI—THE ORGANS OF STATE ADMINISTRATION
OF THE UNION REPUBLICS

ART. 79—The highest executive and administrative organ of the state power of a Union Republic is the Council of Ministers of the Union Republic.

* As amended by the Supreme Soviet, October 12, 1967, to
   add to the lists of all-Union and Union-Republic ministries.—*Ed.'s note.*

ART. 80—The Council of Ministers of a Union Republic is responsible and accountable to the Supreme Soviet of the Union Republic, or, in the intervals between sessions of the Supreme Soviet of the Union Republic, to the Presidium of the Supreme Soviet of the Union Republic.

ART. 81—The Council of Ministers of a Union Republic issues decisions and orders on the basis and in pursuance of the laws in operation of the U.S.S.R. and of the Union Republic, and of the decisions and orders of the Council of Ministers of the U.S.S.R., and verifies their execution.

ART. 82*—The Council of Ministers of a Union Republic has the right to suspend decisions and orders of the Councils of Ministers of its Autonomous Republics and to annul decisions and orders of the Executive Committees of the Soviets of Working People's Deputies of its Territories, Regions and Autonomous Regions.

ART. 83—The Council of Ministers of a Union Republic is appointed by the Supreme Soviet of the Union Republic and consists of:

The Chairman of the Council of Ministers of the Union Republic; the Vice-Chairmen of the Council of Ministers; the Ministers; the Chairmen of the state committees and commissions and directors of other agencies of the Council of Ministers set up by the Supreme Soviet of the Union Republic in accordance with the constitution of the Union Republic.

ART. 84—The Ministers of a Union Republic direct the branches of state administration which come within the jurisdiction of the Union Republic.

ART. 85—The Ministers of a Union Republic, within the limits of the jurisdiction of their respective Ministries, issue orders and instructions on the basis and in pursuance of the laws of the U.S.S.R. and of the Union Republic,

* As amended by the Supreme Soviet, December 19, 1963, to add after "Autonomous Regions" the phrase "and also decisions and orders of the republics Council of the National Economy" and, October 2, 1965, to delete that phrase and the phrase following it: "and the economic councils of the economic administrative areas."—*Ed.'s note.*

of the decisions and orders of the Council of Ministers of the U.S.S.R. and the Council of Ministers of the Union Republic, and of the orders and instructions of the Union-Republican Ministries of the U.S.S.R.

ART. 86—The Ministries of a Union Republic are either Union-Republican or Republican Ministries.

ART. 87—Each Union-Republican Ministry directs the branch of state administration entrusted to it, and is subordinate both to the Council of Ministers of the Union Republic and to the corresponding Union-Republican Ministry of the U.S.S.R.

ART. 88—Each Republican Ministry directs the branch of state administration entrusted to it and is directly subordinate to the Council of Ministers of the Union Republic.*

CHAPTER VII—THE HIGHER ORGANS OF STATE POWER IN THE AUTONOMOUS SOVIET SOCIALIST REPUBLICS

ART. 89—The highest organ of state power in an Autonomous Republic is the Supreme Soviet of the Autonomous Republic.

ART. 90—The Supreme Soviet of an Autonomous Republic is elected by the citizens of the Republic for a term of four years on a basis of representation established by the Constitution of the Autonomous Republic.

ART. 91—The Supreme Soviet of an Autonomous Republic is the sole legislative organ of the Autonomous Republic.

ART. 92—Each Autonomous Republic has its own Constitution, which takes account of the specific features of the Autonomous Republic and is drawn up in full conformity with the Constitution of the Union Republic.

ART. 93—The Supreme Soviet of an Autonomous Republic elects the Presidium of the Supreme Soviet of the Autonomous Republic and appoints the Council of Ministers of the Autonomous Republic, in accordance with its Constitution.

* As amended by the Supreme Soviet, December 19, 1963, to delete Articles 88a and 88b pertaining to the economic councils of the economic administrative areas.—*Ed.'s note.*

Chapter VIII—The Local Organs of State Power

Art. 94—The organs of state power in Territories, Regions, Autonomous Regions, Areas, Districts, cities and rural localities (stanitsas, villages, hamlets, kishlaks, auls) are the Soviets of Working People's Deputies.

Art. 95—The Soviets of Working People's Deputies of Territories, Regions, Autonomous Regions, Areas, Districts, cities and rural localities (stanitsas, villages, hamlets, kishlaks, auls) are elected by the working people of the respective Territories, Regions, Autonomous Regions, Areas, Districts, cities or rural localities for a term of two years.

Art. 96—The basis of representation for Soviets of Working People's Deputies is determined by the Constitutions of the Union Republics.

Art. 97—The Soviets of Working People's Deputies direct the work of the organs of administration subordinate to them, ensure the maintenance of public order, the observance of the laws and the protection of the rights of citizens, direct local economic and cultural affairs and draw up the local budgets.

Art. 98—The Soviets of Working People's Deputies adopt decisions and issue orders within the limits of the powers vested in them by the laws of the U.S.S.R. and of the Union Republic.

Art. 99—The executive and administrative organ of the Soviet of Working People's Deputies of a Territory, Region, Autonomous Region, Area, District, city or rural locality is the Executive Committee elected by it, consisting of a Chairman, Vice-Chairmen, a Secretary, and members.

Art. 100—The executive and administrative organ of the Soviet of Working People's Deputies in a small locality, in accordance with the Constitution of the Union Republic, is the Chairman, the Vice-Chairman and the Secretary elected by the Soviet of Working People's Deputies.

Art. 101—The executive organs of the Soviets of Working People's Deputies are directly accountable both to the Soviets of Working People's Deputies which elected them and to the executive organ of the superior Soviet of Working People's Deputies.

CHAPTER IX—THE COURTS
AND THE PROCURATOR'S OFFICE

ART. 102—In the U.S.S.R. justice is administered by the Supreme Court of the U.S.S.R., the Supreme Courts of the Union Republics, the Courts of the Territories, Regions, Autonomous Republics, Autonomous Regions and Areas, the Special Courts of the U.S.S.R. established by decision of the Supreme Soviet of the U.S.S.R., and the People's Courts.

ART. 103—In all Courts cases are tried with the participation of people's assessors except in cases specially provided for by law.

ART. 104—The Supreme Court of the U.S.S.R. is the highest judicial organ. The Supreme Court of the U.S.S.R. is charged with the supervision of the judicial activities of the judicial organs of the U.S.S.R. and of the Union Republics within the limits established by law.

ART. 105—The Supreme Court of the U.S.S.R. is elected by the Supreme Soviet of the U.S.S.R. for a term of five years.

ART. 106—The Supreme Courts of the Union Republics are elected by the Supreme Soviets of the Union Republics for a term of five years.

ART. 107—The Supreme Courts of the Autonomous Republics are elected by the Supreme Soviets of the Autonomous Republics for a term of five years.

ART. 108—The Courts of Territories, Regions, Autonomous Regions and Areas are elected by the Soviets of Working People's Deputies of the respective Territories, Regions, Autonomous Regions or Areas for a term of five years.

ART. 109—People's Courts are elected by the citizens of the districts on the basis of universal, direct and equal suffrage by secret ballot for a term of three years.

ART. 110—Judicial proceedings are conducted in the language of the Union Republic, Autonomous Republic or Autonomous Region, persons not knowing this language being guaranteed the opportunity of fully acquainting themselves with the material of the case through an interpreter and likewise the right to use their own language in court.

ART. 111—In all Courts of the U.S.S.R. cases are heard in public, unless otherwise provided for by law, and the accused is guaranteed the right to defense.

ART. 112—Judges are independent and subject only to the law.

ART. 113—Supreme supervisory power to ensure the strict observance of the law by all Ministries and institutions subordinated to them, as well as by officials and citizens of the U.S.S.R. generally, is vested in the Procurator-General of the U.S.S.R.

ART. 114—The Procurator-General of the U.S.S.R. is appointed by the Supreme Soviet of the U.S.S.R. for a term of seven years.

ART. 115—Procurators of Republics, Territories, Regions, Autonomous Republics and Autonomous Regions are appointed by the Procurator-General of the U.S.S.R. for a term of five years.

ART. 116—Area, district and city procurators are appointed by the Procurators of the Union Republics, subject to the approval of the Procurator-General of the U.S.S.R., for a term of five years.

ART. 117—The organs of the Procurator's Office perform their functions independently of any local organs whatsoever, being subordinate solely to the Procurator-General of the U.S.S.R.

CHAPTER X—FUNDAMENTAL RIGHTS AND DUTIES
OF CITIZENS

ART. 118—Citizens of the U.S.S.R. have the right to work, that is, the right to guaranteed employment and payment for their work in accordance with its quantity and quality.

The right to work is ensured by the socialist organization of the national economy, the steady growth of the productive forces of Soviet society, the elimination of the possibility of economic crises, and the abolition of unemployment.

ART. 119—Citizens of the U.S.S.R. have the right to rest and leisure.

The right to rest and leisure is ensured by the establishment of an eight-hour day for industrial, office, and professional workers, the reduction of the working day to seven or six hours for arduous trades and to four hours in shops where conditions of work are particularly arduous; by the institution of annual vacations with full pay for industrial, office, and professional workers, and by the provision of a wide network of sanatoria, holiday homes and clubs for the accommodation of the working people.

ART. 120—Citizens of the U.S.S.R. have the right to maintenance in old age and also in case of sickness or disability.

This right is ensured by the extensive development of social insurance of industrial, office, and professional workers at state expense, free medical service for the working people, and the provision of a wide network of health resorts for the use of the working people.

ART. 121—Citizens of the U.S.S.R. have the right to education.

This right is ensured by universal and compulsory eight-year education; by the extensive development of secondary general polytechnical education, technical vocational education, and specialized secondary and higher education on the basis of a link between training and life and production; by the comprehensive development of evening and correspondence education; by free education in all types of schools; by a system of state stipends; by instruction in the schools in the native languages; and by the organization at plants and state and collective farms of free vocational, technical, and agronomic training for the working people.

ART. 122—Women in the U.S.S.R. are accorded equal rights with men in all spheres of economic, government, cultural, political and other public activity.

The possibility of exercising these rights is ensured by women being accorded an equal right with men to work, payment for work, rest and leisure, social insurance and education, and by state protection of the interest of mother and child, state aid to mothers of large families and unmarried mothers, maternity leave with full pay, and the provision of a wide network of maternity homes, nurseries and kindergartens.

ART. 123—Equality of rights of citizens of the U.S.S.R., irrespective of their nationality or race, in all spheres of economic, governmental, cultural, political and other public activity, is an indefeasible law.

Any direct or indirect restriction of the rights of, or, conversely, the establishment of any direct or indirect privileges for, citizens on account of their race or nationality, as well as any advocacy of racial or national exclusiveness or hatred and contempt, are punishable by law.

ART. 124—In order to ensure to citizens freedom of conscience, the church in the U.S.S.R. is separated from the state, and the school from the church. Freedom of religious worship and freedom of anti-religious propaganda is recognized for all citizens.

ART. 125—In conformity with the interests of the working people, and in order to strengthen the socialist system, the citizens of the U.S.S.R. are guaranteed by law:

a) freedom of speech;

b) freedom of the press;

c) freedom of assembly, including the holding of mass meetings;

d) freedom of street processions and demonstrations.

These civil rights are ensured by placing at the disposal of the working people and their organizations printing presses, stocks of paper, public buildings, the streets, communications facilities, and other material requisites for the exercise of these rights.

ART. 126—In conformity with the interests of the working people, and in order to develop the organizational initiative and political activity of the masses of the people, citizens of the U.S.S.R. are guaranteed the right to unite in public organizations; trade unions, co-operative societies, youth organizations, sport and defense organizations, cultural, technical and scientific societies; and the most active and politically-conscious citizens in the ranks of the working class, working peasants and working intelligentsia voluntary unite in the Communist Party of the Soviet Union, which is the vanguard of the working people in their struggle to build a communist society and is the leading core of all organizations of the working people, both public and state.

ART. 127—Citizens of the U.S.S.R. are guaranteed inviolability of the person. No person may be placed under arrest except by decision of a court or with the sanction of a procurator.

ART. 128—The inviolability of the homes of citizens and privacy of correspondence are protected by law.

ART. 129—The U.S.S.R. affords the right of asylum to foreign citizens persecuted for defending the interests of the working people, or for scientific activities, or for struggling for national liberation.

ART. 130—It is the duty of every citizen of the U.S.S.R. to abide by the Constitution of the Union of Soviet Socialist Republics, to observe the laws, to maintain labor discipline, honestly to perform public duties, and to respect the rules of socialist intercourse.

ART. 131—It is the duty of every citizen of the U.S.S.R. to safeguard and fortify public, socialist property as the sacred and inviolable foundation of the Soviet system, as the source of the wealth and might of the country, as the source of the prosperity and culture of all the working people.

Persons committing offenses against public, socialist property are enemies of the people.

ART. 132—Universal military service is law.

Military service in the Armed Forces of the U.S.S.R. is an honorable duty of the citizens of the U.S.S.R.

ART. 133—To defend the country is the sacred duty of every citizen of the U.S.S.R. Treason to the Motherland—violation of the oath of allegiance, desertion to the enemy, impairing the military power of the state, espionage—is punishable with all the severity of the law as the most heinous of crimes.

CHAPTER XI—THE ELECTORAL SYSTEM

ART. 134—Members of all Soviets of Working People's Deputies—of the Supreme Soviet of the U.S.S.R., the Supreme Soviets of the Union Republics, the Soviets of Working People's Deputies of the Territories and Regions, the Supreme Soviets of the Autonomous Republics, the Soviets of Working People's Deputies of the Autonomous Regions, and the Area, District, City and rural (stanitsa, village, hamlet, kishlak, aul) Soviets of Working People's Deputies—are chosen by the electors on the basis of universal, equal and direct suffrage by secret ballot.

ART. 135—Elections of deputies are universal: all citizens of the U.S.S.R. who have reached the age of eighteen, irrespective of race or nationality, sex, religion, education, domicile, social origin, property status or past activities have the right to vote in the election of deputies, with the exception of persons who have been legally certified as insane.

Every citizen of the U.S.S.R. who has reached the age of twenty-three is eligible for election to the Supreme Soviet of the U.S.S.R., irrespective of race or nationality, sex, religion, education, domicile, social origin, property status or past activities.

ART. 136—Elections of deputies are equal: each citizen has one vote; all citizens participate in elections on an equal footing.

ART. 137—Women have the right to elect and be elected on equal terms with men.

ART. 138—Citizens serving in the Armed Forces of the U.S.S.R. have the right to elect and be elected on equal terms with all other citizens.

ART. 139—Elections of deputies are direct: all Soviets of Working People's Deputies, from rural and city Soviets of Working People's Deputies to the Supreme Soviet of the U.S.S.R., are elected by the citizens by direct vote.

ART. 140—Voting at elections of deputies is secret.

ART. 141—Candidates are nominated by election districts.

The right to nominate candidates is secured to public organizations and societies of the working people: Communist Party organizations, trade unions, co-operatives, youth organizations and cultural societies.

ART. 142—It is the duty of every deputy to report to his electors on his work and on the work of his Soviet of Working People's Deputies, and he may be recalled at any time upon decision of a majority of the electors in the manner established by law.

Chapter XII—Arms, Flag, Capital

Art. 143—The arms of the Union of Soviet Socialist Republics are a sickle and hammer against a globe depicted in the rays of the sun and surrounded by ears of grain, with the inscription "Workers of All Countries, Unite!" in the languages of the Union Republics. At the top of the arms is a five-pointed star.

Art. 144—The state flag of the Union of Soviet Socialist Republics is of red cloth with the sickle and hammer depicted in gold in the upper corner near the staff and above them a five-pointed red star bordered in gold. The ratio of the width to the length is 1:2.

Art. 145—The Capital of the Union of Soviet Socialist Republics is the City of Moscow.

Chapter XIII—Procedure for Amending the Constitution

Art. 146—The Constitution of the U.S.S.R. may be amended only by decision of the Supreme Soviet of the U.S.S.R. adopted by a majority of not less than two-thirds of the votes in each of its Chambers.

2. STATUTES OF THE COMMUNIST PARTY OF THE SOVIET UNION, 1961 [1]

The Communist Party of the Soviet Union is the tried and tested militant vanguard of the Soviet people, uniting on a voluntary basis, the more advanced the more socially conscious section of the working class, collective-farm peasantry and intelligentsia of the USSR.

Founded by V. I. Lenin as the vanguard of the working class, the Communist Party has travelled a glorious

[1] This text is based on the translation published in the supplement to *Moscow News,* August 12, 1961, with some revisions to incorporate the changes made in the draft by the Twenty-second Party Congress as reported in *Current Digest of the Soviet Press,* December 20, 1961. The Statutes were adopted at the Twenty-second Congress of the CPSU, November 1961. A resolution authorizing amendments to the Statutes was voted by the Twenty-third Congress of the CPSU, April 8, 1966. The changes made in pursuance of that resolution have been translated from an official handbook of the Statutes.

road of struggle, and brought the working class and the working peasantry to the victory of the Great October Socialist Revolution and to the establishment of the dictatorship of the proletariat in the USSR. Under the leadership of the Communist Party, the exploiting classes were abolished in the Soviet Union, and the moral and political unity of Soviet society has taken shape and grown in strength. Socialism has triumphed completely and finally. The Communist Party, the party of the working class, has today become the party of the Soviet people as a whole.

The Party exists for, and serves, the people. It is the highest form of socio-political organization, and is the leading and guiding force of Soviet society. It directs the great creative activity of the Soviet people and imparts an organized, planned, and scientifically-based character to their struggle to achieve the ultimate goal, the victory of communism.

The CPSU bases its work on the unswerving adherence to the Leninist standards of Party life—the principle of collective leadership, the promotion in every possible way of inner-party democracy, the activity and initiative of the Communists, criticism and self-criticism.

Ideological and organizational unity, monolithic solidarity of its ranks, and a high degree of conscious discipline on the part of all Communists are an inviolable law of the CPSU. All manifestations of factionalism and clique activity are incompatible with Marxist-Leninist Party principles and with Party membership. *The Party purges itself of those who violate the Program and Statutes of the CPSU and, dishonor by their behavior the lofty name of Communist.**

In all its activities, the CPSU is guided by Marxist-Leninist theory and the Program based on it, which define the fundamental tasks of the Party for the period of the construction of communist society.

In creatively developing Marxism-Leninism, the CPSU vigorously combats all manifestations of revisionism and dogmatism, which are profoundly alien to revolutionary theory.

* As amended, 1966, by the addition of the italicized sentence.—*Ed.'s note.*

The Communist Party of the Soviet Union is an integral part of the international Communist and working-class movement. It firmly adheres to the tried and tested Marxist-Leninist principles of proletarian internationalism; it actively promotes the unity of the international Communist and working class movement as a whole, and of the fraternal ties with the great army of Communists of all countries.

1. Party Members, Their Duties and Rights

1. Membership in the CPSU is open to any citizen of the Soviet Union who accepts the Program and Statutes of the Party, takes an active part in communist construction, works in one of the Party organizations, carries out Party decisions, and pays membership dues.

2. It is the duty of a Party member:

(a) to work for the creation of the material and technical basis of communism; to serve as an example of the Communist attitude toward labor; to raise labor productivity; to take the initiative in all that is new and progressive; to support and propagate advanced methods; to master techniques, to improve his skills; to protect and increase public, socialist property, the mainstay of the might and prosperity of the Soviet country;

(b) to put Party decisions firmly and steadfastly into effect; to explain the policy of the Party to the masses; to help strengthen and multiply the Party's bonds with the people; to be considerate and attentive toward people; to respond promptly to the wants and needs of the working people;

(c) to take an active part in the political affairs of the country, in the administration of state affairs, and in economic and cultural development; to set an example in the fulfillment of his public duty; to assist in developing and strengthening Communist social relations;

(d) to master Marxist-Leninist theory, to improve his ideological knowledge, and to contribute to the molding and education of the man of Communist society; to combat resolutely all manifestations of bourgeois ideology, remnants of a private-property psychology, religious prejudices, and other survivals of the past; to observe the principles of Communist morality, and to give public interests precedence over his own;

(e) to be an active proponent of the ideas of socialist internationalism and Soviet patriotism among the masses of the working people; to combat survivals of nationalism and chauvinism; to contribute by word and by deed to the consolidation of the friendship of the peoples of the USSR and the fraternal bonds linking the Soviet people with the peoples of the socialist countries and with the proletarians and other working people in all countries;

(f) to strengthen the ideological and organizational unity of the Party in every way; to safeguard the Party against the infiltration of people unworthy of the lofty name of Communist; to be truthful and honest with the Party and people; to display vigilance, to guard Party and state secrets;

(g) to develop criticism and self-criticism, boldly to lay bare shortcomings and strive for their removal; to combat ostentation, conceit, complacency and parochial tendencies; to rebuff firmly all attempts at suppressing criticism; to resist all actions injurious to the Party and the state, and to give information about them to Party bodies, up to and including the Central Committee of the Communist Party of the Soviet Union;

(h) to implement undeviatingly the party's policy with regard to the proper selection of personnel according to their political and professional qualifications; to be uncompromising whenever the Leninists principles of the selection and training of personnel are violated;

(i) to observe Party and state discipline, which is equally binding on all Party members. The Party has one discipline, one law, for all Communists, irrespective of their past services or the positions they occupy.

(j) to help in every way to strengthen the defense might of the USSR, to wage a tireless struggle for peace and friendship among peoples.

3. A Party member has the right:

(a) to elect and be elected to Party bodies;

(b) to discuss freely questions of the Party's policies and practical activities at Party meetings, conferences and congresses, at the meetings of Party committees and in the Party press; to introduce motions; openly to express and uphold his opinion as long as the organization concerned has not adopted a decision;

(c) to criticize any Communist, irrespective of the position he holds, at Party meetings, conferences and congresses and at the plenary meetings of Party committees. Those guilty of suppressing criticism or persecuting anyone for criticism are responsible to and will be penalized by the Party, up to and including expulsion from the CPSU;

(d) to take part in person in all Party meetings and all bureau and committee meetings that discuss his activities or conduct;

(e) to address questions, statements or proposals to any Party body, up to and including the Central Committee of the CPSU, and to demand an answer on the substance of his address.

4. Applicants are admitted to Party membership only individually. Membership in the Party is open to politically conscious and active workers, peasants, and representatives of the intelligentsia, devoted to the cause of communism. New members are admitted from among the candidate members who have passed through the established probationary period.

Persons may join the Party on attaining the age of eighteen. Young people up to the age of *twenty-three** inclusive may join the Party only through the Young Communist League.

The procedure for the admission of candidate members to full Party membership is as follows:

(a) applicants for Party membership must submit recommendations from three Party members who have a Party standing of not less than *five** years and who know the applicants from having worked with them, professionally and socially, for not less than one year.

Note 1. In the case of members of the YCL applying for membership in the Party, the recommenda-

* As amended, 1966, to substitute "twenty-three" for "twenty" and "five" for "three."—*Ed.'s note.*

tion of a district or city committee of the YCL is equivalent to the recommendation of one Party member.

Note 2. Members and alternate members of the Central Committee of the CPSU shall refrain from giving recommendations.

(b) applications for Party membership are discussed and a decision is taken by the general meeting of the primary Party organization; the decision of the latter *requires a two-thirds vote of the members present at the meeting and* takes effect after endorsement by the district Party committee, or by the city Party committee in cities with no district divisions.*

The presence of those who have recommended an applicant for Party membership at the discussion of the application concerned is optional;

(c) citizens of the USSR who formerly belonged to the Communist or Workers' Party of another country are admitted to membership of the Communist Party of the Soviet Union in conformity with the rules established by the Central Committee of the CPSU.

Former members of other parties are admitted to membership of the CPSU in conformity with the regular procedure, except that their admission must be endorsed by a regional or territorial committee or the Central Committee of the Communist Party of a union republic.

5. Communists recommending applicants for Party membership are responsible to Party organizations for the impartiality of their description of the political, work, and moral qualifications of those they recommend.

6. Tenure of membership dates from the day when the general meeting of the primary Party organization decides to accept them as full members.

7. The procedure of registering members and candidate members of the Party, and of transferring them from one organization to another is determined by the appropriate instructions of the Central Committee of the CPSU.

8. If a Party member or candidate member fails to pay membership dues for three months in succession without sufficient reason, the matter shall be discussed by the primary Party organization. If it is revealed as a

* As amended, 1966, to add the italicized words.—*Ed.'s note.*

result that the Party member or candidate member in question has virtually lost contact with the Party organization, he shall be regarded as having ceased to be a member of the Party; the primary Party organization shall pass a decision thereon and submit it to the district or city committee of the Party for endorsement.

9.* A Party member or candidate member who fails to fulfill his duties as laid down in the Statutes or commits other offenses shall be called to account, and may be subjected to the penalty of admonition, by reprimand (or severe reprimand), with entry in the registration card. The highest Party penalty is expulsion from the Party.

In the case of minor offenses, measures of Party education and influence should be applied—in the form of comradely criticism, Party censure, warning, or reproof.

When the question of expelling a member from the Party is discussed, the maximum thoughtfulness must be shown, a thorough investigation must be conducted, *and the Communist must be informed of the charges against him.***

10.† The decision to expel a Communist from the Party is made by the general meeting of a primary Party organization. The decision of the primary Party organization expelling a member is regarded as adopted if not less than two-thirds of the Party members attending the meeting have voted for it, and it is endorsed by the district or city Party committee.

Until the decision to expel him is endorsed by a district or city Party committee, the Party member or candidate retains his membership or candidates' card and is entitled to attend closed Party meetings.

An expelled Party member retains the right to appeal, within two months, to the higher Party bodies, up to and including the Central Committee of the CPSU.

11. The question of calling a member or alternate

* As amended, 1966, to delete a paragraph that authorized Party organizations to reduce members to candidate member status.—*Ed.'s note.*
** As amended, 1966, to add the italicized words.—*Ed.'s note.*
† As amended, 1966, to eliminate a review procedure.—*Ed.'s note.*

member of the Central Committee of the Communist Party of a union republic, of a territorial, regional, area, city or district Party committee, or of an auditing commission, to account before the Party is discussed by primary Party organizations.

Party organizations pass decisions imposing penalties on members or alternate members of the said Party committees, or on members of auditing commissions, in conformity with the regular procedure.

A Party organization which proposes expelling a Communist from the CPSU communicates its proposal to the Party committee of which he is a member. A decision to expel from the Party a member or alternate member of the Central Committee of the Communist Party of a union republic or a territorial, regional, area, city or district Party committee, or a member of an auditing commission, is taken at the plenary meeting of the committee concerned by a majority of two-thirds of the membership.

The decision to expel from the Party a member or alternate member of the Central Committee of the CPSU, or a member of the Central Auditing Commission, is made by the Party congress, and in the interval between two congresses, by a plenary meeting of the Central Committee, by a majority of two-thirds of the membership.

12. Should a Party member commit an indictable offense, he shall be expelled from the Party and prosecuted in conformity with the law.

13. Appeals against expulsion from the Party or against the imposition of a penalty, as well as the decisions of Party organizations on expulsion from the Party shall be reviewed by the appropriate Party bodies within not more than one month from the date of their receipt.

2. Candidate Members

14. Those joining the Party pass through a probationary period as candidate members which is essential in order that they familiarize themselves with the Program

and Statutes of the CPSU and prepare for admission to full membership of the Party. Party organizations must assist candidates to prepare for admission to full membership of the Party and test their personal qualities. Probationary membership shall be for one year.

15. The procedure for the admission of candidate members (individual admission, submission of recommendations, decision of the primary organization on admission, and its endorsement) is identical with the procedure for the admission of Party members.

16. On the expiration of a candidate member's probationary period, the primary Party organization discusses and decides on his application for admission to full membership. Should a candidate member fail, in the course of his probationary period, to prove himself and cannot, because of his personal qualities, be admitted to membership in the CPSU, the Party organization shall pass a resolution rejecting his admission to membership in the Party; after endorsement of that decision by the district or city Party committee, he shall cease to be considered a candidate member of the CPSU.

17. Candidate members of the Party participate in all the activities of their Party organizations; they shall have a consultative voice at Party meetings. They may not be elected to any executive Party body, nor may they be delegates to a Party conference or congress.

18. Candidate members of the CPSU pay membership dues at the same rate as full members.

3. Organizational Structure of the Party (Inner-Party Democracy)

19. The guiding principle of the organizational structure of the Party is democratic centralism, which means:

    (a) election of all leading Party bodies, from the lowest to the highest;

    (b) periodic accountability of Party bodies to their Party organizations and to higher bodies;

    (c) strict Party discipline and subordination of the minority to the majority;

(d) that the decisions of higher bodies are obligatory for lower bodies.

20. The Party is built on the territorial-industrial principle: Primary organizations are established at places where Communists are employed, and are associated territorially in district, city, etc., organizations. An organization serving a given area is higher than any Party organization serving part of that area.

21. All Party organizations are autonomous in deciding local questions, unless their decisions conflict with Party policy.

22. The highest executive body of a Party organization is the general meeting (in the case of primary organizations); the conference (in the case of district, city, area, regional or territorial organizations); or the congress (in the case of the Communist Parties of union republics and the Communist Party of the Soviet Union).

23. The general meeting, conference or congress elects a bureau or committee which acts as its executive body and directs all the current work of the Party organization.

24.* Party bodies shall be elected by secret ballot. In an election, all Party members have the unlimited right to challenge candidates and to criticize them. Each candidate shall be voted upon separately. A candidate is considered elected if more than one half of those attending the meeting, conference or congress has voted for him.

The principle of systematic renewal of the composition of Party bodies—*from the primary organizations to the Central Committee of the CPSU*—and of continuity of leadership shall be observed in the election of those bodies.

25. A member or alternate member of the Central Committee of the CPSU must by his entire activity justify the great trust placed in him by the Party. A member or alternate member of the Central Committee of the CPSU who does not uphold his honor and dignity may

* As amended, 1966, to add the italicized phrase and to delete four following paragraphs that elaborated on and qualified the rule on the renewal of Party leadership.—*Ed.'s note.*

not remain a member of the Central Committee. The question of the removal of a member or alternate member of the Central Committee of the CPSU from that body shall be decided by a plenary meeting of the Central Committee by secret ballot. The decision is regarded as adopted if not less than two-thirds of the membership of the Central Committee of the CPSU vote for it.

The question of the removal of a member or alternate member of the Central Committee of the Communist Party of a union republic, or of a territorial, regional, area, city or district Party committee from the Party body concerned is decided by a plenary meeting of that body. The decision is regarded as adopted if not less than two-thirds of the membership of the committee in question vote for it by secret ballot.

A member of the Central Auditing Commission who does not justify the great trust placed in him by the Party shall be removed from that body. This question shall be decided by a meeting of the Central Auditing Commission.

The decision is regarded as adopted if not less than two-thirds of the membership of the Central Auditing Commission vote by secret ballot for the removal from that body of the member or alternate member concerned.

The question of the removal of a member from the auditing commission of a republican, territorial, regional, area, city or district Party organization shall be decided by a meeting of the appropriate commission according to the procedure established for members and alternate members of Party committees.

26. The free and business-like discussion of questions of Party policy in individual Party organizations or in the Party as a whole is the inalienable right of every Party member and is an important principle of inner-Party democracy. Only on the basis of inner-Party democracy is it possible to develop criticism and self-criticism and to strengthen Party discipline, which must be conscious and not mechanical.

Discussion of controversial or insufficiently clear issues may be held within the framework of individual organizations or the Party as a whole.

General Party discussion is necessary:

(a) if the necessity is recognized by several Party organizations at regional or republican level;

(b) if there is not a sufficiently solid majority in the Central Committee on major questions of Party policy;

(c) if the Central Committee of the CPSU considers it necessary to consult the Party as a whole on any particular questions of policy.

Wide discussion, especially discussion on a countrywide scale, of questions of Party policy must be carried out in such a way as to ensure for Party members the free expression of their views and preclude attempts to form factional groupings destroying Party unity or attempts to split the Party.

27. The highest principle of Party leadership is collectivity of leadership, which is an absolute requisite for the normal functioning of Party organizations, the proper education of personnel, and the promotion of the activity and initiative of Communists. The cult of the individual and the violations of inner-Party democracy connected with it must not be tolerated in the Party; they are incompatible with the Leninist principles of Party life.

Collective leadership does not absolve persons in office of their responsibility for the job entrusted to them.

28. In the period between congresses and conferences the Central Committees of the Communist Parties of union republics, and territorial, regional, area, city and district Party committees shall periodically inform Party organizations of their work.

29. Meetings of the *aktiv* of district, city, area, regional and territorial Party organizations and of the Communist Parties of union republics shall be held to discuss major decisions of the Party and to work out measures for their execution, as well as to examine questions of local significance.

4. Higher Party Organs

30. The supreme organ of the CPSU is the Party congress. Regular congresses are convened by the Central

Committee at least once in four years. The convocation of a Party congress shall be announced at least six weeks before the congress. Extraordinary congresses are convened by the Central Committee of the Party on its own initiative or on the demand of not less than one-third of the total Party membership represented at the preceding Party congress. Extraordinary congresses shall be convened on two months' notice. A congress is considered properly constituted if not less than one half of the total Party membership is represented at it.

The rates of representation at a Party congress are fixed by the Central Committee.

31. Should the Central Committee of the Party fail to convene an extraordinary congress within the period specified in article 30, the organizations which demanded it have the right to form an organizing committee which shall enjoy the powers of the Central Committee of the Party with respect to the convocation of the extraordinary congress.

32. The congress:

(a) hears and approves the reports of the Central Committee, of the Central Auditing Commission, and of the other central organizations:

(b) reviews, amends and endorses the Program and the Statutes of the Party;

(c) determines the line of the Party in matters of domestic and foreign policy, and examines and decides the most important questions of communist construction;

(d) elects the Central Committee and the Central Auditing Commission.

33. The number of members to be elected to the Central Committee and to the Central Auditing Commission is determined by the congress. In the event of vacancies occurring in the Central Committee, they are filled from among the alternate members of the Central Committee of the CPSU elected by the congress.

34. Between congresses the Central Committee of the CPSU directs the activities of the Party, the local Party bodies, selects and appoints executive functionaries, directs the work of central government bodies and public organizations of working people through the Party groups in them, sets up various Party organs, institutions and enter-

prises and directs their activities, appoints the editors of the central newspapers and magazines operating under its control, and distributes the funds of the Party budget and controls its execution.

The Central Committee represents the CPSU in its relations with other parties.

35. The Central Committee of the CPSU shall keep the Party organizations regularly informed of its work.

36. The Central Auditing Commission supervises the expeditious and proper handling of business by the central bodies of the Party, and audits the treasury and the enterprises of the Central Committee of the CPSU.

37. The Central Committee of the CPSU shall hold not less than one plenary meeting every six months. Alternate members of the Central Committee shall attend its plenary meetings with consultative voice.

38.* The Central Committee of the CPSU elects a *Politburo* to direct the work of the Central Committee between plenary meetings and a Secretariat to direct current work, chiefly the selection of personnel and the verification of the fulfillment of Party decisions.

39. The Central Committee of the CPSU organizes the Party Control Committee of the Central Committee.

The Party Control Committee of the Central Committee:

(a) verifies the observance of Party discipline by members and candidate members of the CPSU, and takes action against Communists who violate the program and the Statutes of the Party, and Party or state discipline, and against violators of Party ethics;

(b) considers appeals against decisions of Central Committees of the Communist Parties of union republics or of territorial and regional Party committees to expel members from the Party or impose Party penalties upon them.

40.** *In case of need, the Central Committee of the CPSU may convene an all-union Party conference between Party congresses for the discussion of current prob-*

---

* As amended, 1966, to substitute "Politburo" for "Presidium" and to a closing phrase that authorized a CC CPSU Bureau for the Russian Republic.—*Ed.'s note.*
** Article 40 added, 1966.—*Ed.'s note.*

lems concerning Party policies. The organization of the all-union Party conference is determined by the Central Committee of the CPSU.

5. Republican, Territorial, Regional, Area, City and District Organizations of the Party

41. The republican, territorial, regional, area, city and district Party organizations and their committees take guidance in their activities from the Program and the Statutes of the CPSU, conduct all work for the implementation of Party policy and organize the fulfillment of the directives of the Central Committee of the CPSU within the republics, territories, regions, areas, cities and districts concerned.

42. The chief duties of republican, territorial, regional, area, city and district Party organizations, and of their executive bodies, are:

(a) political and organizational work among the masses, mobilization of the masses for the fulfillment of the tasks of Communist construction, for the maximum development of industrial and agricultural production, for the fulfillment and over-fulfillment of state plans; solicitude for the steady improvement of the material and cultural standards of the working people;

(b) organization of ideological work, propaganda of Marxism-Leninism, promotion of the Communist awareness of the working people, guidance of the local press, radio and television, and control over the activities of cultural and educational institutions;

(c) guidance of Soviets, trade unions, the YCL, the cooperatives and other public organizations through the Party groups in them, and increasingly broader enlistment of working people in the activities of these organizations, development of the initiative and activity of the masses as an essential condition for the gradual transition from socialist statehood to public self-government under communism.

Party organizations must not act in place of government, trade-union, cooperative or other public organizations of the working people; they must not allow either the merging of the functions of Party and other bodies or undue parallelism in work;

(d) selection and appointment of executive cadres, their education in the spirit of Communist ideology, honesty and truthfulness, and a high sense of responsibility to the Party and the people for the work entrusted to them;

(e) large-scale enlistment of Communists in the conduct of Party activities as unsalaried workers, as a form of public work;

(f) organization of various institutions and enterprises of the Party within the bounds of the respective republic, territory, region, area, city or district, and guidance of their activities; distribution of Party funds within the given organization; systematic information of the higher Party body and accountability to it for their work.

Executive Bodies of Republican, Territorial and Regional Party Organizations

43. The highest body of regional, territorial and republican Party organizations is the respective regional or territorial Party conference or the congress of the Communist Party of the union republic, and in the interim between their meetings the regional committee, territorial committee or the Central Committee of the Communist Party of the union republic.

44.* A regular regional or territorial conference is convened by a regional or territorial committee once every two years. A regular congress of a Communist Party of a union republic is convened by the Central Committee of the Communist Party not less than every four years. Extraordinary conferences and congresses are convened by decision of regional or territorial committees, or the Central Committees of the Communist Parties of union republics, or on the demand of one-third of the total membership of the organizations belonging to the regional, territorial or republican Party organization.

* As amended, 1966, to set a uniform maximum interval between congresses of union republic Parties and to add the italicized paragraph.—*Ed.'s note.*

The rates of representation at regional and territorial conferences and at congresses of Communist Parties of union republics are fixed by the respective Party committees.

Regional and territorial conferences and congresses of the Communist Parties of union republics hear and act upon the reports of the respective regional or territorial committee, or the Central Committee of the Communist Party of the union republic, and of the Auditing Commission; discuss at their own discretion other matters of Party, economic and cultural development, and elect the regional or territorial committee or Central Committee of the union republic, the Auditing Commission and the delegates to the congress of the CPSU.

In case of need in the interval between congresses of the Communist Parties of the union republics, the Central Committees of the Communist Parties may convene union republic Party conferences to discuss major problems concerning the activities of the Party organizations. The organization of the union republic Party conferences is determined by the Central Committee of the Communist Party of the union republics.

45. The regional and territorial committees, and the central Committees of the Communist Parties of union republics elect bureaus, which also include secretaries of the committees. The secretaries must have Party tenure of not less than five years. The plenary meetings of the committees also confirm the chairmen of Party commissions, heads of departments of these committees, editors of Party newspapers and magazines.

Regional and territorial committees and the Central Committees of the Communist Parties of union republics may set up secretariats to handle current business and verify the execution of decisions.

46. The plenary meetings of regional and territorial committees and the Central Committees of the Communist Parties of union republics shall be convened at least once every four months.

47. The regional and territorial committees and the Central Committees of the Communist Parties of union republics direct the activities of area, city and district Party organizations, inspect their work and regularly

hear reports of area, city and district Party committees.

Party organizations in autonomous republics, and in autonomous and other regions forming parts of territories or union republics, function under the guidance of the respective territorial committees or Central Committees of the Communist Parties of union republics.

Executive Bodies of Area, City and District (Urban and Rural) Party Organizations

48. The highest body of an area, city or district Party organization is the area, city and district Party conference or the general meeting of Communists convened by the area, city or district committee at least once in two years, and the extraordinary conference convened by decision of the respective committee or on the demand of one-third of the total membership of the Party organization concerned.

The area, city or district conference (general meeting) hears reports of the committee and audit commission, discusses at its own discretion other questions of Party, economic and cultural development, and elects the area, city and district committee, the audit commission and delegates to the regional, and territorial conference or the congress of the Communist Party of the union republic.

The rates of representation at the area, city, or district conference are fixed by the Party committee concerned.

49. Each area, city or district committee elects a bureau, including the committee secretaries, and confirms the appointment of heads of committee departments and newspaper editors. The secretaries of the area, city and district committees must have Party tenure of at least three years. The committee secretaries are confirmed by the respective regional or territorial committee, or the Central Committee of the Communist Party of the union republic.

50. The area, city or district committee organizes and confirms the primary Party organizations, directs their work, regularly hears reports concerning the work of Party organizations, and keeps a record of Communists.

51. The plenary meeting of the area, city or district committee is convened at least once in three months.

52. The area, city or district committee has unsalaried instructors, sets up standing or ad hoc commissions on various aspects of Party work and uses other ways to draw Communists into the activities of the Party committee as a social duty.

6. Primary Party Organizations

53. The primary Party organizations are the foundation of the Party.

Primary Party organizations are formed at the places of work of Party members—in factories, on state farms and at other enterprises, collective farms, units of the Soviet Army, offices, educational establishments, etc., wherever there are not less than three Party members. Primary Party organizations may also be organized on the residential principle in villages and in apartment house administrations.

54. Shop, sectional, farm, team, departmental, etc., Party organizations may be formed as units of the general primary Party organization, with the authorization of the area, city or district committee, at enterprises, collective farms and institutions with over 50 Party members and candidate members.

Within shop, sectional, etc., organizations, and also within primary Party organizations having less than 50 members and candidate members, Party groups may be formed in the teams and other production units.

55.* The highest organ of the primary Party organization is the Party meeting, which is held at least once a month. *In Party organizations having shop organizations the general Party meeting takes place not less often than once every two months.*

In large Party organizations with more than 300 Communists a general Party meeting is convened when necessary at times fixed by the Party committee or on

* As amended, 1966, to add the italicized sentence.—*Ed.'s note.*

the demand of a number of shop or departmental Party organizations.

56. For the conduct of current business the primary, shop or departmental Party organization elects a bureau for the term of one year. The number of its members is fixed by the Party meeting. Primary, shop and departmental Party organizations with less than 15 Party members do not elect a bureau. Instead, they elect a secretary and deputy secretary of the Party organization.

Secretaries of primary, shop and departmental organizations must have Party tenure of at least one year.

Primary Party organizations with less than 150 Party members shall have, as a rule, no salaried functionaries released from their regular work.

57. In large factories and offices with more than 300 members and candidate members of the Party, and in exceptional cases in factories and offices with over 100 Communists by virtue of special production conditions and geographic dispersion, subject to the approval of the regional committee, territorial committee or Central Committee of the Communist Party of the union republic, Party committees may be formed, the shop and departmental Party organizations at these factories and offices being granted the status of primary Party organizations.

The Party organizations of collective farms may set up Party committees if they have a minimum of 50 Communists.

The Party committees are elected for the term of one year. The number of members is fixed by the general Party meeting or conference.

58.* *Party committees of those primary organizations having more than 1,000 Communists may be granted, with the approval of the Central Committee of the Communist Party of the union republic, the rights of a district party with respect to its enrollment in the Communist Party of the Soviet Union, the keeping of a register of the members and candidate members of the Party, investigation into the personal affairs of the Communists.*

* Article 58 added, 1966.—*Ed.'s note.*

In exceptional cases, Party committees in factories may be established within those organizations and the Party organizations of the included sections are granted the rights of primary party organizations.

Party committees which have been granted the rights of district committees of the Party are elected for the term of two years.

59. In its activities the primary Party organization takes guidance from the Program and the Statutes of the CPSU. It conducts its work directly among the working people, rallies them around the Communist Party of the Soviet Union, organizes the masses to carry out the Party policy and to work for the building of communism.

The primary Party organization:

(a) enrolls new members in the CPSU;

(b) educates Communists in a spirit of loyalty to the Party cause, ideological conviction and communist ethics;

(c) organizes the study by Communists of Marxist-Leninist theory in close connection with the practice of communist construction and opposes all attempts to introduce revisionist distortions into Marxism-Leninism and its dogmatic interpretation;

(d) ensures the vanguard role of Communists in the sphere of labor and in the socio-political and economic activities of enterprises, collective farms, institutions, educational establishments, etc;

(e) acts as the organizer of the working people for the performance of the current tasks of communist construction; heads socialist competition for the fulfillment of state plans and undertakings of the working people; rallies the masses to disclose and make the best use of untapped resources at enterprises and collective farms, and on a broad scale to apply in production the achievements of science, engineering and the experience of leading workers; works for the strengthening of labor discipline, the steady increase of labor productivity and improvement of the quality of production, and shows concern for the protection and increase of social wealth at enterprises, state and collective farms;

(f) conducts agitational and propaganda work

among the masses, educates them in the communist spirit, helps the working people to acquire proficiency in administering state and social affairs;

(g) on the basis of extensive criticism and self-criticism, combats cases of bureaucracy, parochialism, and violations of state discipline, thwarts attempts to deceive the state, acts against negligence, waste and extravagance at enterprises, collective farms and offices;

(h) assists the area, city and district committees in their activities and is accountable to them for its work.

The Party organization must see to it that every Communist should observe in his own life and cultivate among working people the ethical principles set forth in the Program of the CPSU in the ethical code of the builder of communism:

—loyalty to the communist cause, love of the socialist homeland and of other socialist countries;

—conscientious labor for the benefit of society: He who does not work, neither shall he eat;

—concern on everyone's part for the protection and increase of public wealth;

—a lofty sense of public duty, intolerance of violations of public interests;

—collectivism and comradely mutual assistance: one for all and all for one;

—humane relations and mutual respect among people: Man is to man a friend, comrade and brother;

—honesty and truthfulness, moral purity, unpretentiousness and modesty in public and personal life;

—mutual respect in the family circle and concern for the upbringing of children;

—intolerance of injustice, parasitism, dishonesty, careerism and money-grubbing;

—friendship and fraternity among all peoples of the USSR, intolerance of national and racial hostility;

—intolerance of the enemies of communism, peace, and the freedom of peoples;

—fraternal solidarity with the working people of all countries with all peoples.

60. Primary Party organizations of industrial enterprises and trading establishments; state and collective farms; and design organizations, drafting offices and re-

search institutes directly related to production enjoy the
right to control the work of the administration.

The Party organizations at ministries, state committees, economic councils and other central and local
government or economic agencies and departments, which
do not have the function of controlling the administration,
must actively promote improvement of the apparatus,
cultivate among the personnel a high sense of responsibility for work entrusted to them, work to strengthen
state discipline and for the better servicing of the population, firmly combat bureaucracy and red tape, inform
the appropriate Party bodies in good time of shortcomings in the work of the respective offices and individuals,
regardless of the posts they occupy.

7. The Party and the Young Communist League

61. The Leninist YCL of the Soviet Union is an independent public organization of young people, an active
helper and reserve of the Party. The YCL helps the Party
educate the youth in the communist spirit, draws it into
the work of building a new society, trains a rising gen-
eration of harmoniously developed people who will live
and work and administer public affairs under communism.

62. YCL organizations enjoy the right of broad initiative in discussing and submitting to the appropriate Party
organizations questions related to the work of enterprises,
collective farms and offices. They must be really active
in the implementation of Party directives in all spheres
of communist construction, especially where there are no
primary Party organizations.

63. The YCL works under the guidance of the Communist Party of the Soviet Union. The work of the local
YCL organizations is directed and controlled by the appropriate republican, territorial, regional, area, city and
district Party organizations.

In their communist educational work among the
youth, local Party organs and primary Party organizations rely on the support of the YCL organizations, and
uphold and promote their useful undertakings.

64. Members of the YCL who are admitted to the Party cease to belong to the YCL the moment they join the Party, provided they do not hold executive posts in YCL organizations.

8. Party Organizations in the Soviet Army

65. Party organizations in the Soviet Army take guidance in their work from the Program and the Statutes of the CPSU and operate on the basis of instructions issued by the Central Committee.

The Party organizations of the Soviet Army ensure the implementation of the policy of the Party in the Armed Forces; rally servicemen around the Communist Party; educate them in the spirit of Marxism-Leninism and boundless loyalty to the socialist homeland; actively further the unity of the army and the people; work for the strengthening of discipline; rally servicemen to carry out the tasks of military and political training and acquire skill in the use of new techniques and weapons, and irreproachably to carry out their military duty and the orders and instructions of the command.

66. The guidance of Party work in the Armed Forces is exercised by the Central Committee of the CPSU through the Chief Political Administration of the Soviet Army and Navy, which functions as a department of the Central Committee of the CPSU.

The chiefs of the political administrations of military areas and fleets and chiefs of the political administrations of armies must be Party members of five-years' tenure, and the chiefs of political departments of military formations must be Party members of three years'. tenure.

67. The Party organizations and political bodies of the Soviet Army maintain close contact with local Party committees, and keep them informed about political work in the military units. The secretaries of military Party organizations and chiefs of political bodies participate in the work of local Party committees.

9. Party Groups in Non-Party Organizations

68. At congresses, conferences and meetings and in the elective bodies of Soviets, trade unions, cooperatives and other mass organizations of the working people, having at least three Party members, Party groups are formed for the purpose of strengthening the influence of the Party in every way and carrying out Party policy among non-Party people, strengthening Party and state discipline, combatting bureaucracy, and verifying the fulfillment of Party and government directives.

69. The Party groups are subordinate to the appropriate Party bodies: Central Committee of the CPSU, the Central Committees of the Communist Parties of union republics, territorial, regional, area, city or district Party committees.

In all matters the groups must strictly and unswervingly abide by decisions of the executive Party bodies.

10. Party Funds

70. The funds of the Party and its organizations are derived from membership dues, income from Party enterprises and other revenue.

71. The monthly membership dues for Party members and candidate members are as follows:

Monthly Earnings	Dues (Percentage of Monthly Earnings)
up to 50 rubles	10 kopeks
from 51 to 100 rubles	0.5 percent
from 101 to 150 rubles	1.0 percent
from 151 to 200 rubles	1.5 percent
from 201 to 250 rubles	2.0 percent
from 251 to 300 rubles	2.5 percent
over 300 rubles	3.0 percent

72. An entrance fee of 2 percent of monthly earnings is assessed on acceptance into the Party as a candidate member.

ADDENDA

EMERGENCY POWERS AMENDMENTS (1968) TO THE BASIC LAW OF THE FEDERAL REPUBLIC OF GERMANY *

(Italicized lines are explanatory and are not part of the document.)

The following amendments to the Basic Law were enacted by the West German parliament in early June 1968:

1. Addition at the end of Art. 9 (3):
Measures taken under Art. 12a (2) and (3), Art. 87a (4), and Art. 91 may not be directed against labor strikes that are called by the organizations described in the first sentence of this paragraph to safeguard and improve working and economic conditions.

2. Revision of Art. 10:
(1) Secrecy of the mail and secrecy of posts and telecommunications are inviolable.

(2) Restrictions may be ordered only pursuant to a law. If the restriction serves to protect the free democratic basic order or to preserve or secure the Federation or one of the *Laender,* the law may provide that the subject not be informed and that instead of the legal proceedings the evidence may be presented to the representatives of the people by the department or agency concerned.

3. Revision of Art. 11 (2):
(2) This right may be restricted only by a law and only in cases in which an adequate basis of existence is lacking and special burdens would arise to the community as a result thereof or in which the restriction is necessary for protection against imminent danger to the existence of the free democratic basic order of the Federation or the *Laender* or for combatting the danger of epidemics or natural catastrophes or especially serious accidents or for the protection of the young from neglect or from unlawful actions.

4. Addition at the end of Art. 12 (1):
or on the basis of a law.

---

* Translated from *Schriftlicher Bericht des Rechtsausschusses, Deutscher Bundestag 5. Wahlperiode, Drucksache V/2873;* and *Zusammenstellung des Entwurfs . . . mit den Beschlüssen des Bundestages in zweiter Beratung, Deutscher Bundestag 5. Wahlperiode, Drucksache V/2917,* by the editor and Mrs. Eliese Hetler.

5. *Deletion from Art. 12 (2):*

Anyone who . . . Armed Forces.

6. *Deletion from Art. 12 (3) and renumbering of Art. 12 (4) to become Art. 12 (3).*

7. *Addition of Art. 12a:*

(1) Men over 18 years may be compelled to serve in the Armed Forces, the Federal border patrol, or in some form of civil defense.

(2) Anyone who refuses on conscientious grounds to render war service involving the use of arms, may be required to render an alternative service. The duration of this alternative service shall not exceed the duration of military service. Details shall be regulated by a law which shall not prejudice freedom of conscience and shall provide also for the possibility of an alternative service having no connection with any unit of the Armed Forces or the Federal border patrol.

(3) In the event of a defense emergency, conscriptees who cannot be conscripted under (1) or (2) above may be compelled by a law or on the basis of a law to perform civil defense service including the protection of the civilian population; this obligation may be met in the civil administration only by service in police duties or other such highly important tasks that can be performed only in the civil administration. Service under sentence 1 above may be performed in either the Armed Forces in their supply units or in the civil administration; service in the area of supply for the civilian population is permitted only to ensure its survival or its protection.

(4) If the need for civilian personnel in civilian hospitals and health services and in permanent military hospitals in a defense emergency cannot be met by volunteers, women from 18 through 55 may be conscripted by law or on the basis of a law. Under no circumstances shall they bear arms.

(5) Prior to a defense emergency, service under (3) above may be based upon the provisions of Art. 80a (1). In order to prepare for service under (3) above for which special knowledge or training is required, participation in a training program may be required by a law or on the basis of a law. Sentence 1 above does not apply in that case.

(6) If the need for workers described in (3) sentence 2 above cannot be met by volunteers, the freedom of Germans to choose their trade or profession or their place of work can be suspended by a law or on the basis of a law. Prior to a defense emergency, (5) above applies.

8. *Addition at the end of Art. 19 (4):*

Art. 10 (2) sentence 2 does not apply.

9. *Addition to Art. 20.*

(4) All Germans have the right, if no other means exist, to

resist any person who undertakes to destroy the constitutional order.

10.   *Addition to Art. 35:*

(2) To help in the event of a natural catastrophe or an especially serious accident, a *Land* police force can summon from other *Laender* forces and equipment of other jurisdictions as well as those of the Federal border patrol and Armed Forces.

(3) If the catastrophe or accident endangers the territory of more than one *Land,* the Federal Government, if necessary, may summon the police forces of other *Laender* as well as units of the Federal border patrol and the Armed Forces to support their police forces. Measures taken by the Federal Government under sentence 1 above must be withdrawn immediately when the danger has passed or the Bundestag so requests.

11.   *Addition after Art. 53:*

TITLE IVa.   THE JOINT COMMISSION

Art. 53a—(1) The Joint Commission consists two-thirds of deputies from the Bundestag and one-third of members of the Bundesrat. The deputies are elected so as to represent proportionately the strength of the party caucuses. They may not be members of the Federal Government. Each *Land* selects a member of the Bundesrat to represent it; these members may not be bound by instructions. The formation of the Joint Commission and its proceedings are regulated by the standing orders of the Bundestag as accepted by the Bundesrat.

(2) The Federal Government must inform the Joint Commission of its plans in case of defense emergency. The rights of the Bundestag and its committees as set forth in Art. 43 (1) are not affected.

12.   *Repeal of Art. 59a.*

13.   *Repeal of Art. 65a (2).*

14.   *Deletion from Art. 73, clause 1:*
both military service for males over 18 years.

15.   *Addition after Art. 80:*

Art. 80a—(1) This Basic Law or a Federal law concerning defense including the protection of the civilian population shall provide that the decrees under the provisions of this article may be given effect, except in case of defense emergency, only when the Bundestag has declared that an emergency has begun or has consented expressly to their application. A two-thirds majority of the votes cast is necessary to declare that an emergency has begun or to give express consent to the application of Art. 12a (5) sentence 1 and Art. 12a (6) sentence 2.

(2) Deviation from (1) above in giving effect to decrees is permitted also on the basis and the authority of a resolution

passed by an international organization within the framework of a treaty to which the Federal Government has consented.

(3) Measures taken under (1) and (2) above must be suspended when a majority of the members of the Bundestag so request.

16.   *Revision of Art. 87a:*

(1) The Federation establishes Armed Forces for defense. Their numerical strength and general organization must be determined by the budget.

(2) Except in case of defense emergency, these Armed Forces may be used only as this Basic Law provides.

(3) The Armed Forces are obliged to protect civil property in case of defense emergency or disorder and have the task of controlling traffic to the extent necessary for defense. Furthermore, the Armed Forces may be assigned to perform police duties to protect civil property in case of defense emergency or disorder; in such cases, the Armed Forces shall cooperate with the appropriate civil officials.

(4) In case of imminent danger to the existence of the free democratic basic order of the Federation or a *Land,* the Federal Government can call upon the Armed Forces when the conditions described in Art. 91 (2) exist and the police forces and the Federal border patrol are not sufficient. The Armed Forces will aid the police and the Federal border patrol to protect civil property and to combat organized, militarily-armed rioters. The use of the Armed Forces shall cease if the Bundestag or the Bundesrat so requests.

17.   *Addition at end of Art. 91 (1):*
as well as forces and equipment of other governments and the Federal border patrol.

18.   *Insertion in Art. 91 (2) between* "Laender" *and* "under":
as well as units of the Federal border patrol.

19.   *Addition at end of Art. 91 (2):*
If the danger extends beyond the territory of one *Land,* the Federal Government may issue instructions to the *Land* Governments to the extent necessary for effective defense; sentences 1 and 2 above are not affected.

20.   *Addition after Art. 115:*

TITLE Xa. EMERGENCY POWERS

Art. 115a.—(1) The declaration that the territory of the Federation is under armed attack or that such attack is imminent shall be made by a resolution passed by the Bundestag with the consent of the Bundesrat. The resolution shall be initiated by the Federal Government and requires for passage a majority of at least two-thirds of the votes cast, including the votes of at least a majority of the members of the Bundestag.

(2) If the situation requires immediate action and unsurmountable obstacles prevent an early meeting of the Bundestag or if the Bundestag is unable to reach a decision, the Joint Commission may pass the resolution, provided it receives a majority of two-thirds of the votes cast, including the votes of a majority of its members.

(3) The resolution shall be published in the Federal Gazette in accordance with the provisions of Art. 82. If this is not possible immediately, the announcement must be made in some other way; as soon as conditions permit, the resolution must be published in the Federal Gazette retroactively.

(4) If the Federal territory is attacked by armed force and the Federal governmental organs are unable to pass a resolution under (1) sentence 1 above, the resolution is regarded as having been passed, its effective date being the time the attack began. The Federal President will announce the date as soon as circumstances permit.

(5) If a defense emergency resolution is passed and the territory of the Federation is attacked by armed force, the Federal President with the consent of the Bundestag, can issue a declaration under international law concerning the existence of a defense emergency. In the conditions described in (2) above, the Joint Commission acts in place of the Bundestag.

Art. 115b.—With the declaration of defense emergency, the command of and authority over the Armed Forces shall be transferred to the Federal Chancellor.

Art. 115c.—(1) In a defense emergency, the Federation may pass concurrent legislation in areas which belong normally to the legislative authority of the *Laender*. These laws require the consent of the Bundesrat.

(2) To the extent required by the conditions of the defense emergency, for the period of the defense emergency, Federal legislation can

1. expropriate property without regard to Art. 14 (3) sentence 2, which regulates compensation otherwise.
2. permit deprivation of liberty without regard to Art. 104 (2) sentence 3 and (3) sentence for a period no longer than four days if no judge is available to assume jurisdiction during the period of time normally allowed.

(3) To the extent necessary to prepare for defense against actual or imminently-threatened attack, the Governments and the fiscal administrations of the Federation and the *Laender* may disregard, in case of a defense emergency, the provisions of Title VIII and Arts. 106 through 115 by Federal law with the agreement of the Bundesrat if this is necessary in order to pre-

serve the viability of the *Laender,* communes, and associations of communes especially with respect to financial matters.

(4) Federal laws under (1) and (2) clause 1 above may be put into effect prior to a defense emergency in order to prepare for it.

Art. 115d.—(1) The provisions of (2) and (3) apply to legislation by the Federation except that enacted under Art. 76 (2), Art. 77 (1) sentence 2 and (2) through (4), Art. 78, and Art. 82 (1).

(2) Proposals for legislation by the Federal Government which are considered urgent shall be submitted to the Bundestag and the Bundesrat at the same time. The Bundestag and the Bundesrat will discuss them jointly without delay. When the consent of the Bundesrat is necessary for a law the agreement of a majority of its votes is necessary to pass the law. The latter is regulated by the procedures which shall be decided upon by the Bundestag with the agreement of the Bundesrat.

(3) For the proclamation of the law, Art. 115a (3) sentence 3 is applicable.

Art. 115e.—(1) If, in a defense emergency, the Joint Commission decides by a two-thirds majority of the votes cast, including at least a majority of its members, that obstacles prevent rapid convocation of the Bundestag or that the Bundestag is unable to reach a decision, the Joint Commission can act in place of the Bundestag and the Bundesrat and can assume their rights.

(2) Laws of the Joint Commission may neither partially nor completely change nor suspend the Basic Law. The Joint Commission is not authorized to suspend laws under Art. 24 (1) and Art. 29 by decree.

Art. 115f.—(1) As far as required by the situation in a defense emergency, the Federal Government can

1. deploy the Federal border patrol throughout the territory of the Federation,
2. give instructions not only to the Federal administration but also to the *Laender* Governments when it believes this to be necessary and the *Laender* officials will transmit those instructions to the appropriate members of the *Laender* Governments.

(2) The Bundestag, Bundesrat, and Joint Commission must be notified immediately when measures are taken under (1) above.

Art. 115g.—The constitutional position and responsibility with respect to the constitutional duties of the Federal Constitutional Court and its judges may not be affected. The law concerning the Constitutional Court may be changed by a law of the Joint Commission only when, in the opinion of the Federal

Constitutional Court, this is necessary in order to maintain the ability of the court to function. Until such a law is passed the Federal Constitutional Court can take the steps necessary to maintain the operation of the court. Decisions under sentences 2 and 3 above can be reached only in agreement with a majority of the judges present.

Art. 115h.—(1) All elections for the Bundestag and *Laender* popular consultations regularly scheduled to fall during a period of defense emergency shall be postponed until six months after the end of the defense emergency. If the term of office of the Federal President expires as well as if the President of the Bundesrat assumes the powers of the President of the Federation because the office has fallen vacant prematurely during the period of defense emergency, the office shall be relinquished within nine months after the defense emergency ends. The term of office of a member of the Federal Constitutional Court which expires during a defense emergency shall end six months after the emergency ends.

(2) If an election of the Federal Chancellor by the Joint Commission must be held, the Federal Chancellor must receive the votes of a majority of its members; the Federal President proposes a nomination to the Joint Commission. The Joint Commission can express its lack of confidence in the Federal Chancellor only by electing a successor by a two-thirds majority of its members.

(3) The Bundestag may not be dissolved during a defense emergency.

Art. 115i.—(1) If the appropriate Federal governmental organs are unable to take the necessary measures to avert the danger, or if the situation requires unavoidable and expeditious independent handling in particular parts of the Federal territory, the *Laender* governments or those officials designated by them are empowered to take measures under Art. 115f (1) in the areas of their jurisdiction.

(2) Measures taken by the *Laender* administrations and by the Federal administration under (1) above may be suspended by the Federal Government acting through the Minister Presidents of the *Laender*.

Art. 115k.—(1) For the duration of their applicability, laws under Art. 115c, 115e, and 115g, and decrees which are based on those laws shall override conflicting laws. This does not apply to earlier laws which were issued under Arts. 115c, 115e, and 115g.

(2) Laws containing provisions that disregard Arts. 106 and 107 expire no later than the end of the second fiscal year after the defense emergency ends. They can be changed by Federal law with the concurrence of the Bundesrat at the end of the de-

fense emergency in order to provide a transition to regulations under Title X.

Art. 115l.—(1) With the concurrence of the Bundesrat, the Bundestag can suspend laws of the Joint Commission at any time. The Bundesrat can demand that the Bundestag take such action. Other measures which were taken by the Joint Commission or the Federal Government to avert the danger shall be suspended when the Bundestag and the Bundesrat so decide.

(2) With the concurrence of the Bundesrat, the Bundestag can declare at any time that the Federal President should proclaim that the defense emergency has ended. The Bundesrat can demand that the Bundestag so decide. The defense emergency must be declared over immediately when the conditions that created it no longer exist.

(3) Peace is concluded by Federal law.

21. Repeal of Art. 142a and Art. 143.

STATISTICAL APPENDIX

Great Britain

TABLE 1

POLITICAL EVENTS SINCE 1918

1918	Property qualifications for voting abolished; **Partial** women's suffrage introduced.
1921	Clynes becomes Labour Leader; Bonar Law **resigns;** A. Chamberlain becomes Conservative leader.
1922	Conservative backbenchers form 1922 Committee, force Chamberlain to resign; Bonar Law re-elected Leader; MacDonald becomes Labour Leader.
1923	Free trade abandoned.
1924	First Labour government; Red scare and "Zinoviev letter" affair.
1926	General Strike fails.
1929	Financial crisis; Gold standard abandoned.
1931	Labour-Liberal coalition collapses; "National" government formed; Statute of Westminster enacted; Henderson becomes Labour Leader.
1932	Lansbury becomes Labour Leader.
1935	Attlee becomes Labour Leader.
1936	Edward VIII abdication crisis.
1937	Ministers of the Crown Act passed.
1938	N. Chamberlain agrees to Munich Pact.
1939-	
1945	World War II; "National" coalition government.
1945	Nationalization program begins.
1947	Empire becomes Commonwealth.
1948	Representation of the People Act passed.
1949	Parliament Act passed.
1953	Steel industry denationalized.
1955	Gaitskell becomes Labour Leader.
1958	Life Peerages Act passed.
1962	National Economic Development Council established.
1963	Wilson becomes Labour Leader.
1965	Heath becomes Conservative Leader.
1967	Steel renationalized; Elimination of hereditary House of Lords proposed.

TABLE 2

PARTY REPRESENTATION IN THE HOUSE OF COMMONS

Date of General Election	Conservative and Unionist	Labour	Liberal
October 1900	402	11	185
January 1906	158	41	387
January 24, 1910	273	40	275
December 24, 1910	272	42	272
December 15, 1918	382[a]	74[b]	161[c]
November 15, 1922	347	142	118[d]
December 6, 1923	258	191	151
October 29, 1924	414	150	39
May 30, 1929	260	287	59
October 27, 1931	471	65[e]	72[f]
November 14, 1935	387	166[g]	54[h]
July 5, 1945	189	396[i]	25[j]
February 23, 1950	298[k]	315	9
October 25, 1951	320[l]	296	6
May 26, 1955	344[l]	277	6
October 8, 1959	365	258	6
October 15, 1964	303	317	9
March 31, 1966	253	363	12

[a] Including 48 Non-Coalition Unionists.
[b] Including 63 Non-Coalition Labour.
[c] Including 28 Non-Coalition Liberals.
[d] Liberal National 59; Liberal 59.
[e] National Labour 13 (MacDonald); Labour 52 (Henderson).
[f] Liberal National 35 (Simon); Liberal 33 (Samuel); 4 (Lloyd George).
[g] Labour 154; National Labour 8; I.L.P. 4.
[h] Liberal National 33; Liberal 21.
[i] Labour 393; I.L.P. 3.
[j] Liberal National 13; Liberal 12.
[k] Includes National Liberal.
[l] Includes Associates.

Source: *Whitaker's Almanack* (London, 1959 and 1967) Vol. 91 and 99.

TABLE 3

POPULAR VOTE FOR THE HOUSE
OF COMMONS SINCE 1945

Election	Conservative and Associate	Labour	Liberal	Other	Total
1945	8,693,858	11,985,733	2,253,197	2,085,605[a]	25,018,393
1950	11,166,026	13,265,610	2,621,489	1,716,352[b]	28,769,477
1951	13,718,069	13,949,105	730,552	198,969	28,596,695
1955	13,311,938	12,405,246	722,395	321,175	26,760,754
1959	13,750,965	12,195,765	1,661,262	255,346	27,863,338
1964	12,002,407	12,205,581	3,093,316	348,914	27,656,149
1966	11,418,433	13,064,951	2,327,533	452,689	27,263,606

[a] Includes Liberal National 759,884 and Ulster Unionist 441,108.

[b] Includes National Liberal and Conservative 983,623 and Ulster Unionist 352,334.

Source: *Whitaker's Almanack.*

TABLE 4

SOVEREIGNS SINCE 1837

Sovereign	Regnal Year
Victoria	1 June 20, 1837-June 19, 1838
	64 June 20, 1900-January 22, 1901
Edward VII	1 January 22, 1901-January 21, 1902
	10 January 22, 1910-May 6, 1910
George V	1 May 6, 1910-May 5, 1911
	26 May 6, 1936-January 20, 1936
Edward VIII	1 January 20, 1936-December 11, 1936
George VI	1 December 11, 1936-December 10, 1937
	16 December 11, 1951-February 6, 1952
Elizabeth II	1 February 6, 1952-February 5, 1953

Source: *Whitaker's Almanack.*

TABLE 5

PRIME MINISTERS SINCE 1895

Prime Minister	Assumed Office	Government Parties
Marquess of Salisbury	July 2, 1895	Conservative
Sir H. Campbell-Bannerman	December 5, 1905	Liberal
H. H. Asquith	April 8, 1908	Liberal
H. H. Asquith	May 26, 1915	Liberal, Conservative
D. Lloyd George	December 7, 1916	Liberal, Conservative
A. Bonar Law	October 23, 1922	Conservative
S. Baldwin	May 22, 1923	Conservative
J. R. MacDonald	January 22, 1924	Labour
S. Baldwin	November 2, 1924	Conservative
J. R. MacDonald	June 8, 1929	Labour
J. R. MacDonald	August 25, 1931	National (Conservative)
S. Baldwin	June 7, 1935	Conservative
N. Chamberlain	May 28, 1937	Conservative
W. S. Churchill	May 11, 1940	Conservative, Labour, Liberal
W. S. Churchill	May 23, 1945	Conservative
C. R. Attlee	July 26, 1945	Labour
Sir W. S. Churchill	October 26, 1951	Conservative

TABLE 5 (*Continued*)

PRIME MINISTERS SINCE 1895

Prime Minister	Assumed Office	Government Parties
Sir A. Eden	April 6, 1955	Conservative
H. Macmillan	January 13, 1957	Conservative
Sir A. Douglas-Home	October 19, 1957	Conservative
J. H. Wilson	October 16, 1964	Labour

Source: *Whitaker's Almanack.*

TABLE 6

PEERS SERVING UNDER THE LIFE PEERAGES ACT OF 1958

Year	Life Peers	Life Peeresses	Total Membership of House of Lords
1959	10	4	884
1960	14	4	889
1961	19	5	899
1962	28	6	903
1963	34	7	924
1964	37	7	957
1965	44	9	962
1966	87	15	994
1967	103	16	1020

Source: *Whitaker's Almanack* (London: 1959-1967) Vols. 91 through 99.

France

TABLE 1

POLITICAL PERIODS

before 1789	Monarchy
1789-1792	Revolution
1792-1795	First Republic, Convention
1795-1799	Directory
1799-1804	Consulate
1804-1814	First Empire
1814	First Restoration Monarchy, Napoleon's "Hundred Days"
1815-1830	Second Restoration Monarchy
1830-1848	July Monarchy
1848-1852	Second Republic
1852-1870	Second Empire
1871-1940	Third Republic
1940-1944	French State/Free France
1944-1946	Provisional Government
1946-1958	Fourth Republic
1958-	Fifth Republic

TABLE 2

IMPORTANT EVENTS SINCE 1918

1923	France invades Ruhr to demand reparations
1924	Cartel des Gauches wins election
	President Millerand attempts to dissolve Assembly
1925	Briand becomes Premier
	Conciliation with republican Germany
1926	Poincaré receives special economic powers
1928	Cartel des Gauches breaks up
	Social insurance legislation passed
1930	Allies evacuate Rhineland
1932	Family allowances established
1934	Stavisky affair

TABLE 2 (*Continued*)

1935	Saar returned to Germany
1936	Radicals, Socialists, and Communists win "Popular Front" election
1937	Blum resigns in financial crisis
	Chautemps wins plenary powers
1940	French Army defeated
	Pétain signs Armistice
	De Gaulle escapes to England
1941	French National Committee established
1943	French Committee of National Liberation succeeds French National Committee
1944	Paris Liberated
	French State abolished
	Provisional government takes power
1945	Women's suffrage introduced
	Constituent assembly elected
	De Gaulle becomes Premier
1946	De Gaulle resigns
	Draft Constitution rejected
	New Constituent Assembly elected
	Fourth Republic Constitution approved
1947	De Gaulle forms RPF
	Communists go into opposition
	Monnet Plan undertaken
1950	Schuman plan adopted
1953	RPF dissolved
1954	Indochina War ends
	Algerian War begins
	EDC rejected
1955	Poujadism emerges as a political force
1956	French Union reformed by Defferre law
1958	De Gaulle returns as Premier with emergency transitional powers
	UNR formed
	Constitution of Fifth Republic approved
	De Gaulle becomes President of the Republic and of the French Community
1961	Abortive military putsch in Algiers
1962	Algeria becomes independent
1963	France vetoes British entry into Common Market
1966	France withdraws from NATO military committee
1967	Leftwing parties unite in parliamentary election
1968	General strike
	Parliamentary elections

TABLE 3

DISTRIBUTION OF NATIONAL ASSEMBLY SEATS AND VOTES
IN NATIONAL ASSEMBLY ELECTIONS SINCE 1945

	Oct. 1945	June 1946	Nov. 1946	June 1951	Jan. 1956	Nov. 1958	Nov. 1962	Mar. 1967	June 1968
Communist	146	146	164	97	145	10	41	71	33
(mil. votes)	4.3	5.2	5.4	4.9	5.4	3.7	4.0	5.0	4.4
Extreme Left	—	—	—	—	—	2	2	4	0
(mil. votes)	0.7	—	—	0.1	0.1	—	0.4	0.5	0.9
SFIO	113	115	91	94	88	40	65	114[1]	57[8]
(mil. votes)	4.5	4.2	3.4	2.8	3.2	2.5	2.3	4.2	3.7
Radicals, allies[2]	45	39	53	83	71	35	42		
(mil. votes)	1.4	2.3	2.4	2.5	3.3	1.4	1.4		
MRP	139	160	156	82	71	57[3]	36		
(mil. votes)	4.6	5.6	5.1	2.5	2.4	1.4	1.7		
Conservatives[4]	64	62	75	81	95	132	28	30[7]	29[9]
(mil. votes)	2.9	2.5	2.5	1.9	3.1	4.3	1.4	2.9	2.3

Gaullists	—	—	5	107	16	189	249[5]	230[5]
(mil. votes)			0.3	4.0	0.9	4.8	6.9	8.5
Other	11	11	—	—	54[6]	1	2	20
(mil. votes)	0.1	0.1	0.1	0.1	2.5	—	0.2	1.3
Total	518	522	544	544	544	465	465	470
(mil. votes)	18.5	19.9	19.2	19.1	20.9	18.1	18.3	22.4

(final column) Gaullists 346 / 10.1; Other 8 / 0.9; Total 943 / 44.7

1 SFIO and Radicals presented joint lists as Federation of the Democratic and Socialist Left.
2 Includes UDSR and dissident Radicals.
3 Includes dissident MRP.
4 Includes Peasant Party.
5 Includes Independent Republicans.
6 Includes 51 Poujadists.
7 MRP and Conservatives presented joint lists as the Democratic Center.
8 SFIO and Radical Socialists presented joint lists in 1968 as the Federation of the Democratic and Socialist Left (FGDS).
9 The Democratic Center became the Progress and Modern Democracy (PDM) in 1968.

Sources: *L'Année politique*, election issues of *Le Monde, Les élections législatives du 17 juin 1951, La Documentation française*, Paris, 1953. Figures on voting. since 1958 refer to first-round balloting. *Le Monde*, June 25, 1968, and July 2, 1968.

TABLE 4

DISTRIBUTION OF SENATE SEATS
AFTER EACH ELECTION SINCE 1945

	1946	1948	1952	1955	1958	1959	1962	1965
Communists	88	18	16	14	16	14	14	14
SFIO	64	62	56	56	56	51	53	52
Radicals and allies	42	87	73	74	65	64	50	50
MRP	77	21	24	24	26	34	35	38
Conservatives	33	69	80	83	90	94	84	81
Gaullists	—	57	46	36	39	44	31	30
Others	11	6	25	32	24	6	6	9
	315	320	320	319	316	307	273	274

Sources: *Le Conseil de la République,* La Documentation
française, Paris, 1954; *L'Année politique.* Elections for
all seats were held in 1946, 1948, and 1959, for one
third in 1952, 1955, 1958, 1962, and 1965. Before 1958,
the Senate was named the Council of the Republic.

TABLE 5

RESULTS OF REFERENDA SINCE 1945

			(millions)	
Date	Subject	Registered votes	Yes	No
October 21, 1945	Constituent Assembly	25.718	18.585	0.699
October 21, 1945	Restricting Constituent Assembly power	25.718	12.795	6.449
May 5, 1946	Draft Constitution	24.657	9.110	10.273
October 13, 1946	Draft Constitution (Fourth Republic)	25.073	9.039	7.830
September 28, 1958	Draft Constitution (Fifth Republic)	26.603	17.689	4.625
January 8, 1961	Algerian policies	27.184	15.200	4.996
April 8, 1962	Algerian Independence	26.992	17.509	1.795
October 28, 1962	Direct Presidential Election	27.582	12.809	7.933

Source: *L'Année politique.*

TABLE 6

RESULTS OF ELECTIONS FOR PRESIDENT OF THE REPUBLIC SINCE 1947

January 16, 1947 (Elected by Parliament, 1st ballot)

Vincent Auriol	452
Champetier de Ribes	242
Others	189

December 23, 1953 (Elected by Parliament, 13th ballot)

René Coty	477
Marcel-Edmond Naegelen	329
Others	65

December 21, 1958 (Elected by Electoral College, 1st ballot)

Charles de Gaulle	63,394
Georges Marrane	10,355
Albert Châtelet	6,721

December 19, 1965 (Elected by popular vote, 2nd ballot)

Charles de Gaulle	13,083,699
François Mitterrand	10,619,735
Registered voters	28,902,704

Source: *L'Année politique.*

TABLE 7

PRIME MINISTERS SINCE 1944

September 1944	Charles de Gaulle	non-party
January 1946	Félix Gouin	Socialist
June 1946	Georges Bidault	MRP
December 1946	Léon Blum	Socialist
January 1947	Paul Ramadier	Socialist
November 1947	Robert Schuman	MRP
July 1948	André Marie	Radical
September 1948	Robert Schuman	MRP
September 1948	Henri Queuille	Radical
October 1949	Georges Bidault	MRP
July 1950	Henri Queuille	Radical
July 1950	René Pleven	UDSR
March 1951	Henri Queuille	Radical
August 1951	René Pleven	UDSR
January 1952	Edgar Faure	Radical
March 1952	Antoine Pinay	Conservative
January 1953	René Mayer	Radical
June 1953	Joseph Laniel	Conservative
June 1954	Pierre Mendès-France	Radical
February 1955	Edgar Faure	Radical
February 1956	Guy Mollet	Socialist
June 1957	Maurice Bourgès-Maunoury	Radical
November 1957	Félix Gaillard	Radical
May 1958	Pierre Pflimlin	MRP
June 1958	Charles de Gaulle	non-party
January 1959	Michel Debré	UNR
April 1962	Georges Pompidou	non-party Gaullist

MRP-*Mouvement républicain populaire* (Christian Democrats)

UDSR-*Union démocratique et socialiste de la Résistance*

UNR-*Union pour la nouvelle république* (Gaullists)

Source: Through 1958, Philip M. Williams, *Crisis and Compromise* (Garden City, New York, Doubleday and Company, Inc. 1966 edition), pp. 587–588.

Germany

TABLE 1

IMPORTANT EVENTS SINCE 1917

1917	End of three class voting; equal, direct and secret suffrage introduced
1918	Revolt at Kiel; Emperor abdicates; Republic proclaimed
	Armistice signed
1919	National constituent assembly elected; Wiemar Constitution adopted; Kapp monarchist putsch fails
1921	Allied reparation terms accepted
1923	France occupies Ruhr
	Munich "Beer Hall Putsch" fails
1925	Hindenberg elected President
1930	National Socialists emerge as major party
1931	Economy collapses
1932	Von Papen forms the "ministry of barons"
	Reichstag dissolved
1933	Hitler becomes Chancellor
	Reichstag building burns; civil liberties suspended
	Enabling Act passed; Nazi dictatorship established; National Socialists become only party
1934	Great Blood Purge
1938	Austria and Czechoslovakia annexed and occupied
1939	War declared by England and France
1945	German provisional government established and surrenders; Military government established
1946	Länder constituent assemblies elected
1947	Länder legislatures elected in first postwar elections
1948	Berlin airlift; Soviet delegates walk out of Allied Control Council
	London Agreements signed
	Parliamentary Council elected; deliberates on Basic Law
	Free market economy established
1949	Basic Law adopted
1951	Occupation Statute replaced by Peace Contract
	Federal Constitutional Court established

1952	Neo-Nazi party declared illegal
1955	West Germany becomes sovereign; joins NATO
1956	Communist Party outlawed
1961	Berlin Wall constructed
1962	Spiegel affair
1966	Black and red coalition formed

TABLE 2

PARTY REPRESENTATION IN THE BUNDESTAG SINCE 1949 [1]

Election	CDU/ CSU	SPD	FDP	DP	Other	Total
August 14, 1949	139	131	52	17	63[2]	402
September 6, 1953	243	151	48	15	30[3]	487
September 15, 1957	270	169	41	17	0	497
September 17, 1961	242	190	66	0	0	499
September 19, 1965	245	202	49	0	0	496

[1] Excluding Berlin.
[2] Includes Bavarian Party 17, Center 10, Communist 15.
[3] Includes Refugee League 27, Center 2.

Source: *Statistisches Jahrbuch für die Bundesrepublik Deutschland.*

TABLE 3

POPULAR VOTE FOR THE BUNDESTAG SINCE 1949

		Percentages			
Year	Total Vote	CDU/CSU	SPD	FDP	Other
1949	24,495,600	31.0	29.2	11.9	27.8
1953	28,479,600	45.2	28.8	9.5	16.5
1957	31,072,900	50.2	31.8	7.7	10.3
1961	33,849,600	45.3	36.2	12.8	5.7
1965	33,416,200	47.6	39.3	9.5	3.6

Source: *Statistisches Jahrbuch für die Bundesrepublik Deutschland.*

TABLE 4

APPROXIMATE COMPOSITION OF STATE
DELEGATIONS TO THE BUNDESRAT
SINCE 1949

Date	CDU	SPD	Unknown	Total
September 1949	3	10	30	43
August 1950	12	6	25	43
June 1951	16	15	12	43
April 1952	18	15	5	38
October 1953	23	15	—	38
1954	26	12	—	38
April 1955	26	12	—	38
February 1956	21	17	—	38
November 1957	26	15	—	41
July 1958	31	10	—	41
May 1959	26	15	—	41
July 1960	26	15	—	41
January 1, 1961	26	15	—	41
January 1, 1962	26	15	—	41
January 1, 1963	26	15	—	41
January 1, 1964	26	15	—	41
January 1, 1965	26	15	—	41
January 1, 1966	26	15	—	41
January 1, 1967	26	15	—	41

Source: Through 1960; Edward L. Pinney, *Federalism, Bureaucracy and Party Politics in Western Germany,* Chapel Hill: University of North Carolina Press 1963 p. 98. After 1960: *Statistisches Jahrbuch für die Bundesrepublik Deutschland.*

TABLE 5

COMPOSITION OF STATE DIETS AFTER
EACH ELECTION SINCE 1949

	CDU/CSU	SPD	FDP	Other
Baden-Wurttemberg				
1952	50	38	23[1]	10
1956	56	36	21	7
1960	52	44	18	7
1964	59	47	14	0

[1] FDP/DVP.

TABLE 5 (*Continued*)

	CDU/CSU	SPD	FDP	Other
Bavaria				
1950	64	63	12	65
1954	85	61	12	46
1958	102	62	8	30
1962	108	79	9	8
1966	110	79	0	15
Berlin				
1950	34	61	32	0
1954	42	63	12	10
1958	55	78	0	0
1963	41	89	10	0
1967	46	79	9	0
Bremen				
1951	9	43	12[2]	36
1955	18	62	8	18
1959	16	61	7	16
1963	31	57	8	4
1967	32	50	10	8
Hamburg				
1949	40[4]	65	3	15
1953	0	58	0	62[3]
1957	41	69	10	0
1961	36	72	12	0
1966	38	74	8	0
Hesse				
1950	12	47	21	0
1954	24	44	20	8
1958	32	48	9	7
1962	28	51	11	6
1966	26	52	10	8
Lower Saxony				
1951	35	64	12	47
1955	44	57	11	47
1959	51	65	8	33
1963	62	73	14	0
1967	62	73	14	0

[2] FDP/BDV.
[3] Hamburg Bloc.
[4] VBM (CDU and FDP).

TABLE 5 (*Continued*)

	CDU/CSU	SPD	FDP	Other
North Rhineland-Westphalia				
1950	93	68	26	28
1954	89	76	26	9
1958	104	81	15	0
1962	96	90	14	0
1966	86	99	15	0
Rhineland-Palatinate				
1951	43	38	19	0
1955	51	36	13	0
1959	52	37	10	1
1963	46	43	11	0
1967	49	39	8	4
Saar				
1955	24	8	16	2
1960	19	16	7	8
1965	23	21	4	2
Schleswig-Holstein				
1950	16	9	8	26
1954	25	25	5	14
1958	33	26	3	7
1962	34	29	5	1
1967	34	30	4	5

Source: *Statistisches Jahrbuch für die Bundesrepublik Deutschland* and *Facts on File*.

TABLE 6

PRESIDENTIAL ELECTIONS SINCE 1949

Votes in the Federal Assembly for Principal Candidates

September 12, 1949	Theodor Heuss (FDP)	416
	Kurt Schumacher (SPD)	312
July 17, 1954	Theodor Heuss (FDP)	871
July 1, 1959	Heinrich Lubke (CDU)	526
	Carlo Schmid (SPD)	486
	Max Becker (FDP)	99
July 1, 1964	Heinrich Lubke (CDU)	710
	Ewald Bucher (FDP)	123

Source: *New York Times*.

TABLE 7

CHANCELLORS SINCE 1949

September 15, 1949	Konrad Adenauer (CDU)
October 16, 1963	Ludwig Erhard (CDU)
December 1, 1966	Kurt Kiesinger (CDU)

Soviet Union

TABLE 1

IMPORTANT EVENTS SINCE 1917

1917	March (April) revolution
	Abdication of Czar
	Formation of Provisional Government
	October (November) revolution; Bolsheviks overthrow Provisional Government
1918	Treaty of Brest Litovsk
	First Soviet Constitution promulgated after adoption by 5th Bolshevik Congress
1918-	
1920	Civil War
1921	Introduction of New Economic Policy (NEP)
1922	Famine
	Lenin's first stroke
1924	Lenin dies
	Eclipse of Trotsky
	Defeat of Zinoviev and Kamenev by Stalin
1928	Trotsky goes into exile
	First Five Year Plan; begins major effort to industrialize
	Beginning of collectivization
1930-	
1931	Famine
1934	Kirov murdered
1935-	
1938	Great Purge and Treason Trials
1936	Stalin Constitution adopted
1938	First meeting of the Supreme Soviet
1941	Germany invades; State Committee of Defense formed
1946	First general election since 1937
1947	Cominform established
1953	Doctors' Plot
	Stalin dies; Malenkov becomes Prime Minister and key Secretariat member
	Khrushchev becomes First Secretary

231

1954	Virgin lands campaign
1955	Malenkov falls
1956	Khrushchev's secret speech denounces Stalin
1957	Industry decentralized
	Anti-party group ousted
1958	Khrushchev becomes Premier
1961	Further attacks on Anti-party group
1964	Khrushchev ousted; collective leadership develops
	Centralization reestablished

Table 2

MEMBERS, C.P.S.U.*

	Full Members	Candidate Members
1918	390,000	none
1919	350,000	none
1920	611,978	not counted
1921	732,521	not counted
1922	410,430	117,924
1923	381,400	117,700
1924	350,000	122,000
1925	440,365	361,439
1926	639,652	440,162
1927	786,288	426,217
1928	914,307	391,547
1929	1,090,508	444,854
1930	1,184,651	493,259
1931	1,369,406	842,819
1932	1,769,773	1,347,477
1933	2,203,951	1,351,387
1934	1,826,756	874,252
1935	1,659,104	699,610
1936	1,489,907	586,935
1937	1,453,828	527,869
1938	1,405,879	514,123
1939	1,514,181	792,792
1940	1,982,743	1,417,232
1941	2,490,479	1,381,986
1942	2,155,336	908,540
1943	2,451,511	1,403,190
1944	3,126,627	1,791,934

* *Source: Partiinaya Zhizn,* No. 19, October 1967, p. 10. As of
March 1918, 1919, 1920, and 1921. As of January 1 for
each subsequent year.

TABLE 2 (*Continued*)

	Full Members	Candidate Members
1945	3,965,530	1,794,839
1946	4,127,689	1,383,173
1947	4,774,886	1,277,015
1948	5,181,199	1,209,082
1949	5,334,811	1,017,761
1950	5,510,787	829,396
1951	5,658,577	804,398
1952	5,853,200	854,339
1953	6,067,027	830,197
1954	6,402,284	462,579
1955	6,610,238	346,867
1956	6,767,644	405,877
1957	7,001,114	493,459
1958	7,296,559	546,637
1959	7,622,356	616,775
1960	8,017,249	691,418
1961	8,472,396	803,430
1962	9,051,934	839,134
1963	9,581,149	806,047
1964	10,182,916	839,453
1965	10,811,443	946,726
1966	11,548,287	809,021
1967	12,135,103	549,030

TABLE 3

SECRETARIES OF THE COMMUNIST PARTY SINCE 1917

Date designated

November 1917	Y. M. Sverdlov[1]
March 1919	N. M. Krestinskii[2]
March 1920	N. M. Krestinskii[3]
April 1922	J. V. Stalin[4]
March 7, 1953	G. M. Malenkov[3]
March 14, 1953	N. S. Khrushchev[3]
September 1953	N. S. Khrushchev[5]
October 1964	L. I. Brezhnev[5]
March 1966	L. I. Brezhnev[4]

[1] Chairman of the Executive Committee
[2] Secretary
[3] The senior secretary
[4] General Secretary
[5] First Secretary

TABLE 4
MEMBERS OF THE COMMUNIST PARTY POLITBURO SINCE 1917*

Year	Stalin	Kamenev	Trotsky	Lenin	Zinoviev	Sokol'nikov	Bubnov	Kalinin	Kuibyshev	Kossior	Ordzhonikidze	Beria	Shvernik	Voronov	Polianskii
1917	Stalin	Kamenev	Trotsky	Lenin	Zinoviev	Sokol'nikov	Bubnov								
1919	"	"	"	"	Krestinskii										
1921	"	"	"	"	Zinoviev										
1922	"	"	"	"	"	Tomskii	Rykov								
1924	"	"	"	Bukharin	"	"	"								
1926	"	Voroshilov	Rudzutak	"	Molotov	"	"	Kalinin	Kuibyshev						
1927	"	"	"	"	"	"	"	"	"						
1929	"	"	"	"	"	"	"	"	"						
1930	"	"	"	Kaganovich	"		Kirov	"	"	Kossior	Ordzhonikidze				
1932	"	"	Andreev	"	"		"	"	"	"	"				
1934	"	"	"	"	"		"	"	"	"	"				
1935	"	"	"	"	"		Mikoyan	"	Chubar'	"	"				
1937	"	"	"	"	"		"	"	Zhdanov	"					
1939	"	"	"	"	"	Khrushchev	"	"	"	"					
1946	"	"	"	"	"	"	"		"	Malenkov		Beria	Shvernik		
1947	"	"	"	"	"	"	"		"	"	Voznesenskii	"	"		
1948	"	"	"	"	"	"	"	Bulganin	Kosygin	"	"	"	"		
1952¹	"	"	Saburov	"	"	"	"	"	Kuusinen	"	Perrihin	"	"		
1953	"	"	"	"	"	"	"	"	"	"	"		"		
1955	Suslov	"	"	"	"	"	"	"	"	Kirichenko	"		"		
1957²	"	"	Kozlov	Brezhnev		"	"	Podgornyi	Mukhitdinov	"	"		"		
1958	"	"	"	"		"	"	"	"	"	"		"		
1960	"	Kosygin	"	"		"	"	"	"	"	"		"		
1961	"	"	"	"		"	"	"	"	"	"		"	Voronov	
1962	"	"	"	"		"	"	Kirilenko	"	"	"		"	"	
1964	"	"	"	"		Shelepin	"	"	Shelest	"	"		"	"	
1965	"	"	Mazurov	"		"	"	"	"	"	"		"	"	
1966	"	"	"	"	Pelse	"	"	"	"	"	"		"	"	Polianskii

* As of December 31 of every year in which changes occurred. Politburo known as Presidium, 1952–64.

[1] Also Andrianov, Aristov, Ignat'ev, Korotchenko, Kuznetsov, Kuusinen, Malyshev, Mel'nikov, Mikhailov, Ponomarenko, Chesnokov, Shvernik, Shkiriatov were members, October 1952–March 1953.

[2] Also Zhukov was a member, June–November 1957, and Aristov, Beliaev, Ignatov, and Furtseva were members, June 1957–October 1961.

TABLE 5

CHAIRMEN OF THE COUNCIL OF MINISTERS (PRIME MINISTERS) SINCE 1917

Date designated

November 19, 1917	V. I. Lenin
February 2, 1924	A. I. Rykov
January 8, 1930	V. M. Molotov
May 6, 1941	J. V. Stalin
March 15, 1953	G. M. Malenkov
February 8, 1955	N. A. Bulganin
March 27, 1958	N. S. Khrushchev
October 15, 1964	A. N. Kosygin

TABLE 6

CHAIRMEN OF THE PRESIDIUM OF THE SUPREME SOVIET (CHIEF OF STATE) SINCE 1917

Dates designated

November 21, 1917	Y. M. Sverdlov
March 19, 1919	M. I. Kalinin
March 19, 1946	N. M. Shvernik
March 15, 1953	K. E. Voroshilov
May 7, 1960	L. I. Brezhnev
July 15, 1964	A. I. Mikoyan
December 9, 1965	N. V. Podgornyi

TABLE 7

DATES OF PARTY CONFERENCES AND CONGRESSES SINCE 1898

First Congress	March 1-3, 1898 Minsk
Second Congress	July 17-August 10, 1903 Brussels-London
Third Congress	April 12-27, 1905 London
Conference of Social-Democratic Organizations in Russia	September 7-9, 1905 Riga
First Conference	December 12-17, 1905 Tammerfors
Fourth (Unification) Congress	April 10-25, 1906 Stockholm
First All-Russian Conference	November 3-7, 1906 Tammerfors
Fifth Congress	April 30-May 19, 1907 London
Second All-Russian Conference	July 21-23, 1907 Ketka, Finland
Third All-Russian Conference	November 5-12, 1907 Helsingfors
Fifth All-Russian Conference	December 21-27, 1908 Paris
Sixth All-Russian Conference	January 5-17, 1912 Prague
Foreign Sections Conference	February 14-19 Berne
Seventh All-Russian Conference	April 24-29, 1917 Petrograd
Sixth Congress	July 26-August 3, 1917 Petrograd
Seventh Congress	March 6-8, 1918 Petrograd
Eighth Congress	March 18-23, 1919 Moscow
Eighth All-Russian Conference	December 2-4, 1919 Moscow
Ninth Congress	March 29-April 5, 1920 Moscow
Ninth All-Russian Conference	September 22-25, 1920 Moscow
Tenth Congress	March 8-16, 1921 Moscow
Tenth "All-Russian" Conference	May 26-28, 1921 Moscow
Eleventh "All-Russian" Conference	December 19-22, 1921 Moscow
Eleventh Congress	March 27-April 2, 1922 Moscow
Twelfth "All-Russian" Conference	August 4-7, 1922 Moscow
Twelfth Congress	April 17-25, 1923 Moscow

TABLE 7 (*Continued*)

Thirteenth Conference	January 16-18, 1924 Moscow
Thirteenth Congress	May 23-31, 1924 Moscow
Fourteenth Conference	April 27-29, 1925 Moscow
Fourteenth Congress of the AUCP(B)	December 18-31, 1925 Moscow
Fifteenth Conference	October 26-November 3, 1926 Moscow
Fifteenth Congress	December 2-19, 1927 Moscow
Sixteenth Conference	April 23-29, 1929 Moscow
Sixteenth Congress	June 26-July 13, 1930 Moscow
Seventeenth Conference	January 30-February 4, 1932 Moscow
Seventeenth Congress	January 26-February 10, 1934 Moscow
Eighteenth Congress	March 10-21, 1939 Moscow
Eighteenth Conference	February 15-20, 1941 Moscow
Nineteenth Congress of the CPSU	October 5-14, 1952 Moscow
Twentieth Congress	February 14-25, 1956 Moscow
Twenty-first (Extraordinary) Congress	January 27-February 5, 1959 Moscow
Twenty-second Congress	October 17-27, 1961 Moscow
Twenty-third Congress	March 29-April 8, 1966 Moscow

Note: Party titles and dates adopted were:
      1898 Russian Social Democratic Labor Party.
      1918 All-Russian Communist Party (Bolsheviks).
      1925 All-Union Communist Party (Bolsheviks).
      1952 Communist Party of the Soviet Union.

Source: Through 1959, Robert Maxwell, ed., *Information, USSR*. Dates before 1918 follow Old Style (Gregorian) Calendar.

COMPARATIVE DATA

	Germany	Great Britain	France	Soviet Union	United States
Total population[1] (millions)	57.5 (1966)	54.7 (1966)	49.4 (1966)	230.6[a] (1965)	196.9 (1966)
Area in square miles[2] (thousands)	95.7	94.2	211.2	8,649.5	3,615.2
Population per square mile	601	581	234	27	54
Gross National Product[3] (billions of dollar equivalents)	116.2 (1966)	100.0 (1966)	98.0 (1966)	329.4[4] (1966)	718.1 (1966)
GNP per capita[3]	1,945	1,817	1,984	1,429[4]	3,648
Private Consumption as a percent of GNP[3]	57	64	64	64[5]	63
National Defense as a percent of GNP[6]	3.6	6.4	4.4	8.9	9.2
Agricultural workers as a percent of labor force[7]	10.9	5.1	19.8	35.2	6.2
Manufacturing workers as a percent of labor force[7]	37.5	26.9	26.9	Not available	25.6
Service workers as a percent of labor force[7]	20.5	23.7	20.1	Not available	27.6

Members of Armed Forces as a Percent of population[8]	.8	.8	1.0	1.4	1.7
Students in Higher or teacher training education as a Percent of population[9]	0.4	0.6	1.0	3.0	2.8
Jews as a Percentage of population[10]	.04	0.8	1.1	1.1	2.9
Catholics as a Percentage of population[11]	47.6	8.3	82.6	4.4	23.7
Percentage of Registered Voters Voting	86.8 (1965)	75.8 (1966)	79.9 (1967)	99.9 (1967)	76.0* (1964)
Chief Executive	Chancellor	Prime Minister	President	General Secretary, CPSU	President
Highest Court	Federal Constitutional Court	House of Lords	Supreme Court of Appeal	Supreme Court	Supreme Court
Principal Legislative Assembly	Bundestag	House of Commons	National Assembly	Supreme Soviet	Congress
Institutional Organization	Federal	Unitary	Unitary	Federal	Federal
Date of Present Written Constitution	1949	None	1958	1936	1787

(Footnotes on p. 240.)

Footnotes for Comparative Data

[1] Source: International Monetary Fund, *International Financial Statistics*, (December, 1967).

[2] Source: *Statistical Abstract of the United States*.

[3] Source: Agency for International Development, *Gross National Product* (March 31, 1967) Except USSR 1965 Dollar Equivalents.

[4] Joint Economic Committee of the US Congress, 1966 *New Directions in the Soviet Economy*, Part IIA, p. 107 updated.

[5] Based on Net Material Product.

[6] Institute for Strategic Studies (London): *The Military Balance, 1967-1968*.

[7] ILO. *Yearbook of Labour Statistics, 1966*.

[8] Institute for Strategic Studies (London): *The Military Balance, 1967-1968*.

[9] *United Nations Statistical Yearbook, 1966*.

[10] *American Jewish Yearbook, 1967*.

[11] *National Catholic Almanac, 1967*.

[*] Source: *Book of the States, 1967*. Based on States for which registration data is available.